The Politics of
Japan's Energy Strategy
Resources—Diplomacy—Security

A publication of the
Institute of East Asian Studies,
University of California,
Berkeley

The Research Papers and Policy Studies Series is one of several publications series sponsored by the Institute of East Asian Studies in conjunction with its three constituent units—the Center for Chinese Studies, the Center for Japanese Studies, and the Center for Korean Studies. The others include the China Research Monograph Series, whose first title appeared in 1967, a new Japan Research Monograph Series, and the Korea Research Monograph Series. The Institute sponsors also a Faculty Reprint Series.

Correspondence may be sent to:
Director of Publications
Institute of East Asian Studies
University of California
Berkeley, California 94720

RESEARCH PAPERS AND POLICY STUDIES　　3

INSTITUTE OF EAST ASIAN STUDIES
UNIVERSITY OF CALIFORNIA · BERKELEY

The Politics of Japan's Energy Strategy

Resources—Diplomacy—Security

Ronald A. Morse, Editor

Although the Institute of East Asian Studies is responsible for the selection and acceptance of manuscripts in this series, responsibility for the opinions expressed and for the accuracy of statements rests with their authors.

©1981 by the Regents of the University of California
ISBN 0–912966–45–9
Library of Congress Catalog Number 81–83220
Printed in the United States of America
$7.00

Contents

Foreword

If there is such a thing as a "recurrent surprise," then surely one example is the reaction one has when one sees beneath the surface of a well-established stereotype. In the case of the Japanese energy situation, the standard story goes something like the following:

> Japan is an island nation with no energy resources—a fragile blossom whose very existence is threatened by the prospect of oil supply disruptions. The Japanese strategy is to shift to less energy-intensive industries (steel to computers), and to convert the economy to nuclear power (the latter change being possible only after a painful process of consensus formation). This restructuring is being carried out by Japan, Inc.—which is a seamless web of banks and industries operating under the direction of the Ministry of International Trade and Industry (MITI).

As is often the case with stereotypes, this one contains a grain of truth; indeed, some of its aspects are fostered by the Japanese themselves—sometimes for tactical reasons, but most often because the image is widely shared. The surprise comes when we see some of the details of how things actually work, and we begin to realize how wrong one can be if the shorthand description is used as a basis for judgment about specific policies and actions.

This volume of essays is highly valuable in this regard, for it is the first attempt, to date, to look into the linkages between international military and trade issues, domestic Japanese politics and bureaucratic structure, and the decisions now being made about energy demand and supply and the future structure of the Japanese energy sector. Moreover, it has the advantage of having been researched and written by scholars who all speak Japanese.

Some deeper understanding of the energy scene is of crucial importance to U.S. scholars and policymakers, because there are several areas of important (and not always very friendly) interaction between the U.S. and Japan as regards energy questions. For one thing, we are competitors in a rapidly changing world oil market. Only a few years ago, oil imports to Japan were handled via third-party sales by the international oil companies, most of which are U.S.-based. As a result of changes stimulated by the Iranian revolution, these arrangements were terminated or drastically curtailed; Japanese trading organizations and oil companies, with substantial involvement by MITI, were forced into oil markets in order to cover the loss. The result has been a wholly different set of relationships between Japan, the world market, and other consuming nations. Moreover, Japanese foreign policy with regard to the Middle East is strongly influenced by the desire to maintain healthy commercial relations with oil-exporters, and issues of joint military security cannot be separated from the perceptions and concerns that motivate Japanese oil policy.

As if U.S.-Japan relations were not tangled enough on the oil front, we, along with a host of other nations, are involved in a complex set of international emergency planning schemes organized under the aegis of the International Energy Agency. The success of U.S. policy with regard to the IEA must depend on a clear understanding of the Japanese perceptions of the IEA, and of other mechanisms that might be used to moderate oil shock.

Nuclear policy is another area where there are close and complex relations between our two countries. Japan has been a customer for U.S. technology and fuel cycle services, and has been caught up in the American policy with regard to nonproliferation and the associated attempts to control trade in sensitive materials and technologies. According to many Japanese observers, events in the U.S.—including the shifting policies regarding nonproliferation and the events surrounding the Three Mile Island accident—have a substantial effect on the ability of Japanese authorities to carry out the current government and industry policy with regard to nuclear power development.

Yet another point of interaction, and not always a happy one, is in Japan-U.S. cooperation on energy research and development. As a result of an initiative by Prime Minister Fukuda in May 1978, there has been a program of joint activities in the areas of fusion, synthetic fuels, and solar power. These cooperative agreements have been affected by the drastic shift in government priorities and expenditure patterns brought about by the Reagan Administration; major programs appear likely to be canceled, much to the dismay of many Japanese involved in this work—both from the technical and the policy perspective.

Because of the language barrier and a dearth of serious scholarship on Japanese institutions, politics, and public viewpoints, we in the U.S.

lack in-depth knowledge that is needed to inform discussions of long-term oil policy and preparation for short-term emergencies, nuclear issues, and R&D cooperation. Nor is this a one-way street. It is important for Japanese scholars, industry, and government officials to read what is being written about Japan and the United States and begin a flow of correction about those matters which we may misperceive. And there should be a flow in the other direction: with Japanese scholars studying and writing about the U.S. energy scene, and receiving comments and criticism from the U.S. side about Japanese impressions of what drives U.S. actions.

No one book can fill such a wide gap, but it is encouraging to have such a good offering as a beginning, and one may hope that it is the start of a continuing flow of research and scholarly writing about the Japanese energy sector. We have every reason to expect that in the next twenty years world energy will be as great a source of international stress as it has been in the last eight. This is a world where "surprise" about a country as important as Japan can prove very costly to all of us.

Henry D. Jacoby
Professor, Sloan School of Management
Associate Director of the Energy Laboratory
Massachusetts Institute of Technology

Cambridge, Mass.
July 1981

Editor's Preface

This book has been compiled, at least in part, to fill what we consider an important gap in the available information on Japan's energy policies, strategies, and objectives. This is an important subject, and it deserves more serious treatment than it has received to date. All of the chapters here are by experts with a special knowledge of and interest in Japan. More importantly, we have a special interest in the foreign policy implications of Japan's energy strategies. This perspective is reflected in the various chapters, each of which attempts to link the domestic Japanese policy process to the broader international energy context. The complexities of the domestic public policy process in Japan are examined in detail. The authors generally agree that Japan has been somewhat less successful in the energy area than is generally perceived. Indeed, read carefully, the book suggests that opportunities for cooperation and coordination may have been lost because of the priorities of Japanese energy policies.

The chapters, as they appear here, are revised versions of papers prepared for a panel at the annual convention of the Association of Asian Studies, held in Toronto, Canada, in March 1981. The essay "Japan's Energy Policies and Options" has been added to give the general reader the information necessary to fully understand the more specialized chapters. The basic intention of the volume is to stimulate a more meaningful dialogue on the interrelationships between Japan's energy strategies and the global energy scene.

Japan, as we know, is not unique in having had difficulty in getting its energy policies in order. To date, no major energy importing nation has come up with an effective strategy for managing present high energy costs. Japan, as one of these nations, is naturally interested in obtaining secure and reliable energy supplies at reasonable prices. How Japan goes about accomplishing its future energy goals will also have an impact on the availability of world energy supplies and the stability of the international economic order. It was with these and other issues in mind that we have put together what we consider a thoughtful but critical overview of the energy situation in Japan.

Energy policies change quickly, and data are always sensitive to time. Because of the special efforts provided by the Institute of East Asian Studies at Berkeley, it required only four months to make this volume available to the public. This cooperation and the assistance of many others have been greatly appreciated. While everyone cannot be mentioned individually, I would especially like to thank Guy Caruso, John Despres, Mike Gaffen, Jeffrey Hartman, Lucian Pugliaresi, and Robert M. Weiss, all of the Department of Energy. Professor Henry Rowen of Stanford University and Norio Tanaka of the Institute for Energy Economics were also cooperative at critical times. To the many others who helped make the volume possible, we all express our sincere thanks.

Ronald A. Morse

Washington, D.C.
July 1981

Contributors

MARTHA CALDWELL is currently working on international competitiveness and energy policy at the International Security and Commerce Program of the Congressional Office of Technology Assessment. Her doctoral work at the University of Wisconsin focused on state and industry in the formation of Japanese petroleum policy.

ROGER W. GALE writes for the *Energy Daily*, Washington, D.C. He is currently working on a book on Japanese energy policy, and was a visiting professor at the University of Tsukaba, Japan.

RONALD A. MORSE is Director of the East Asia Program at the Woodrow Wilson International Center for Scholars, in Washington, D.C. Since 1974, when he received his Ph.D. in Japanese studies from Princeton University, he has held several U.S. government positions. He was with the Department of Energy until February 1981.

PETER A. PETRI, an international economist, is an associate professor of economics at Brandeis University. He has written several papers on U.S.-Japan trade, including studies for various branches of the U.S. government. A book describing his detailed quantitative model of U.S.-Japan trade will be published in 1982 by Harvard University Press.

RICHARD J. SAMUELS is an assistant professor of political science and a research associate in the Energy Laboratory at the Massachusetts Institute of Technology. He was a Fulbright and Japan Foundation Research Fellow at the University of Tokyo from 1977 to 1979. Currently, he is working on a comparative study of public energy corporations.

RICHARD P. SUTTMEIER is an associate professor of government and chairman of the Department of Government at Hamilton College. He was a Fulbright Research Fellow in Japan in 1976–77, studying Japanese nuclear policies. He is currently working as a National Fellow at the Hoover Institution, where he is preparing a book on U.S. relations with China and Japan in the areas of science and technology.

The Politics of
Japan's Energy Strategy
Resources—Diplomacy—Security

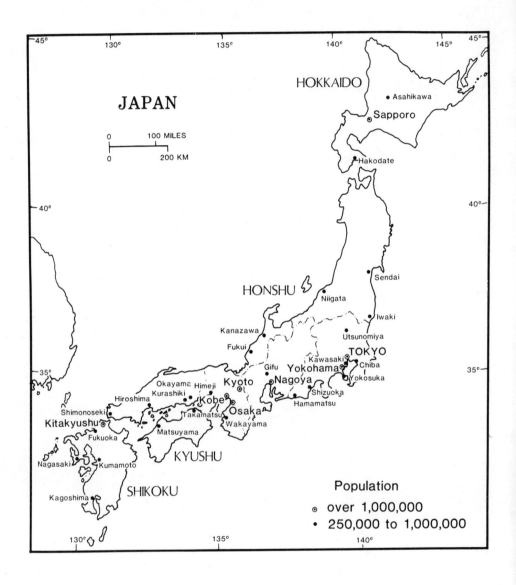

Introduction: Japan's Energy Policies and Options

Ronald A. Morse

Japan has moved into the decade of the 1980s convinced that effective government-business cooperation to lower Japan's energy demand and diversify its sources of energy supply will be the only way to ensure the nation's continued economic survival and prosperity. The essays in this volume explore Japan's energy strategy, assess the domestic economic and political costs of these decisions, and examine the implications of Japan's policies for the world in economic and strategic terms.[1]

Japan's national energy policy took a dramatic turn with the 1973–74 oil crisis. The new policy, which involves greater government involvement in oil and other energy markets, has the following basic elements:

1. The promotion of overseas oil development and better use of potential domestic energy sources.

2. The development of short-run non-oil energy alternatives: coal, nuclear power, and liquefied natural gas (LNG).

3. The diversification of oil supply sources and the encouragement of direct and government-to-government oil deals with the producing nations.

4. The encouragement of conservation and the commercialization of new energy technologies.

---

[1] A number of recent publications, each with a particular perspective, have taken up the subject of Japan's energy options. In particular, see *Oil and the Atom: Issues in U.S.-Japan Energy Relations*, edited by Michael Blaker (East Asian Institute, Columbia University, 1980); *Japan and the World Energy Problem*, by Herbert I. Goodman (Stanford University Press, 1980); the *Report of the Japan–United States Economic Relations Group* (January 1980); and *U.S.-Japan Energy Relationships in the 1980s* (Policy Paper of the Atlantic Council, June 1981).

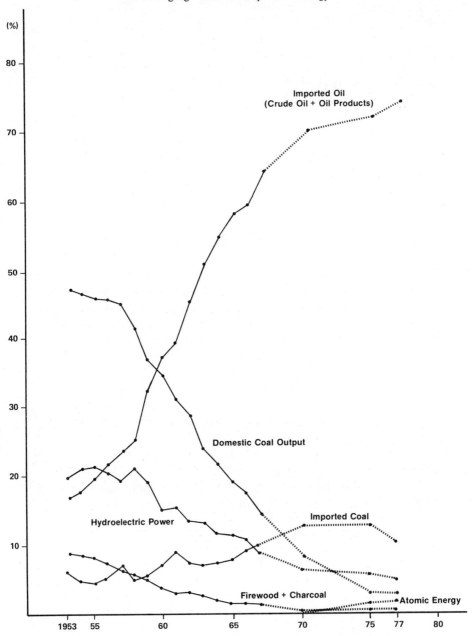

FIGURE 1

The Changing Pattern of Japanese Energy Use

SOURCE: Agency of Natural Resources and Energy, *Sōgo energy tōkei* [Energy Statistics], 1978 edition.

2

Table 1

ADVANCED NATIONS' ENERGY IMPORT DEPENDENCE, 1979

Country	Percent of Total Energy	Petroleum (%)	Net Oil Imports (*millions of barrels per day*)
Japan	88	99.8	5.64
Federal Republic of Germany	59	96.8	2.92
United Kingdom	13	19.1	0.38
France	76	99.0	2.44
Italy	82	98.4	2.00
Canada	Net Exporter	3.7	0.07
United States	20	42.7	7.99

5. The preparation of energy emergency-management procedures and the buildup of petroleum stockpiles to insulate Japan in the event of a major oil disruption.

These policies reflect the dominant views of Japan's ruling conservative Liberal Democratic Party, which has dominated Japanese politics for over two decades. Various aspects of Japanese party policies are examined throughout this volume as they relate to energy policy.

PETROLEUM DEPENDENCE

Japan has practically no oil or natural gas and only limited coal, geothermal, and hydropower resources. It is dependent on petroleum for 75 percent of its energy needs, and nearly three-quarters of that comes from the Persian Gulf, through the Strait of Hormuz and across thousands of miles of undefended sea-lanes. With nearly half of its imports consisting of energy, it is particularly sensitive to trends in world economic growth and fluctuations in export markets.

Japan's energy policy has been characterized by vigorous competition among importers and refiners, minimum domestic regulation, and a great deal of expediency in securing supplies vital to the national interest. By most estimates, Japan has managed its oil dependency better during the recent crisis than it did in 1973–74. During the recent crisis, wage increases were kept in line with low inflation rates, the national economy and the budget deficit were managed well, and the necessary adjustments were made for higher oil prices.

By most standards, Japan's economy handled its oil dependency well during the crises of 1973 and 1979. The reasons for this strong

Table 2

WORLD OIL PRODUCTION
(thousands of barrels per day)

Year	Non-OPEC Production	% Change	OAPEC Production*	% Change	Non-Arab OPEC Production†	% Change	Communist Production	% Change	Total World Production	% Change
1960	8,890	—	4,480	—	4,366	—	3,342	—	21,078	—
1965	10,365	3.1/yr	8,336	16.8/yr	6,149	7.1	5,320	9.7/yr	30,170	7.4/yr
1969	13,094	6.0/yr	12,812	11.3/yr	8,348	7.9/yr	7,123	7.6/yr	41,377	8.2/yr
1970	13,796	5.4	14,223	11.0	9,087	8.9	7,917	11.1	45,023	8.8
1971	14,137	2.5	15,053	5.8	10,756	18.4	8,608	8.7	48,554	7.8
1972	14,377	1.7	16,004	6.3	11,496	6.9	9,171	6.5	51,048	5.1
1973	14,580	1.4	18,111	13.2	13,199	14.8	9,972	8.7	55,862	9.4
1974	14,251	-2.3	17,810	-1.7	13,246	0.4	10,886	9.2	56,193	0.6
1975	13,886	-2.6	16,192	-9.1	11,462	-13.5	11,794	8.3	53,334	-5.1
1976	13,990	0.7	18,800	16.1	12,511	9.2	12,554	6.4	57,855	8.5
1977	14,842	6.1	19,507	3.8	12,427	-0.7	13,109	4.4	59,885	3.5
1978	15,973	7.6	18,723	-4.0	11,753	-5.4	13,896	6.0	60,345	0.8
1979	17,148	7.4	21,325	13.9	9,987	-15.0	14,206	2.2	62,666	3.8
1980	17,601	2.6	19,569	-8.2	8,012	-19.8	14,488	2.0	59,670	-4.8

SOURCES: *The International Petroleum Encyclopedia*, 1975 and 1980; and "Worldwide Crude Oil and Gas Production," *Oil and Gas Journal*, March 2, 1981, p. 163.

*The Organization of Arab Petroleum-Exporting Countries (OAPEC) includes Abu Dhabi, Algeria, Bahrain, Egypt, Iraq, Kuwait, Libya, Neutral Zone, Qatar, Saudi Arabia, and Syria. Egypt was suspended from OAPEC in April 1979, but is included for consistency in OAPEC totals for 1979 and 1980.

†The non-Arab members of the Organization of Petroleum-Exporting Countries (OPEC) are Ecuador, Gabon, Indonesia, Iran, Nigeria, Venezuela, Dubai, and Sharjah.

performance and the prospects for adjustment to still higher energy prices in the future are examined in detail in the chapter by Peter A. Petri. The economic dimensions of the problem are staggering: in 1979, Japan paid $33 billion for its imported oil, up sharply from $23 billion a year earlier. But Petri shows that Japan's competitive trade position, its emerging ability to attract substantial foreign investment, and its heavy investment in new technology enabled it to adjust with unusual success during the 1970s. In turn, the diversification of Japan's exports (across products as well as country destinations) and imports will contribute to its ability to adjust, if necessary, to an even more unfavorable future environment. Still, Japan faces difficult problems in its export offensives in the United States, Europe, and the Third World.

OIL POLITICS

At its most fundamental level, the present energy problem is the availability and acquisition of oil—the issue that Martha Caldwell addresses in her chapter about trading company policy and the dilemmas of Japanese oil diplomacy. Caldwell places the history and significance of the bilateral Iran-Japan Petrochemical Project within the context of Japan's tilt toward the oil-producing states and the problems that this position has created for Tokyo's relations with the United States. This project, which figured so prominently during the Iranian crisis and the Iran-Iraq war, is symbolic of Japan's tactical approach on oil issues. It also illustrates the relationship between business and government in Japan's Middle East policies.

It was not until 1963 that Japan's oil imports reached the level of 50 percent of its total energy needs. This increased oil dependence was part of a worldwide historical process of adaptation to changing energy availability and supply costs. Until the 1950s, Japan was nearly self-sufficient in energy, relying primarily on coal, hydropower, firewood, and charcoal. It was only in the 1960s, with the rapid rise in the production of synthetics and the dramatic rise of energy consumption that oil came to dominate Japanese energy use.

Along with this dependence on oil and the omnipresence of oil and oil by-products in the industrial process, the number of interest groups and government agencies involved in the energy policy process has increased dramatically. The Ministry of International Trade and Industry (MITI), traditionally involved directly in domestic market policy, has found it necessary to take on a larger international role in world energy markets. As oil costs have taken on major importance for the health of the economy, the Ministry of Finance has become more involved in energy budgeting. Fuel economy is managed by the Ministry of Transportation. Nuclear policy, as noted in the chapters by Suttmeier and Samuels, goes

Table 3

THE ENERGY ESTABLISHMENT*

Prime Minister	Key Cabinet Actors	Parliament
Science and Technology Council	Comprehensive Security Council	(Lower House) Energy and Minerals Resources Subcommittee
Atomic Energy Commission	Ministerial Council on Overall Energy Policy (ad hoc)	(Upper House) Energy Measures Committee
Nuclear Safety Commission	Ministry of Finance	Liberal Democratic Party and Other Party Energy Policy Committees
Electric Power Development Coordination Council	Ministry of Foreign Affairs	
Atomic Power Policy Discussion Group	Ministry of International Trade and Industry (Agency for Natural Resources and Energy)	
	Ministry of Transportation	
	Science and Technology Agency (Power Reactor and Nuclear Fuel Development Corp.)	
	Economic Planning Agency	

Environmental/Consumer	Lobbyists	Vested Interests	Research Groups
Environmental Agency	Japan Federation of Economic Organizations	Oil Companies	National Institute for Research Advancement
Industrial Pollution Control Association of Japan	Energy Policy Promotion Committee	Trading Companies	Nomura Research Institute
Consumer's Union of Japan	Petroleum Association of Japan	Japan Development Bank	Mitsubishi Research Institute
Council of Environmental Groups	Japan Coal Association	Atomic Power Commission	Committee for Energy Policy Promotion
	Association of Petrochemical Industries in Japan	Japan Atomic Industrial Forum, Inc.	Institute of Energy Economics
		Electric Industries Association	Energy Conservation Center
		Japan National Oil Co.	Research Institute for Ocean Economics
		Japan Tanker Oil Stockpiling Association	New Energy Development Organization
		Japan Offshore Petroleum Development Association	

*For a more comprehensive listing, see the *Japan Petroleum and Energy Yearbook* (Japan Petroleum Consultants, Ltd.).

Table 4

CHANGES IN SHARE OF ENERGY SOURCES*
(*percent*)

Year	Electric Power	Coal	Oil	Natural Gas
1905	0.2	92.4	7.4	0.0
1920	4.2	91.0	2.8	2.0
1935	13.6	73.7	12.6	0.1
1950	24.9	69.9	5.1	0.2
1965	10.1	29.6	59.1	1.2
1978	8.4	13.7	73.0	4.7

SOURCE: *Enerugii Foramu*, January 1981, p. 152.

*Electric power = water and nuclear; oil = oil imports and LPG; natural gas = natural gas and LNG.

beyond the jurisdiction of the Science and Technology Agency. Along with the increase of government involvement in energy policy, private enterprise and business groups have organized to protect their interests. Roger Gale challenges the conventional wisdom about MITI's role by examining the case of the Tokyo Electric Power Company. Another theme examined by the authors of this volume is the role of the Japanese bureaucracy as a major element in the "energy establishment" and in energy policy formation. While Japanese bureaucrats are influential and are certainly masters of routine, the incoherence and the weakness of top political leadership in the energy policy area can also be attributed to them.

THE CURRENT SITUATION

In 1980, Japan's oil imports were about 4.9 million barrels per day (MM B/D), slightly below the original projected target of 5.4 MM B/D. Recent private and government forecasts for Japan's oil imports for 1985 have ranged from 5.9 to 6.5 MM B/D, but even these projections may be too high, given what we have seen in the world economic slowdown and the impact of conservation measures. The most recent government forecast puts the number at 5.7 MM B/D.

ENERGY FORECASTING

Forecasting, a risky enterprise even under stable conditions, has proved even more difficult in recent years. Government energy forecasts by MITI,

Table 5

OIL CONSUMPTION AND IMPORTATION, 1980

	Japan*	United States
Oil Consumption	5.08 MM B/D	17.0 MM B/D
Oil Imports	4.9 MM B/D	6.2 MM B/D
Government Emergency Oil Stockpile (*at year's end*)	33.00 MMB	108.0 MMB

*Japan's current oil and gas production, totaling 55,000 B/D in crude oil equivalent, accounts for only 0.9 percent of Japan's total primary energy supply. This figure is expected to rise to 1.4 percent by 1985.

which often include optimistic economic growth factors and vague political considerations, have been revised nearly every six months since 1977. The interim report of the most recent review of long-range energy supply-demand estimates was done in May 1981; the final version of the report will be out in the Fall. In view of recent developments, especially the weakening of oil demand, the government now plans to reduce price controls on oil products (gasoline, kerosene) and devise ways to encourage private oil companies to coordinate policies more closely.

Table 6

JAPANESE CRUDE OIL IMPORTS BY SOURCE
(*thousands of barrels per day*)

Source Country	1973 (*pre-crisis*)	1979
Algeria	—	6
Iraq	—	262
Kuwait	488	466 (10%)
Libya	31	7
Qatar	—	140
Saudi Arabia	1,148	1,672 (35%)
United Arab Emirates	511	494 (10%)
Indonesia	638	699 (14%)
Iran	1,554	468 (10%)
Nigeria	101	—
Venezuela	7	8
Total OPEC	4,478	4,222
Other	397	624
Total	4,875	4,846

The annual projections announced by MITI in May 1981 for crude oil imports were, in millions of barrels of oil per day (MM B/D): 4.98 (1981), 5.21 (1982), 5.36 (1983), 5.54 (1984) and 5.71 (1985). In January 1981, the Institute of Energy Economics (IEE) made the following comparison between earlier MITI goals and its own rough predictions for the year:

Table 7

MITI VERSUS IEE PROJECTIONS FOR 1980

	Oil Imports (*MMB/D*)	Coal Imports (*million tons*)	LNG (*million tons*)	Nuclear (*million KW*)	Growth Rate (*percent*)
MITI	6.3	63	45	51	5.3
IEE	5.0	46	37	36	4.0

DEMAND RESTRAINT AND CONSERVATION

In line with developments in the other advanced nations, Japan has made considerable strides in reducing energy demand. The ratio of energy use to economic growth has declined gradually over the years. Since 1973, Japan's economy has grown with a less than equal increase in energy consumption. In 1979, the economy grew in real terms by 6.0 percent, while energy demand increased by only 3.3 percent.

The government continues to press for energy conservation. In response to the Iran-Iraq war, the government called for increased energy savings. The government sought lower building temperatures (18° Celsius or less) and encouraged citizens to reduce driving. A 10-point proposal was announced to reduce oil consumption by 7 percent in 1980. On January 23, 1981, the government Overall Energy Policy Committee set the conservation target for fiscal year 1981 (beginning in April) at 8 percent. This would mean a potential saving of 157 million barrels of oil (25 million kiloliters).[2]

The Japanese government has implemented a variety of demand restraint measures, including voluntary guidelines and investment incentives to utilize energy-efficient equipment and increase conservation. Of a total conservation budget of $22 million for fiscal year 1979, a considerable portion was directed for research and development. The highlights of the conservation effort have been as follows:

[2] The 25 million kiloliters were allocated as follows: 11.2 million for households, 2.8 million for transportation, and 11.0 million for industry.

• 1946: Cabinet decision on heat control measures.

• 1951: Heat Control Law.

• 1972: Establishment of Japan Thermal Energy Technology Association.

• 1973: Large-scale increase in price of crude oil, and restrictions on OPEC imports.

• 1974: 25th National Heat Control Conference; Energy Conservation Exhibition.

• 1975: First National Energy Conservation Conference.

• 1978: Moonlight Project (Science and Technology Agency's energy conservation project); establishment of the Energy Conservation Center.[3]

• 1979: Law Concerning the Rationalization of Energy Consumption.

While Japan's conservation policies are largely voluntary, the government allows market forces (price) to provide the main stimulus for demand restraint. During 1979, the gasoline tax was raised by about 25 percent, the aviation fuel tax by 100 percent, and kerosene prices were deregulated. Crude oil and imported petroleum products are also subject to a 3.5 percent ad valorem tax. Moreover, toward the end of the year, the government removed all petroleum product prices from its "administrative guidance," thus announcing its intention to let prices be determined solely by market forces.

Japan's energy consumption in the residential/commercial sector (19 percent) is one of the lowest of the major industrial nations; the United States uses more because of its sprawling geography, its many single-family homes, and, until recently, with oil price decontrol, its relatively low energy prices. A *Yomiuri* newspaper poll conducted on June 11, 1979, revealed that 70 percent of Japan's housewives (especially older women) are doing something on a regular basis to reduce energy use (for example, they turn off lights, do not use kerosene heaters or air conditioners, and cut down on TV use). On the other hand, it is predicted that energy consumption in the private sector will rise. Only 17 percent of the polling sample exercised restraint in private vehicle use. February, a peak energy period, has been designated Energy Conservation Month.

---

[3] The Moonlight Project, aimed at researching and developing energy-related technologies, was proposed by the Agency of Industrial Science and Technology of the Ministry of International Trade and Industry on the heels of the Sunshine Project. The proposal calls for programs for energy conservation technology, starting from basic research and continuing through the developmental stage, to be undertaken on a national basis. Areas of concentration are: (1) development of large-scale technologies for energy conservation; (2) development of pioneering, basic technologies for energy conservation; and (3) development of energy-saving technologies for devices used in the household and commercial sectors.

Industry, which uses almost 60 percent of Japan's total consumption, provides the key to the success of Japan's energy conservation policies. Large industrial energy use, as Richard J. Samuels explains below, also accounts for the significant interest in energy research and development. Japan currently provides substantial loans and fiscal incentives to encourage investment in energy-efficient equipment. To speed up Japan's general industrial restructuring drive to reduce oil use, the government has initiated a three-year "Energy Policy Measures Promotion Tax System" to stimulate new investment in energy-saving facilities. The rates of energy use reduction since 1973 have been quite dramatic for nearly every industry. Nevertheless, some analysts believe that the easy phase of energy conservation is over in Japan, and that now significant investment in electronic and computer applications will be required to obtain future energy conservation.

ALTERNATIVE ENERGY

If 1973 marked the beginning of Japan's new Middle East oil diplomatic offensive, 1980 marked the government's full commitment to short- and long-term alternative energy strategies. Japan's experience with industrial success and its faith in technology are the driving forces behind its new fascination with technical solutions to energy problems.

In May 1980, the government passed The Petroleum-Substitute Energy Promotion and Development Law, which was designed to set goals for the development of new energy sources, investigate policies for commercial and technical applications, and establish the New Energy Development Organization (NEDO). NEDO began operation on October 1, 1980, as Japan's equivalent of a synfuels corporation. How this came about and the implications for research and development policy are examined in the chapter by Samuels, who suggests that the link between industrial policy and the potential for the commercialization of energy technology is an important, but somewhat confused, process in Japan.

While the long-range commitment to alternative sources of energy remains firm, the Japanese are still uncertain about the best way to pursue their interests. The development options are: liquefied and gasified coal, oil sand, oil shale, geothermal energy, biomass,[4] and solar energy. It will not be until the twenty-first century that these new sources of energy will have a significant impact on Japan's energy needs.

The Sunshine Project has been at the center of Japan's efforts to develop clean, alternative energy sources to replace oil as the basic resource for Japan's energy needs. Initiated in 1974, it is an extensive technological development program projected on a very long-term basis,

---

[4] A Biomass Policy Committee was formed in 1980.

and covers all areas of new energy-related technology with the exception of nuclear energy. At present there are four important target areas: solar energy, geothermal energy, coal conservation, and hydrogen energy. The project also has plans for the development of such inexhaustible energy sources of the future as the ocean, wind power, and biomass technology.

NEDO now has the task of finding commercial uses for the technology, and has been given new research and development funding.

Coal, nuclear power, and natural gas (primarily LNG) are projected to be the principal sources of alternative energy supply for Japan by 1990. Combined, these sources are expected to supply 4.7 million barrels per day in oil equivalent against a total primary energy supply estimated at 12.0 million barrels per day. To achieve these targets, Japan must increase its coal supply 2.2 times, its nuclear power 4.9 times, and its natural gas supplies 3.7 times. There are serious doubts, however, that a decade will provide adequate time to shift over to these new sources.

The Japanese electric power industry, more optimistic than other groups about meeting its supply targets, expects Japan's energy needs to grow 1.7 times by 1990 over 1978. Meeting future electric power needs alone will require a full nuclear program, a significant increase in LNG imports, and a fivefold increase in coal use.

COAL

Japan's coal strategy, as examined here by Roger W. Gale, has been under review for nearly one year (the first overall review in five years), as Japanese officials examine the relative merits of significant increases in steam coal imports for new electric power and industrial coal-fired facilities. Coal usage in Japan expanded until 1967, when environmental regulations, the high cost of domestic coal production, and the ample supply of inexpensive oil dampened prospects for major increases in coal use. Japan is the world's largest coal importer; its principal suppliers in 1979 were Australia, the United States, and Canada.

Japan's present coal strategy is based upon three pillars:

1. Continued support for a domestic coal production of 15–20 million tons per year.
2. A dramatic increase in coal imports.
3. The promotion of coal gasification and liquefaction technology.

The primary Japanese considerations for coal, as for oil, are diversification of supply and reliable long-term supply commitments. Coal imports provide over 10 percent of Japan's energy consumption. The government anticipates that imports in 1985 will be almost double the present level, providing 14 percent of energy consumption. Increased imports are necessary to supply the additional coal-fired electric plants under construction or planned, and, to a lesser degree, for other industrial uses. However, environmental concerns and the need to develop coal-handling facilities and storage space are likely to add significantly to Japan's electric power generating costs, already among the highest in the world.

LIQUEFIED NATURAL GAS

LNG imports currently represent about 4.5 percent of Japan's energy consumption, and are projected to reach 7 percent of energy consumption by 1985. Japan imported almost 16 million metric tons of liquefied natural gas in 1979, a figure that accounts for 51 percent of world LNG trade (approximately 1.5 percent of world natural gas consumption). Official Japanese projections for increases in LNG imports are comparable to nuclear power development estimates for the same periods. The attainment of these objectives will depend on the availability of government subsidies for additional infrastructure: the construction of liquefaction bases, transportation and distribution systems, and LNG tankers.

Government plans call for further LNG utilization in the generation of electricity and industrial heat. Three-quarters of the LNG now imported is utilized by the major urban electric power companies, largely because of the strict pollution controls they must conform with. Indonesia (7.5 million tons), Brunei (5.1 million tons), Abu Dhabi (2.0 million tons), and Alaska (960,000 tons) have been Japan's major suppliers, but a dozen or so projects now under way in Australia, Malaysia, Qatar, and Siberia could supply an additional 40 million tons in the coming years.

Japan is anxious to exploit the world LNG potential for supply, and has already taken a technological leap in in-ground LNG storage tank construction. It is also moving into cold energy utilization research.

NUCLEAR POWER

The domestic and foreign components of Japan's nuclear energy program are examined by Richard P. Suttmeier. As he points out, the plan for Japan's nuclear energy capacity has frequently been revised downward, thanks to environmental and domestic political constraints. The Japanese themselves are uncertain about the future of nuclear energy. Public opinion surveys give a mixed picture: nearly half of the people surveyed during the last decade think nuclear power will be the principal energy source of the future. Still, an equal number are worried about nuclear safety. An Atomic Energy White Paper released in December 1980 by the Science and Technology Agency (STA) pointed out that the major obstacle to building nuclear power plants was fear by local residents about the safety precautions taken at the facilities.

Nevertheless, nuclear power generation in 1979 was 8 percent above the level in 1978, representing 11 percent of electricity generation. Japanese officials expect that nuclear power will provide 19–20 percent of electricity generation in 1985. To achieve this goal, Japan would have to double its present capacity by 1985 (from 15 to 30 million kilowatts). It is unlikely that additional capacity under construction or authorized will allow Japan to meet this goal.

High-Cost Energy and Japan's International Economic Strategy*

Peter A. Petri

INTRODUCTION

By 1978, only five years after the oil crisis of 1973, Japan's foreign trade was in substantial surplus, and its growth and productivity increase led the industrialized world. Oil prices then doubled in 1979, and while Japanese growth has slowed somewhat, it is now clear that Japan will also adjust to this crisis at least as well as other, more self-sufficient economies. What are the main elements of Japan's success in this era of sharply higher energy costs? Are there limits to Japan's capacity to adjust to perhaps still higher prices in the future? These are some of the questions that will be analyzed here in the context of Japan's international economic strategy. Like the other contributions in this volume, we shall be concerned with policies and adjustment mechanisms that emerged in the past decade, or may emerge in the near future. But while the other chapters deal primarily with the acquisition, production, and consumption of energy, this chapter addresses Japan's capacity to finance its growing energy trade. A key assumption of this analysis—more fully documented in the chapters by Morse and Suttmeier—is that Japan will continue to depend almost entirely on foreign energy in the foreseeable future. Thus, Japan's prosperity will be closely tied to the success of its international trade and finance.

Japan's physical energy vulnerability is well known. But its economic vulnerability to oil shocks extends beyond its direct dependence on

*The author is grateful to Herbert Goodman, Eleanor Hadley, and Edward Lincoln for their constructive comments on previous drafts.

imported energy. As the world's second largest exporter of manufactured goods, Japan is particularly exposed to the global slowdowns that seem to be inevitably associated with increases in energy costs. Furthermore, until very recently, Japan's relatively isolated capital markets have not appeared to participate fully in the investment-oriented recycling of oil revenues. This has meant that adjustment on current account was far more urgently required in Japan than, say, in the United States or some of the major capital centers of Europe.

But adversity is the traditional handmaiden of Japanese economic success. From the viewpoint of its external accounts, the Japanese economy is extremely resilient; its companies diligently track and exploit developments abroad, and its policies, if anything, tend to be overly responsive to the requirements of the external sector.[1] External adaptation—recognition of new opportunities, competitive pricing, and rapid changes in patterns of trade and finance—is, of course, vitally important in a period of economic change. A world with new technological and product requirements thus offers an ideal competitive context for Japan, and promises particularly strong returns on its current technological investments in energy production, energy conservation, information processing, and communications.

Still, a world of scarce energy poses major risks. Japan is adapting to these risks, partly by design and partly through fortunate trends in its economic structure, by diversifying its external economic relationships. An active policy of diversification has been pursued most visibly in the area of oil diplomacy, but rather more successful and important examples of diversification include the emergence of new export industries and the establishment of trade and financial links with developing countries.[2] The outstanding issue, then, is not the character of Japan's long-run international strategy, but rather the speed and scope of its progress in diversification.[3]

It is evident that in some dimensions diversification has been carried just about as far as global political and economic realities permit. Further movements in new directions now often come at the expense of other

---

[1] Gardner Ackley and Hiromitsu Ishi, "Fiscal, Monetary and Related Policies," in *Asia's New Giant*, ed. Hugh Patrick and Henry Rosovsky (Washington, D.C.: Brookings Institution, 1976).

[2] This theme appears in various official documents, including MITI's "Vision for the 1980s," excerpted in *Focus Japan*, April 1980, and in private position papers like Keidanren's "The Japanese Economy: Its Present Phase and Medium-Term Tasks."

[3] While diversification has been practiced at several junctures in Japanese history, it seems to have become official policy in the current period with a MITI paper on the subject in 1971. See Masataka Kosaka, "The International Economic Policy of Japan," in *The Foreign Policy of Modern Japan*, ed. Robert A. Scalapino (Berkeley and Los Angeles: University of California Press, 1977).

valuable opportunities. One example of such trade-offs is the curious but politically important competition for Japanese capital among China, ASEAN, Mexico, the United States, and even the Soviet Union. Japan is also finding it harder to expand exports without accepting additional non-energy imports. And Japanese international economic policy must account ever more carefully for the conflicting political demands of diverse trading partners.

But certain important techniques for coping with future oil problems have not yet been pushed to practical limits. The largest producers of oil will increasingly try to convert current oil sales into future streams of income. This implies a strong emphasis on investment—in their home economies if absorption limits permit, but abroad if necessary. The Japanese economy stands to benefit from both types of investment. Its capital goods and plant exports have already captured a large share of world markets, and, for reasons discussed below, may perform even better if energy prices rise. In addition, sales of Japanese domestic assets and/or general obligations provide a new and relatively underutilized adjustment option. Thus, while Japan's external prospects are limited in some dimensions, they appear to be strong enough in others to survive even highly unfavorable developments in the world energy situation.

Japan's international energy strategy is examined here largely in the context of growing global scarcity. While sharply higher oil prices do not seem imminent at the time of this writing, it is likely that upward price pressures will again intensify within the next five to ten years. By analyzing such a "stressed" energy environment, we can gain a better perspective on Japan's adjustment capacity. Section I of this chapter examines, in rough quantitative terms, what a hypothetical global oil shortage would mean for Japan's external accounts. Section II reviews some practical dimensions of Japan's external adjustment to energy risk. The limits of diversification and the implications of the remaining risk are explored in the context of actual policies. Section III looks at some possible, but improbable, departures from the mainline strategy. Some conclusions are drawn in Section IV.

THE ARITHMETIC OF ENERGY SCARCITY

How large a financial burden would be imposed on Japan by moderate and extreme future energy scarcities? How would these burdens compare with the likely scale of Japanese international transactions in 1985? Obviously, these questions cannot be answered precisely, but some basic quantification is essential for defining the scope of the adjustment problem.

We examine two scenarios: $33/barrel oil and $66/barrel oil in 1985 (in real terms, using 1980 prices). The lower end of this range is the price prevailing in 1981. Despite the fact that oil prices were under considerable downward pressure in 1981, the maintenance of a constant real price to 1985 will require major continuing efforts in conservation, exploration, and/or the production of alternative fuels. A comprehensive analysis of the world oil market is outside the scope of this paper, but the low-price scenario appears to be consistent with global projections that are based on an OPEC export volume of about 26 million barrels per day (mmbd).[4]

The upper price of $66 is rather unlikely, since it is well above the currently estimated cost of many types of synthetics.[5] A price this high would not occur unless OPEC sharply reduced supplies—a scenario consistent with either the deterioration of the political climate in the Middle East or instability in some key supplying country. Assuming that the price elasticity for OPEC oil is about 0.2 (a value at the conservatively low end of the range of current estimates), the $66 price implies OPEC supplies of 20.5 mmbd. (As calculated later in this chapter, the Japanese import levels corresponding to the $33 and $66 extremes are 6.5 and 5.3 mmbd, respectively.) The important role of synthetics and substitutes at the $66 price will be raised again in Section II, below.

In both the low- and high-price scenarios, the 1985 price is treated as relatively permanent, and is assumed to be reached by gradual changes from current price levels. Admittedly, Japan faces not only the risk of such gradually increasing scarcity, but also the risk of physical interruptions in supply. For the U.S. economy, for example, a one-year, 3.5 mmbd import interruption has been estimated to cause a 6.6 percent decline in output, a 2.1 percent increase in unemployment, and a 20 percent increase in the inflation rate.[6] The effects on the Japanese economy are likely to be at least as severe; although, with extreme conservation and fuel-switching, Japan's relatively large oil reserves (now 105 days, with plans for 125 days) could be stretched over eighteen months or more in the event of a similar 33 percent supply cut. This period is probably long enough to reestablish

---

[4] Two recent projections include: U.S. Central Intelligence Agency, *The World Oil Market in the Years Ahead* (Washington, D.C.: Government Printing Office, August 1979); and Congressional Budget Office (CBO), *The World Oil Market in the 1980s: Implications for the United States* (Washington, D.C.: Government Printing Office, May 1980). The CBO report (p. 34) estimates OPEC exports in 1985 at 25.8 mmbd, given a price of $34 (in 1979 dollars). The CBO estimate for Japan included in these projections is exactly equal to our 6.5 mmbd assumption under low prices.

[5] Estimates of the cost of synthetics from coal, expressed in 1980 prices, range from $15 to $25 per barrel of oil equivalent. See U.S. Congress, Committee on Science and Technology, *Energy Facts: II* (Washington, D.C.: Government Printing Office, August 1975).

[6] Congressional Budget Office, *The Economic Impact of Oil Import Reductions* (Washington, D.C.: Government Printing Office, December 1978), and references in CBO, *World Oil Market*, to a new study, *Strategic Petroleum Reserve: An Analysis*, forthcoming.

some of the lost supply and/or to accelerate emergency conversion to coal. Since this study mainly addresses issues in international economic strategy, it cannot deal in depth with short-term supply interruptions. The ability to withstand such crises depends on internal organizational and social structure, and on timely policies that are often quite different from those required to adjust to permanent energy scarcity.

A convenient point of departure in our analysis is a recent study of U.S.-Japan trade in 1985 by Ron Napier and myself.[7] While this study assumed a more benign energy environment than seems justified today, its "high oil price" scenario, adjusted for the lower Japanese and foreign growth rates that now seem probable, provides a satisfactory "low oil price" alternative for this chapter. These adjusted results are reported in the second column of Table 1, next to comparable data for 1977. The third and fourth columns impose additional, simple adjustments to account for the effects of $66 oil. The details of these adjustments are described in the Appendix; essentially, each type of trade flow is separately modified on the basis of a handful of assumptions about (1) the effect of higher energy prices on Japanese growth, the growth of OPEC imports, and the growth of Japan's trade partners, and (2) the elasticities of Japanese exports and imports with respect to prices and growth rates in Japan and abroad. The results, in billions of 1977 dollars, can be roughly converted to real 1980 dollars by multiplying by 1.25.

The $33 scenario (the $27 amount shown in Table 1 is in 1977 dollars) assumes that Japanese net investment abroad will continue at a $10 billion rate. By 1985, about $2 billion of the current account surplus needed to finance this investment would come from net foreign investment income (a figure arrived at by calculating returns on cumulated past investments), leaving $8 billion to be financed by a surplus in trade and other invisibles. This could be achieved even while the yen appreciates 3 percent relative to its 1977 level vis-à-vis a market basket of currencies. Naturally, the yen would appreciate still further if intense foreign investment in Japan reduces the country's net external investment below the $10 billion level. The projected long-term strength of the Japanese trade account is attributed in our 1979 study to Japan's high and rising market shares in the strongest global markets, in terms of geographical composition (e.g., large market shares in East Asia) as well as product mix (e.g., investment and technology-oriented exports). In March 1980, the yen stood at 312/SDR (special drawing right), representing a 3 percent depreciation relative to its 1977 position, and has appreciated somewhat since. Stable yen exchange rates, therefore, are roughly consistent with $33 oil in 1985, assuming no divergence of future Japanese and average foreign inflation rates.

---

[7] Ron W. Napier and Peter A. Petri, "U.S.-Japan Trade Conflict: The Prospects Ahead," Report to the Department of State, October 1979.

Table 1

EFFECTS OF ALTERNATIVE OIL PRICE
ADJUSTMENT SCENARIOS
(values in billions of 1977 dollars)

	1977 Base Data	Low Oil Prices	1985 Alternatives	
			High Oil Prices	
			Capital Flow Adjustment	Depreciation Adjustment
Assumptions				
Oil Price	13.50	27.0	54.00	54.00
Japanese GNP	100	143	133	133
World GNP	100	128	121	121
Results				
Yen/SDR	100	103	103	89
Exports to OPEC	$12 billion	30	44	51
Other Exports	72	111	105	122
Oil Imports	−25	−65	−105	−105
Other Imports	−40	−54	−56	−48
Invisibles	−8	−14	−13	−11
Capital Outflows less Capital Income	11	8	−25	8

SOURCE: Simulation runs of U.S.-Japan trade model.

With adjustments for $66 oil and for the resulting drop in global economic activity (assumed to be 5 percent abroad and 7 percent in Japan below the $33 scenario level in 1985), a roughly constant yen exchange rate would require net capital inflows of $25 billion (column 3). Alternately, a 14 percent depreciation to 89 percent of the 1977 level could reestablish the $8 billion surplus on trade and invisibles (column 4). Many of the parameters and assumptions of this simple exercise were varied in sensitivity tests; it was difficult, with plausible parameters, to generate financing requirements of over $40 billion or a competitive depreciation requirement above 25 percent.

While these figures represent substantial changes, they are within the range of recent experience: the yen appreciated from 340/SDR at the end of 1976 to 240/SDR in 1978 (up 42 percent), and then depreciated to 312/SDR in early 1980 (down 23 percent). Its movements relative to the dollar have been even sharper. To put the potential asset transfers in perspective, by 1985 Japan's annual investment will be about $250 billion, and its overall capital stock will approach $3,000 billion. On the supply side, the additional annual revenues obtained by OPEC in the event of $66 (instead of $33) oil would amount to $150 billion (these values, except for the price of oil, are in 1977 dollars).

The low- and high-price scenarios assume oil imports of 6.5 mmbd and 5.3 mmbd, respectively. Is such a large drop consistent with a "business as usual" view of external adjustment; and if so, how might it be implemented? In 1985, Japan is projected to consume 10.2 mmbd of energy in oil equivalent.[8] The 7 percent lower output levels hypothesized under $66 oil would automatically reduce these requirements by about 0.7 mmbd. A large part of this, say 0.6 mmbd, would be translated into reduced oil import demand, leaving another 0.6 mmbd to be filled by conservation and fuel substitution. To put this effort in perspective, consider a partial acceleration of MITI's long-term energy program that would compress the more easily implemented aspects of the ten-year plan into the coming five-year period. Specifically, MITI's plan would cut the energy/GNP ratio by an additional 3 percent between 1985 and 1990; if it could be implemented already by 1985, it would yield annual savings of about 0.3 mmbd. Conversion from oil to coal and gas planned for the 1985–1990 period would reduce 1990 oil requirements by 7 percent; if implemented by 1985, it would yield oil savings of 0.5 mmbd. It seems possible, then, to reduce oil imports substantially by accelerating programs which make relatively limited demands on capital, planning time, and new technology.

Of course, such a rough analysis is subject to many unstated assumptions and especially presumes effective internal policies. In the case of an exchange-oriented adjustment policy, for example, Japanese macroeconomic policies would have to engineer a correspondingly large reduction in domestic real consumption and facilitate the conversion of this capacity to export-oriented industries. If this cannot be accomplished smoothly, and serious political or economic problems ensue, it might be impossible for Japan to compete as effectively as trends suggest and as this analysis assumes. A severe deceleration in Japanese productivity and technological leadership would not only endanger the export assumptions of this exercise, but would also make Japanese assets less attractive to foreign investors. Many of these questions cannot be handled adequately within this chapter.

The results do not, however, indicate an export increase large enough to necessarily trigger global protectionism. (Protectionism in the U.S. will be considered in somewhat more detail in Section III, below.) Even if the adjustment to $66 oil is based entirely on depreciation, Japan's

---

[8] The following quantitative estimates are based on MITI's long-term energy plan, announced in the fall of 1979, as reported in *Focus Japan*, March 1980, and by Data Resources, Inc., *Japanese Economic Review*, September 19, 1979.

exports to non-OPEC countries would be just 16 percent higher than in a constant-yen world; overall, the SDR value of these exports would have to grow at a 7.5 percent rate over the 1977–1985 period. This expansion will be supported in part by strong global demand for fuel-efficient capital goods and energy-saving technologies. From the perspective of international and energy aggregates, then, $66 oil implies a massive but not unprecedented adjustment task.

ADJUSTMENT STRATEGIES

Owing to the active international presence of Japan's powerful ministries and the currently popular image of Japan as a tightly planned enterprise, it is natural, but inaccurate, to attribute Japanese economic results directly to national policy. Through a variety of incentives and controls, government policy can and does affect the direction of economic change, but the ultimate engine of adjustment is private industry. Since much of this chapter, too, will be preoccupied with government policy, it is important to start by reviewing the basic, structural trends of the private economy.

Background to Policy

Historically, the Japanese economy has progressed smoothly and rapidly across successive stages of comparative advantage: from labor-intensive products to heavy industry to advanced technologies.[9] Less often recognized is the fact that Japan has become diversified in this process. In the late 1960s, Japan's exports were still concentrated in a few important basic industries; today they encompass a much wider range of intermediate, consumer, and capital goods. Not only is Japan now better equipped to weather changes in the mix of global demand, but it is also able to develop and export production technologies for many types of industries.

The current thrust of the economy is in advanced technology. The transition to these sectors began well before the energy crisis of 1973, and is based on Japan's highly skilled labor force. The demand for these "knowledge-intensive" industries is relatively insensitive to energy price changes, and is in some cases enhanced by the ability of technological products to control or substitute for the use of energy. While Japanese know-how is still not at the forefront in some important areas (e.g., computing software and large-scale integrated circuits), it is advancing rapidly: Fujitsu has recently surpassed IBM in sales to the Japanese market, and the 48 percent annual growth of computer exports during the

---

[9] The rapidity of this change is documented by Gary R. Saxonhouse, "Industrial Restructuring in Japan," *Japanese Studies*, forthcoming, and by U.S. General Accounting Office, *U.S.-Japan Trade: Issues and Problems* (Washington, D.C.: Government Printing Office, September 1979).

1974–1978 period has led to a nearly balanced trade position in this industry.[10]

Japanese investment in technology has been substantial (nearly $20 billion are spent annually on research),[11] but this alone does not explain the impressive technical and productivity gains. More important, perhaps, is the way research is used: it is sharply focused on practical applications in areas like steel or automobiles, and it is often shared through industry research associations. Also, in a fast-growing economy, much research-like learning takes place without being counted as research. But also in the intermediate term, Japan has adapted more successfully to the era of high energy prices than most other industrialized countries. As Table 2 shows, the recent Japanese record is exceptionally strong on productivity progress, export growth, inflation, and energy conservation.

Against this positive background, Japan has addressed the issue of energy risk in several interdependent ways. The resulting collage of international adjustment policies is here reviewed in broader than usual terms, including policies that are aimed not only at (1) assuring adequate energy supplies, but also at (2) financing supply through strong exports and limited non-energy imports, and (3) promoting capital inflows. These three categories are analytically convenient, but do not describe separate, competitive approaches; the presence of trade-offs across different objectives is an essential feature of Japan's international policy dilemma. But while Japan is facing difficult trade-offs in implementing its strategy abroad, it has found it easier than other countries to establish consensus at home. The absence of a significant domestic energy sector, while increasing the need for successful adjustment, seems to have made it easier to establish policies on energy conservation, pricing, and substitution than has been the case in countries with more diverse economic interests.

Assuring Energy Supply

In 1973, most of Japan's oil came from the Middle East through the major international oil companies.[12] Steps have been taken since then to diversify the source of oil across countries, and to assume national control of supplies by so-called "direct" and "government-to-government" deals. Today, more than half of Japan's oil comes through such arrangements, a result due in part to the "Exxon Shock," the cutback of Seven Sisters supplies to Japanese independent refiners following the Iranian revolution.

While the elimination of the "middleman" has been relatively easy,

---

[10] U.S. General Accounting Office, *U.S.-Japan Trade*.

[11] "Industrial Review of Japan," *Japan Economic Journal*, March 1980 (special issue).

[12] Yoshi Tsurumi, "Japan," in *The Oil Crisis*, by Raymond Vernon (New York: W. W. Norton, 1976).

Table 2

COMPARATIVE INDICATORS OF ECONOMIC PERFORMANCE
(*percent change per annum*)

Indicator	Period	Japan	Canada	France	Germany	Italy	U.K.	U.S.
Gross National	1969–73	9.1	5.9	5.5	4.5	4.1	3.7	3.5
Product	1973–75	0.4	2.4	1.8	−0.8	0.3	−1.7	−1.3
	1975–78	5.8	3.8	4.0	3.7	3.5	2.8	5.2
Productivity	1969–73	8.8	5.0	5.4	4.3	3.4	2.3	1.7
(manufactur-	1973–75	−4.7	0.2	−2.0	0.4	−4.6	−4.4	−4.8
ing)	1975–78	9.2	4.4	4.7	5.5	4.3	3.0	3.4
Prices (indus-	1969–73	4.7	5.9	7.1	4.6	7.9	7.2	4.4
trial goods	1973–75	16.3	15.1	10.4	9.0	23.6	22.4	16.7
	1975–78	1.4	7.4	5.7	2.6	16.1	15.3	6.9
Energy/GNP	1969–74	−0.2	−0.2	−1.1	−0.3	0.4	−1.8	−0.8
Ratio	1974–78	−3.5	−1.7	−2.4	−1.2	0.2	−1.5	−2.5
Exchange Rate	1969–73	1.4	−2.9	−0.5	3.1	−4.0	−5.6	−4.9
(relative to	1973–75	−2.8	0.4	3.9	3.0	−4.5	−5.6	1.7
SDR)	1975–78	10.7	−9.2	−1.3	8.1	−10.6	−3.4	−3.6
Exports (dollar	1969–73	24.0	16.6	24.7	23.7	17.4	15.2	17.0
value)	1973–75	21.5	13.7	20.3	15.5	25.2	19.8	22.8
	1975–78	20.8	12.0	14.4	16.5	17.3	17.2	10.1

SOURCES: International Monetary Fund, *International Financial Statistics*; and various energy publications of the United Nations.

geographical diversification has proved difficult and costly. The case of Iran illustrates some of the frustrations involved. In 1977, Japan imported nearly 1.0 mmbd of oil from Iran, partly as a result of a patiently built bilateral relationship; after the revolution, Japan obtained no more than half this supply, despite aggressive spot market purchases by private companies. Walking a tightrope between the U.S. and Iranian governments, the Japanese government sought, with mixed success, to maintain the lowest possible profile, slowing, stopping, and then promising to restart construction on the large Bandar Khomeini petrochemical complex, and developing ingenious restrictions on Iranian trade and finance designed for minimum impact. This intricate maneuvering is described fully in Caldwell's chapter; its end product is a shaky commitment for 0.5 mmbd of future Iranian oil. In the meantime, Japan labors under continuing pressure to accept compromises on the building and running of the Iranian complex.

China and Mexico are two new potential suppliers of energy. Indicative of the importance attached to these sources is Prime Minister Ohira's personal visit to Mexico to negotiate for 0.3 mmbd of oil. But Mexico's price is high. In part it is political: for example, Mr. Ohira was criticized during his visit for having come to Mexico after visiting the U.S., and for apparently discussing with the U.S. the trading of Mexican for Middle Eastern oil.[13] In part it is economic: Mexico wants soft loans for a steel mill, railroads, and ports. Similar problems arose in negotiations with China, which at one time prepared a $5.5 billion list of development projects (equivalent to half of annual Japanese investments abroad) to be financed on concessionary terms (one recent project has been financed at 3 percent interest for thirty years).[14] Japan agreed to much less, and commitments for Chinese oil were limited to 0.8 mmbd by 1985. These commitments are generally regarded as too optimistic, given Chinese production possibilities, and China has already cut back exports below the much smaller intermediate targets set for 1980 and 1981.[15] Even so, the Indonesians have expressed concern over the Chinese negotiations; Chinese crude is heavy, like Indonesian oil, and might strain the limited capacity of appropriate refineries. Indonesia is also concerned about losing future Japanese loans, such as a recent 18-year, 2.5 percent loan for a urea plant.

This treacherous "fuel diplomacy" has absorbed an inordinate share of the government's attention in recent years,[16] with little visible impact on the ultimate sourcing of Japanese imports. In 1960, 80 percent of Japanese oil came from the Middle East; in 1979, 76 percent (see Figure 1). With optimistic assumptions about Mexican and Chinese oil, the Middle Eastern share might be pushed slightly below 70 percent by 1985. And the cost of the new sources is high, since concessionary loans are required for even limited imports from developing countries. To put the best face on the matter, Japan now regards these agreements as part of an ambitious aid effort—a plan for quadrupling Official Development Assistance between 1978 and 1985. These loans do have positive implications for Japanese exports, but, on the whole, supplier diversification is an expensive and fundamentally limited policy.

Diversification across types of fuel imports is more promising. Japan is a leading importer of both petroleum and natural gas, and world gas

---

[13] U.S.-Japan Trade Council, *Japan Insight*, May 16, 1980.

[14] Ibid., May 2, 1980.

[15] See Herbert I. Goodman, *Japan and the World Energy Problem*, Occasional Paper, Northeast Asia–United States Forum on International Policy, Stanford University, July 1980; and "Japan-China Economic Ties Become Seriously Strained," *Japan Economic Journal*, February 10, 1981.

[16] Donald W. Klein, "Japan 1979: The Second Oil Crisis," *Asian Survey*, 20:1 (January 1980).

FIGURE 1

Geographic Distribution of Japan's Oil Imports

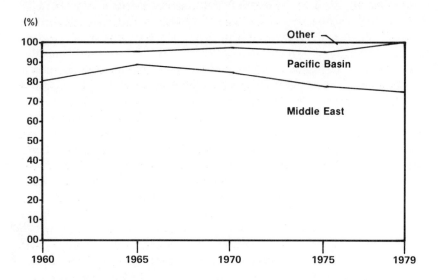

reserves appear to be nearly as high as oil reserves. Because of large infrastructure requirements, however, this option is not likely to make a large impact by 1985. Coal is available from China (the investments mentioned above were made to facilitate coal exports), Australia, Canada, and the United States. Three major coal receiving and processing centers are being developed in Japan, and the scope for coal/oil substitution is significant: nearly half of Japan's electricity generating capacity still operates with oil. As already argued, coal and gas conversion would have to play significant roles in absorbing the oil import difference between the low and high oil price scenarios.

Financing Energy with Trade

The Japanese have historically viewed trade surpluses as insurance against external risk. With imports consisting mainly of raw materials, Japanese import price elasticities are low, and import costs are correspondingly sensitive to price changes abroad. While the recurrent Japanese trade surpluses cannot be traced to any one cause or policy, it is true that quasi-mercantilist policies can be rigorously justified for a severely import-dependent economy. Large foreign exchange reserves, like the full treasuries of mercantilist days, provide a contingency fund for economic or political uncertainty.[17] In fact, the big Japanese trade surpluses of 1978 disappeared quickly after the doubling of oil prices in 1979. Enhanced by the appreciation of the yen, the year-to-year change in the trade balance amounted to about 25 percent of Japanese dollar exports, roughly the relative impact predicted for 1985 under $66 oil. A positive trade account and a less-negative service account thus remain central goals of Japanese policy.

How might the trade account be "insured" against uncertainty about the price of oil? Increased energy risk could be managed in part by shifting exports to products and partners that would remain strong in an energy-scarce environment. Partly because of the nature of its comparative advantage, partly by chance, and partly by policy, Japanese exports were well positioned during the energy crisis of the 1970s. Given its orientation to developing countries and capital goods, Japanese trade benefited greatly from an explosion of investment activity in oil-exporting countries and in East Asia. Will the leading imports of 1985 again concentrate in areas of Japanese strength?

The prospects for Japanese exports under renewed energy scarcity are mixed. To begin with, a third oil crisis is unlikely to bring trade growth paralleling that of the mid-1970s. Some of the most important oil exporters are now near perceived absorption limits; indeed, these very perceptions are usually cited as a reason for potential oil production cutbacks in the future.[18] In addition, many of the rapidly growing developing countries that accounted for a large part of Japan's export success in the 1970s (exports to Korea, for example, grew at an annual rate of 27 percent during 1973–1978) have since accumulated debts large enough to cause international banking concern. The Japanese Ministry of Finance is now itself trying to restrict Japanese loans to developing countries.[19] Since many of these economies are also resource poor, their prospects under still higher oil prices are doubtful.

At the same time, competition will be stiff for the markets of new oil-exporters like China and Mexico, and of countries like Iran, whose development potential remains high. Nothing stirs the imagination quite like the idea of Japanese television sets being used as worker incentives in China, but Chinese policies have changed dramatically toward extreme caution. The trade with Mexico and China does represent real diversifi-

---

[17] For recent related work, see H. O. Schmitt, "Mercantilism: A Modern Argument," *The Manchester School*, 47 (June 1979), 93–111; and John Z. Drabicki and Akira Takayama, "The Classical International Monetary Mechanism and Mercantilism," mimeographed, Purdue University.

[18] CIA, *World Oil Market*.

[19] U.S.-Japan Trade Council, *Japan Insight*, June 13, 1980. See also "A Collapse That Hits Korean Banks Hardest," *Business Week*, May 7, 1979.

cation; it should correlate positively with the price of oil. But this trade now accounts for less than 5 percent of Japanese exports. Thus, geographical diversification is not, on the whole, as promising a strategy for the future as it was for the past.

But trade would not be uniformly stagnant in the event of higher energy prices. Substantial price increases are likely to trigger vast global interest in energy-conserving and oil-substituting technologies, including (1) nuclear power, (2) commercial-scale production of synthetics such as coal gas and liquids, (3) energy-efficient and oil-efficient transportation, including hybrid and electric automobiles, (4) fuel-efficient industrial plants, and (5) modern technology as a substitute for energy (e.g., communications for transportation, biological technology for fertilizer, microcomputer control of energy use, etc.).

Japan is active in all of these fields. As Samuels and Suttmeier report, Japan has an ambitious program to triple nuclear electric generation capacity by 1990, to establish a second fuel recycling plant, to build a uranium enrichment plant with a new, centrifugal technology, and to construct a commercial fast-breeder reactor. Since current U.S. commitments to provide nuclear fuel are judged to be adequate for at least a decade, the Japanese objective is clearly to establish technological parity along the entire fuel cycle. Even if Japan does not fully meet the ambitious nuclear targets that MITI has established, the program is still remarkable in light of the strong public opposition to nuclear power in Japan.

Efforts are also under way in other substitute fuels for oil: a coal liquefaction plant is being built in Australia, Japan is a partner in another project in West Virginia, and $1 billion have been committed to solar and geothermal research.[20] While some observers have noted that Japanese expenditures on these production research activities represent a smaller percentage of GNP than in countries like the U.S., the level of spending is surprisingly large for a country with no significant coal or shale deposits of its own. Moreover, major research spending increases are budgeted for the future.[21]

Mostly through private initiative, Japan has also mounted an impressive effort to conserve energy in industrial applications. Exceptional gains have been reported in the fuel efficiency of steel plants, and waste-heat recovery systems have been designed for a variety of applications. A significant development in the area of consumer products is a hybrid automobile (with a high-efficiency gasoline engine supplemented by electric power), which will be commercially available in the mid-1980s.[22]

---

[20] Data Resources, Inc., *Japanese Economic Review*, November 24, 1979.

[21] See the chapter by Samuels, below; and also "Greater R&D Outlay Is Planned," *Japan Economic Journal*, March 31, 1981.

[22] Paul Aron, "Japanese Export and Overseas Investment Strategies," in *U.S.-Japan Economic Relations in the 1980s*, U.S.-Japan Trade Council, October 1979.

These and other similar thrusts will make Japanese products and process technologies highly competitive in a third energy crisis, particularly if the yen were to depreciate under balance of payments pressure.

The heavy current investment in conservation-oriented technologies and products could prove less advantageous if the high-price scenario does not materialize—for example, because of accelerated fuel switching and conservation in the United States. But, in general, the more that is accomplished abroad in saving energy, the lower is the probability of higher oil prices, and the greater is Japan's potential to expand domestically without serious external constraints. The cost of energy-oriented research is thus not merely an investment but also a form of insurance.

The other side of energy financing is the control of non-energy imports. Here dramatic changes are not possible: Japan is unlikely to retrace its former steady progress toward import liberalization, and it is also unlikely to dismantle the restrictions that remain. The direct, formal controls which restricted manufactured imports in the 1950s and 1960s have now been largely eliminated. Significant concessions have been made in the multilateral trade negotiations (MTN) and bilaterally to the U.S.; and for most manufactured products, Japanese rates of protection are now no higher than those in other industrial countries.[23] To be sure, some of the imports admitted in this process, particularly the labor-intensive manufactures from East Asia, are relatively "safe," in the sense that they tend to collapse—much like big Japanese firms' purchases from domestic subcontractors—during times of adversity, such as 1974–1975.[24]

It is also true that Japan continues to control access to some critical agricultural and technological markets. Domestic agricultural production costs are several times higher than world prices; improbably, Japan is now an exporter of rice. Agricultural protection is due primarily to the disproportionate power of rural voters in the electoral process, and especially in the base of the ruling Liberal-Democratic Party.[25] But agricultural protection also helps to reserve foreign exchange for purchases of essential raw materials. Given perceived constraints on overall exports, and the irreversible specialization effects of free agricultural trade, Japanese policymakers would probably not rush to open agricultural markets even if the politics of the issue were neutral. Further concessions on agricultural

[23] Alan V. Deardorff and Robert M. Stern, "An Economic Analysis of the Effects of the Tokyo Round of Multilateral Trade Negotiations on the U.S. and Other Major Industrialized Countries," U.S. Senate, Committee on Finance (Washington, D.C.: Government Printing Office, June 1979).

[24] Japanese imports from East Asia fell much more sharply than imports from other countries, and formal controls were also instituted on silk textile imports during the 1974–1975 period.

[25] Philip H. Trezise with Yukio Suzuki, "Politics, Government and Economic Growth in Japan," in *Asia's New Giant*, ed. Patrick and Rosovsky.

protection are therefore especially unlikely in an environment of rising energy prices.

Aside from agricultural policy, the main trade barriers that remain involve informal or institutional restrictions—and these cannot be dismantled without wholehearted Japanese cooperation. The cooperative relations between Japanese business and government—e.g., "single tendering" of key contracts to a handful of large firms—and between firms and individuals in complex business and social networks make it hard to "legislate" access to the Japanese market. Complete acceptance of foreign competitors could come in time, but only when Japanese society feels confident of its international environment. In a sense, Japanese trade barriers have now been reduced to the subset most subject to informal manipulation, and these barriers will certainly not be relaxed in adversity.

Promoting the Sale of Assets

Japanese policy has traditionally restricted inward investment, partly to avoid foreign domination of domestic markets, and partly to encourage the flow of technology to domestic producers. Portfolio investment, in turn, has been unattractive because of the limited range of instruments available to foreigners, and because of the low interest rate policy pursued by the government.[26] These issues and controls are becoming irrelevant with the passage of time, and the sale of assets and obligations to oil producers and other foreigners now emerges as a promising policy tool. Japan's recent record on political stability, inflation control, and productivity growth clearly makes such investments attractive by global standards, especially in the not-unlikely event that oil transactions shift away from the dollar.

The Japanese government has begun to actively promote the "internationalization" of the yen through a wide range of measures that make Japanese credit markets more accessible to foreign investors. Some of these measures now permit (1) Japanese companies to issue yen-denominated bonds in foreign markets, (2) Japanese companies to seek "impact" loans in Eurodollar markets, (3) foreign financial companies to participate in Japanese personal credit markets, and (4) foreign investors to buy short-term government bonds. According to some recent reports, foreign bond offerings by Japanese companies, other than financial and utility companies, were about 2.5 times as large as their domestic offerings during fiscal year 1980.[27] The overall effect of these developments is that Japanese capital markets are now beginning to attract a significant part

[26] Wilbur F. Monroe, *Japan: Financial Markets and the World Economy* (New York: Praeger, 1973). Also see Henry C. Wallich and Mable I. Wallich, "Banking and Finance," in *Asia's New Giant*, ed. Patrick and Rosovsky.

[27] "Foreigners' Investments in Bonds and Stocks Prove Extremely Brisk," *Japan Economic Journal*, February 17, 1981.

of the large, oil-related deposits that used to flow mainly into Euro-dollars and into U.S. and British securities. A reinforcing development, the beginnings of which can be traced to the large government financing needs of 1974 and 1975, is the growth of an active open market for government securities with internationally competitive interest rates.

Very recently, the major oil-surplus countries have also begun to place substantial financial resources in Japan. Although Japan had negotiated a $1 billion loan from Saudi Arabia as early as 1974, and Kuwait began substantial purchases of Japanese securities in 1979, it was not until 1980 that the flow of Arab investments became significant in relation to Japan's overall balance of payments.[28] The Ministry of Finance reported that foreign investment in Japanese bonds and stocks amounted to more than $11 billion in 1980; in early 1981, Japan was running an unusual surplus on long-term capital account.[29] There were also reports that the Saudi Arabian Monetary Authority had decided to place 15 percent of its international long-term portfolio into Japanese securities.[30]

The dilemma is that Japan is not only an attractive place for investment but also a major supplier of capital. If Japan finds it difficult, at times, to invest its own savings, how will it be able to accept still larger placements from abroad? In the absence of relevant historical experience, this question cannot be answered with confidence. Yet the environment of $66 oil will create urgent investment opportunities in energy conservation at the same time that it lowers both current and likely future incomes. Even if personal savings rates rise, as happened in 1974–1975, lower business savings and the greater financial requirements of the government could well shift Japanese capital markets from surplus to deficit.

SOME UNLIKELY POSSIBILITIES

Our discussion so far has focused on a mainline strategy, appropriate in the context of a stable pattern of international relationships. This section turns briefly to examples of discontinuous change. The tightly constrained character of the Japanese international economic strategy makes all of these scenarios unlikely, since each would require major qualitative changes in the whole pattern of Japan's international activity.

Japanese-Soviet Economic Rapprochement

The early days of high oil prices, before the blossoming of the potential China trade, held great promise for Japanese-Soviet trade. The Tyumen

[28] "The Japanese Economy Is Disturbed by Petrodollars," *Japan Quarterly*, 28:1 (January–March 1981).
[29] "Japanese Business Borrowings Abroad Surged to Record in Year Ended March 31," *Wall Street Journal*, May 12, 1981.
[30] "Saudi Eyes Japanese Stocks," *Japan Economic Journal*, March 24, 1981.

oil and gas fields in Siberia, in particular, offered an important new route to energy diversification. But the Russian price for Japanese cooperation then escalated in a complicated chain of events. The Japanese eventually sought U.S. involvement, partly to insure future delivery; and when this was not forthcoming, the project collapsed.[31] The incident left ill will on both sides, and the political climate between Japan and the Soviet Union has been deteriorating ever since.

The rationale for Japanese-Soviet cooperation still exists, and is likely to expand in proportion with the apparently increasing isolation of the Soviet Union. While the potential of the Siberian fields is still regarded as limited, the exploration and development of Siberia will become increasingly attractive as the Soviet Union itself encounters energy production constraints in the 1980s. The Soviets can thus be expected to show growing interest in Japanese technology, particularly while their access to U.S. know-how is limited. They have demonstrated a willingness to trade energy for technology and investment aid in negotiations with Western European countries, and, indeed, have threatened the Europeans with switching to Japanese suppliers if the negotiations should fail. Of course, cooperation with Japan would also serve the political objective of possibly weakening the emerging alliance between the U.S., China, and Japan.

The current level of mistrust, however, is high.[32] Since cooperation in energy development involves long lead times, there is little chance that deals will be made soon enough to affect the energy picture by 1985. More importantly, the Japanese will not wish to risk their far greater economic stakes in U.S. and Chinese markets by "tilting" toward the Soviet Union. While the U.S.-Chinese orientation itself has costs (e.g., it diminishes prospects for coal and oil agreements with Vietnam), cooperation with the Soviet Union will develop slowly, if at all, until U.S.-Soviet relations improve.

Collision with the U.S.

Since the mid-1950s, U.S. and Japanese policymakers have faced, and resolved, a number of serious bilateral conflicts. Hugh Patrick has attributed these conflicts to the "leading edge" character of Japanese exports in U.S. markets; the Japanese have been the first to exploit more basic changes in U.S. comparative advantage.[33] In our recent study of U.S.-Japan trade prospects,[34] we found evidence for a changing pattern. Since

---

[31] Gerald R. Curtis, "The Tyumen Oil Development Project and Japanese Foreign Policy Decision-Making," in *The Foreign Policy of Modern Japan*, ed. Robert A. Scalapino.

[32] Donald S. Zagoria, "The Soviet Quandary in Asia," *Foreign Affairs*, January 1978.

[33] Hugh Patrick, "United States–Japan Political Economy: Is the Partnership in Jeopardy?" Lecture at the University of Washington, February 20, 1979.

[34] Napier and Petri, "U.S.-Japan Trade Conflict."

the two economies are converging in their manufacturing profiles—both increasingly emphasize machinery and technology—future trade relations are likely to evolve along European lines; that is, along complementary, intra-industry specialization patterns. One example of this trend is the extensive cross-trade and cross-investment developing within the integrated circuit industry.[35]

Higher resource prices, however, imply greater Japanese exports to the U.S. partly because U.S. capital markets still attract a disproportionate share of financial recycling. (This means that the U.S. tends to settle a larger part of its added energy import bill on the capital account than do other countries.) Japanese exports to the U.S. tend to be more price-elastic than they are to other destinations, and thus would bear a disproportionate share of trade expansion in a high oil price scenario. Nevertheless, in the longer run, the U.S. trade is becoming less important for Japan: the share of Japanese exports destined for American markets fell from 31 percent in 1970 to 26 percent in 1978, and I project it at 20 percent in 1985. Moreover, the U.S. economy would have greater conservation and production opportunities than other countries in a third energy crisis, and it might be willing to expand imports in energy-conserving products such as solar devices and hybrid automobiles.

If U.S. protectionism becomes severe, some of the required adjustment would doubtless spill onto U.S.-Japanese competition in exports to third markets, and onto the capital account (asset sale and borrowing). Even if domestic U.S. markets are protected against Japanese imports, the U.S. trade account would eventually absorb some losses through imports from third countries or through lower exports. In the meantime, Japanese capital assets will become more attractive to investors abroad, and may attract some of the financial recycling originally destined for the U.S. (There are some possible terms of trade benefits to the U.S. from excluding Japanese imports, but these are not large compared to the potential losses from a mutual dismantling of trade.) Because of the increasing *political* importance of the partnership to both countries, and because limits on U.S. sales would not dramatically affect the scale of either the U.S. or the Japanese adjustment task, a serious collision is likely to be avoided.

A Military Road

Japan is under pressure to increase military efforts from both domestic (mainly business) and international sources. The increases currently discussed would raise expenditures from today's 0.9 percent of GNP to

---

[35] There are still conflicting opinions on the strains to come. For background, see Data Resources, Inc., *Japanese Economic Review*, November 24, 1979; U.S. General Accounting Office, *U.S.-Japan Trade;* and U.S.-Japan Trade Council, "U.S.-Japan Competition in Semiconductors, III," March 7, 1980.

not more than 1.9 percent, a level like Switzerland's. In the international economic context, these increased expenditures would affect both weapons imports and exports and would enhance Japanese weapons technology.

Despite a ban on exports of military goods, Japan may already have sold such goods (including ships, radar, and communications equipment) to Korea in the recent past.[36] The Japanese business association Keidanren has advocated some relaxation of MITI's controls on military exports.[37] The President of Kawasaki Heavy Industries puts it more bluntly: "What developing countries are currently in real need of are weapons and foodstuffs. . . . Japanese manufacturers should be allowed to accommodate such countries' needs as long as military equipment is for self defense."[38] Given the potential demand for weapons in a crisis-burdened future, the sale of military technology is also becoming a tool for gaining access to energy; indeed, such sales may have already been addressed in recent Chinese-Japanese military discussions.

Yet, the option of becoming a producer and exporter of military technology is not attractive in the context of Japan's broader economic strategy. Military sales would either conflict with U.S. sales or with U.S. policy, and, given Japan's technological lag, would not be big enough to justify the risk. A higher military profile would reduce maneuverability; countries like Indonesia and China would be compelled to diversify against Japan. Thus, Japan is likely to arm only to the minimal extent necessary for political, rather than economic, objectives. It is also likely to adopt procurement programs with minimum import content (e.g., domestically licensed production of airplanes) and maximum technological spin-off.

CONCLUSIONS

The Japanese economy is growing faster than other industrial economies, and, given stable prices, Japan will import 6.5 mmbd of oil by 1985. This constitutes an annual oil import bill of $80 billion, equivalent to all Japanese imports in 1978. But if energy prices remain stable, this bill would be essentially financed by the growth of Japan's non-energy trade surplus. No new measures would be needed, and the yen's exchange rate could remain at roughly 312/SDR. With $66 oil, after allowing for the

---

[36] Data Resources, Inc., *Japanese Economic Review*, November 24, 1979.
[37] Kazuo Tomiyama, "The Future of Japan's Defense-Related Industries," *Japan Quarterly*, 25:4 (October/December 1978).
[38] Quoted here from "Defense Industry Assumes Cautious Stand, Confident in More Spending," *Japan Economic Journal*, March 10, 1981.

global slowdown likely to be associated with this increase, the Japanese external accounts would show a potential $20–$40 billion deficit, which could be financed, in the extreme, by a competitive devaluation of 12–25 percent. These estimates suggest a large, but not unprecedented, adjustment task.

Efforts to diversify oil supplies now emphasize the Pacific Basin, government-to-government agreements, and negotiations with independent producers like China and Mexico. These arrangements tend to be costly, and, because of the basic realities of global oil output, some 70 percent of Japanese oil—roughly half of Japan's energy requirements—will still come from the Middle East in 1985. Thus, Japan's energy demands will continue to depend on the security of Middle Eastern oil and on Japan's ability to finance its cost.

The natural evolution of the Japanese economy is also carrying it in a direction that tends to reduce its exposure to energy risk. The geographical diversification of Japanese exports—essentially, a strong position in the markets of developing countries—has hastened Japan's adjustment to previous oil crises; but in the third crisis of 1985, this kind of diversification is likely to play a lesser role. Instead, Japanese exports are likely to be strong because Japan's comparative advantage, domestic needs, and government policy all point to the rapid development of a wide range of energy-saving and oil-substituting technologies. Oil priced at $66 would provide a powerful impetus for exports of nuclear technology, synthetic and solar energy technology, fuel-efficient capital goods, and advanced electronics. To a lesser extent, Japan might also curtail its imports, particularly from its East Asian neighbors.

It is also clear that Japan will shift a much larger part of the adjustment burden in future energy crises to the capital account. Through sales of domestic assets, or through large-scale borrowing, Japan could spread the cost of adjustment over a period long enough to develop greater energy independence. Recent experience suggests growing worldwide interest in Japanese assets, and the scale of the financing requirement is not great when compared to either Japanese real wealth or the lending ability of oil-exporters. Such flows presume a growing role for Japanese banks in international finance in general, and in oil revenue recycling in particular.

In many dimensions, Japan's international strategy is closely constrained by the impact of its trade on its partner economies (this is of course true even for its largest partner, the U.S.) and by the political alliances on which Japanese security depends. These constraints lend stability to Japanese economic policy; while Japan will continue to test various economic and political limits, it is unlikely to turn in bold new directions. Rearmament, rapprochement with the Soviet Union, and head-on competition with the United States are examples of strategies that

Japan cannot afford to risk. Japan has, for a long time, pursued the only viable strategy for a resource-poor economy: to produce goods, and now technology, valuable enough to insure access to resources even in times of scarcity. Though the adjustment problems analyzed in this chapter are potentially large, the same strategy, well executed, should enable Japan to buy even costlier energy, or to attract investments in support of conversion to more secure long-term supplies.

Energy and Japan's National Security Strategy

Ronald A. Morse

Throughout most of the postwar era, the Japanese political and economic leadership elite has assumed that trade and economic development would progress naturally and that questions about defense and national security would be taken care of under the arrangements of the United States–Japan mutual security treaty. The success of this approach has ensured the ruling Liberal Democratic Party and their loyal administrators, the bureaucracy, a period of stable political rule unmatched in most other nations. This continuity of leadership and unity of purpose is perhaps the single most important factor in Japan's exceptional postwar economic performance.

Unfortunately, the world today is not as prosperous and tidy as it was a decade ago. Change in political, economic, and strategic terms has been dramatic, especially since 1973, when an era of stable and cheap energy supplies was challenged. Japan, like many nations, was unprepared to make this sudden adjustment and took the path of least resistance, accommodating the oil-producing nations. Today—and this is one of the themes of this chapter, if not the book as a whole—the costs of this accommodation and the risks to alliance politics are being reconsidered. Japan now needs a global strategic vision on security issues that is as systematic and effective as its past economic strategy.

The political instabilities of the Middle East, the current global economic slowdown and inflation, and the uncertain military balance between the United States and the Soviet Union are all forcing Japan to reassess its international policies and strategies. One implication is that Japan can no longer afford the slow and cumbersome bureaucratic style of leadership that has characterized its elite in the past. The recent death of Prime Minister Ohira, the last of a senior generation, made the inadequacies of the Japanese political system evident. For this and other reasons, Japan has not been able to respond quickly to rapidly changing world conditions.

The Japanese leadership still finds it hard to see the world in anything but economic terms, and this is the legacy of an era of virtually no international political or military responsibilities. The adjustment to new realities, given the rigidity of bureaucratic structures, has had to take the form of ad hoc policy fora and partial accommodations to the sharing of political responsibility.

ENERGY AND SECURITY

During the 1970s, with the rise of energy costs and the increasing uncertainties surrounding the uninterrupted flow of oil supplies, energy issues assumed a new prominence. The defense of sea-lanes and the economic impact of supply disruptions must now be given careful consideration in the calculus of economic planning. The high cost of building a strategic crude oil stockpile and the options surrounding further nuclear power plant construction cannot be treated, as in the past, as separate and unrelated issues. As one would expect, the Japanese are still uncomfortable with a concept like "energy security."

This chapter examines the relationships and trade-offs between the three elements in the "energy security" issue: economics, security, and supply. Seeking to avoid the pitfalls of merely reporting the Japanese perspective, I use a broader comparative context within which to raise questions about Japan's pursuit of a low-cost, low-risk geopolitical strategy that has done little to strengthen the economic or political security of the Western alliance. Prime Minister Suzuki's recent reluctance to use the word "alliance" reflects this dilemma. While there are no ready answers to the present international energy crisis, and while the central actor, the United States, seems to be the most confused of nations in arriving at any major conclusions, there are significant questions to be examined with respect to Japan in a global context.

"Energy security" is difficult to define.[1] As used in this chapter, it means the reliability of supply and a strategy to prevent the interruption of oil supplies, reduce vulnerability, and alleviate economic damage. The concept includes a variety of elements: domestic preparations already in place to handle a reduction of supply, the ability to protect supply sources and supply lines, the economic strength to adapt smoothly to higher en-

---

[1] See David A. Deese and Joseph S. Nye, eds., *Energy and Security* (Cambridge, Mass.: Ballinger Press, 1981); Howard Bucknell, III, *Energy and the National Defense* (Lexington: University Press of Kentucky, 1981); *Orbis*, 23:4 (Winter 1980); and Alvin L. Alm, "Energy Supply Interruptions and National Security," *Science*, 211:4489 (March 27, 1981).

Table 1

JAPAN'S PETROLEUM IMPORTS IN RELATION TO
OPEC AND WORLD PRODUCTION
(*millions of barrels per day*)

	1976	1977	1978	1985	1990
Total Oil Imports	5.29	5.35	5.23	5.85	5.86
OPEC Production	31.43	32.09	30.47	30.00	30.00
Free World Production	47.44	49.36	48.90	53.60	55.70
Japan's Imports as a Percent of OPEC Production (*includes LPG*)	16.82	16.68	17.15	19.50	19.53
Japan's Imports as a Percent of Free World Production	11.14	10.84	10.69	10.91	10.52

SOURCE: Institute of Energy Economics, *1990 World Energy Forecast* (in Japanese), 1980, p. 209.

ergy costs, the political will to defend national energy interests, and the intention of strengthening consuming nation leverage vis-à-vis producing nations. Some of these elements are covered in other chapters in this volume.

The concept of energy security as used here is focused on short-run, sudden, or creeping types of disruptions that might take place in the next five to ten years, the period during which oil dependency will remain constant or even increase. The long-run nuclear, coal, and energy R&D options are examined elsewhere in this volume. To the present time, Japan's approach to the energy crisis has been to minimize the domestic economic impact of a severe petroleum cutback. Very little consideration (this is dealt with later) has been given to taking strategic unilateral or coordinated measures to prevent such crises from occurring. It is possible that, given appropriate coordination and consultation, the opportunity exists for the United States and Japan to reduce their mutual vulnerability through joint efforts that would link different but complementary strategic concerns. Forging a combined effort will not be easy (and will require bridging differing assumptions about the nature of the energy issue), but the energy and security benefits of a combined oil strategy far outweigh the benefits of any unilateral actions either side may take. A series of bilateral agreements with Japan and the Europeans would be one way to overcome the diversity and domestic energy policy differences that have blocked effective multilateral coordination to date.

Japanese preparedness for an energy emergency, as one would expect, reflects Tokyo's assumptions about economic policy. While Japan

Table 2

THE RISING COST OF JAPANESE
OIL IMPORTS

Year	Oil Imports (*MMB/D*)	Oil Import Cost (*billions of dollars*)	Actual Growth (*percent*)
1973	5.6	5.9	10.0
1974	5.4	18.9	–0.5
1975	5.0	19.6	1.4
1976	5.2	21.2	6.5
1977	5.4	23.6	5.4
1978	5.3	23.4	6.0
1979	5.6	33.5	5.9
1980	5.1	52.8	5.5

may be better prepared domestically for a major oil disruption than the U.S. or the Europeans, its overall plan is far from adequate. The major flaw, when viewed from the perspective of the need for consuming nation cooperation, is Tokyo's lack of faith in coordinated or international energy strategies. Cooperation seldom takes place during a crisis and is usually ignored during periods of petroleum surpluses; the best time to prepare for cooperation is sometime in between these extremes.

The Japanese private perception of energy emergency preparedness since 1970, based upon several important but rarely articulated assumptions, has significant implications for Tokyo's views about how to handle its energy needs. While public pronouncements may be otherwise, Tokyo believes:

1. The International Energy Agency[2] emergency allocations system will probably not work.

2. Japan cannot rely on the United States or any other nation to come to its assistance.

3. Other cooperative multilateral mechanisms remain unclear.

4. By giving major attention to the Japanese economy, Japan will retain a good competitive economic position vis-à-vis the other major oil-importing nations, even after a severe crisis.

---

[2] Through the International Energy Agency (IEA), consumer countries have addressed the oil distribution issues and designed an oil sharing agreement which is triggered when any of the twenty-one signatory countries suffers a loss of more than 7 percent of total consumption. The IEA countries have also reached agreements on demand restraint, import ceilings, and stockpile policy. The IEA and its parent organization, the Organization of Economic Cooperation and Development (OECD), are located in Paris.

ENERGY CRISES AND MIDDLE EAST POLICY

Japan is a newcomer to Middle East affairs, and its policies have reflected a predictable preoccupation with short-term political costs and benefits. Before 1973, Tokyo had little interest in the region. When the Suez Canal was closed in the crisis of 1956–1957 and the Iraqi pipeline was cut, Japan and other nations experienced a dramatic rise in tanker rates because longer shipping routes had to be used. Again, during the Middle East war in 1967, while Japan was not the target of supply cuts, it did experience an increase in shipping charges.

The domestic energy crisis of October 1973 came as a major "shock" to Japan; the domestic emotional response and toilet paper and soap hoarding caused the sort of panic not experienced since World War II. The foreign policy rush to placate the Arab oil-producing nations produced a policy aimed at direct contacts with the producers, a disassociation from U.S. pro-Israel policy, and major Japanese government involvement in Middle East policy.[3] After seven years of catering to producing nation interests, at the cost of damaged relations with its allies, Tokyo has only recently, and somewhat reluctantly, begun to reevaluate its strategy. Tokyo's policy to embark on a more active foreign policy in the Middle East has had few practical consequences for the Arab-Israel peace process. On balance, Japan's efforts to cultivate good will in the Middle East have not prevented Soviet expansionism, ensured the security of sea-lanes, or prevented the interruption of oil supplies. Until 1979, Tokyo was confident that it could barter technology and assistance for oil. Recent events, however, have proved that Japan is vulnerable to oil cutoffs and increased prices despite this policy of accommodation.

The actual decline in Japanese oil supplies in 1973 (October, 5%; November, 9%; December, 0.1%; January, 13%; and February, 14%) was not as dramatic as the response to that decline. Petroleum product stocks dropped from thirty-two to twenty-five days, and crude supply dropped from twenty-six to twenty-one days—forty-six days' supply being only one day more than the amount required to maintain forty-five days of running stocks. The crisis did, however, produce the management legislation, regulations, and price guidelines that today provide the foundation for Japan's emergency preparedness.[4]

The Iran crisis (late 1978–early 1979) produced quite a different reaction. Actual reductions in supply accelerated the already evident trends in Japan's Middle East diplomacy. The major supply cuts were to the Japanese oil companies that are not directly affiliated with, but are

---

[3] Today, nearly 25 percent of Japan's development assistance goes to the Middle East. It was 2.7 percent in 1975.

[4] Norio Tanaka, "Waga kuni enerugii kyokyu no anzenhosho to Kinkyuji tai-saku," *Enerugii Keizai*, 4:11 (February 1979).

dependent upon, the international oil majors.[5] The companies cut off then scrambled to the spot market to make up shortfalls. This kind of "disruption competition" drove up the spot market price for oil and strained relations among consuming nations.

The Japanese government responded to the cutbacks in two ways. MITI encouraged its domestic oil companies and trading firms to secure crude directly from the oil-producing states.[6] In 1979, direct deals accounted for about one-third of Japan's total imports, about 1.5 million barrels per day (MMB/D), an increase of 600,000 barrels per day compared to 1978. Direct deals under contract for 1980 were slightly higher, and it is anticipated that Japan will increase its direct deals further. Secondly, MITI raised the price ceiling for spot purchases. Thus, in 1978, about 4 percent (0.2 MMB/D) of Japan's petroleum was purchased on the spot market. This figure doubled by 1979 to 8 percent (0.4 MMB/D) of Japan's imports and ranged from 6 to 10 percent in 1980 (0.3–0.5 MMB/D). The figures for spot purchases in November and December 1979 and January 1980 were between 14 and 18 percent. Japan's reluctance to go along with sanctions against Iran over the U.S. hostage issue was another manifestation of strain. The real significance of the Iranian episode—higher oil prices, inadequate responses, and divisive tensions between traditional allies—was the price Tokyo was willing to pay for the commercial benefit of a "special" relationship with the oil producers.

DOMESTIC CRISIS MANAGEMENT PREPAREDNESS

There is little agreement among the advanced nations about the need for and effectiveness of a domestic oil disruption management scheme. The Reagan Administration has now decided that the international oil market can best handle price and allocation problems. The Japanese agree with this, but for their own reasons they have developed an elaborate crisis management strategy that is similar in some respects to U.S. energy policy under the Carter Administration.

Japan's crisis management plan involves moderate government intervention in the oil market—a natural approach, given their views toward international cooperation schemes. The Japanese have in place a set of regulations and established bureaucratic procedures to deal with an energy

---

[5] The seven international majors are British Petroleum, Royal Dutch/Shell, and five U.S.-based companies: Exxon, Mobil, Standard Oil of California, Texaco (the four partners in Aramco, the producer of Saudi Arabia's oil), and Gulf. In 1980, the majors accounted for less than 40 percent of Japan's crude oil imports. Iranian production fell from 5.5 million barrels per day (B/D) in October 1978 to 400,000 B/D in January 1979.

[6] In 1973, a total of 1.5 million B/D (5 percent of the total) was sold in government-to-government sales. In 1979, the figure was 5 million B/D (17 percent).

emergency. Nevertheless, the ad hoc nature of the past energy decision-making process and the tradition of Japanese institutional reluctance to accept political responsibility in a crisis could paralyze the Japanese government if a real crisis came. As plans now stand, the Japanese government privately believes that existing multilateral arrangements (within the framework of the IEA) will not work, that domestic crisis management mechanisms will not be required for a short-run crisis (and would not work in a sustained major crisis), and that Japan's only defense is to have adequate oil stocks to protect itself. This reflects a more general view, held even outside Japan, that the world oil market cannot be relied on to distribute oil during a supply emergency.

Diagrams of the key elements in the energy emergency process and the formal steps and laws available to administrators for coping with an energy emergency can be found in Figure 1. The key crisis regulation is the Petroleum Supply and Demand Adjustment Law, which was hastily compiled to cope with the 1973 crisis. Specific measures under the law include petroleum supply targets, marketing and import plans submitted by refiners and importers, authority to modify such plans, authority to promulgate restrictions on the use of petroleum, provision for mediation in disputes concerning oil allocation, and authority to impose allocation and rationing schemes. The law covers crude oil, gasoline, naphtha, jet fuel, kerosene, gas oil, fuel oil, and LPG.

The initial phase of a crisis would be managed through government "administrative guidance"—i.e., extralegal (moral) persuasion to get all groups to cooperate. This period of voluntary restraint would include all actions through Article 11 in Figure 2, the only leverage on violators being the publication of the names of those unwilling to follow official guidelines. It takes a cabinet decision to impose supply quotas and institute allocation and rationing systems; this would be phase two of the process. The preliminary research for handling rationing in the private and industrial sectors has been carried out by MITI under contract with private research institutions. The necessary rationing coupons have been printed, and they could be openly exchanged by those receiving them. It is hoped that this would prevent the development of a black market for fuel and other supplies.

The Institute for Energy Economics did the research for allocation in the private (gasoline and kerosene) sector. Because of the private/business mix in small and medium-sized companies, their allocations would be treated in the same way as those of private households. The Industry Oil Products Quota and Allocation System study done for MITI by the Nomura Research Institute is still unpublished.[7] Reports suggest, somewhat

---

[7] Hiroaki Fukami, "Keizaikiki kanri seisaku no taikei to arikata," *Kokusai Mondai*, July 1980, p. 23.

FIGURE 1

Key Components in the Japanese Oil Emergency Process

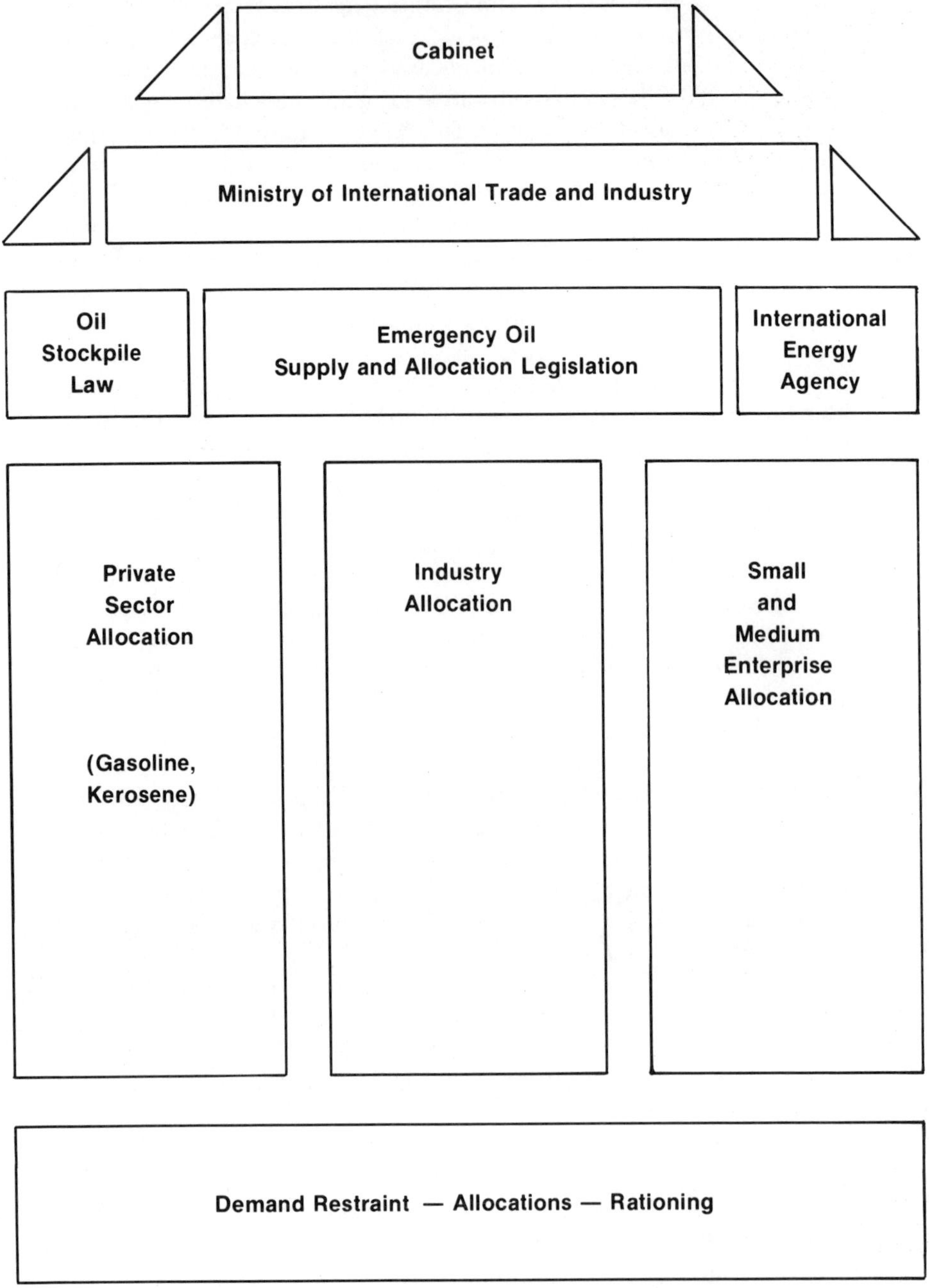

FIGURE 2

Laws and Procedures for Countering an Energy Supply Disruption

SOURCE: Norio Tanaka, "Waga kuni enerugii kyokyu no anzenhosho to Kinkyuji taisaku," *Enerugii Keizai*, 4:11 (February 1979), 55.

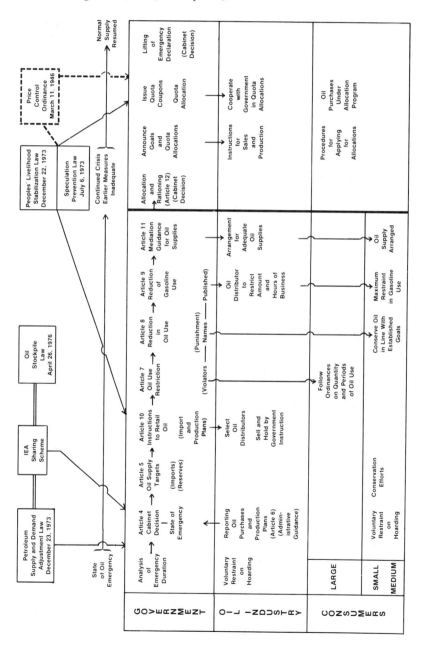

optimistically, that in each major sector industry associations representing major firms could administer the shortage in an equitable manner.

Beyond this, there are still a number of issues concerning emergency preparedness that have to be addressed. Japan's situation is not all that different from the situation in the United States. There is no central control command structure to manage the flow of oil, implement government policies, and distribute rationing coupons. How private and government oil stockpile drawdowns would be coordinated remains unclear. The Japanese, like the Americans, still have limited experience with fuel switching and power supply sharing. Used to high energy prices, the Japanese have also not given consideration to possible coordinated oil-consuming nation tariff schemes to limit imports. The Japanese do currently have an elaborate set of crude oil, heavy oil, and gasoline taxes that are used to finance highways, domestic coal production, and new energy development. These taxes add significantly to the price of petroleum products and make the Japanese government reluctant to discuss new forms of taxation, quotas, or import tariffs.

OIL STOCKPILE POLICY

Japan is willing to pay the price for crude oil and product storage. Japan's petroleum stockpiling program effort is managed by the independent governmental corporation, the Japan National Oil Company (JNOC). In 1978, the overseas oil development responsibilities of the Japan Petroleum Development Corporation (established in 1967) were combined with the national stockpile effort, and the new JNOC absorbed both responsibilities. The Japanese government plan to increase its oil stocks entered a new phase recently with the start of construction of a permanent 35-million-barrel oil storage facility in northern Japan. Due to be completed in March 1983, the 70 percent government-owned facility is the first in a series of eleven government-owned oil storage projects, including floating storage complexes in which Japan's shipbuilding technology will be employed. Until these facilities are completed, Japan will continue its policy of offshore tanker stockpiling. Onshore permanent storage will cost about two-thirds the cost of VLCC (very large crude carriers) floating storage, and is much cheaper over the long run.[8]

The momentum for increased stockpiles has come directly from MITI and indirectly from JNOC. Tokyo has continued to make stockpile purchases, even under tight oil market conditions. Less concerned with price and Japanese reliance on international disruption sharing schemes

---

[8] For further details, see Edward N. Krapels, *Oil Crisis Management* (Baltimore: Johns Hopkins University Press, 1980).

Table 3

JAPAN'S PETROLEUM STOCKPILES*
(*in kiloliters*)

Year	Private Stocks	Days Supply	Government Stocks	Days Supply
1971	28,360,000	45	—	—
1972	35,053,000	50	—	—
1973	—	—	—	—
1974	42,597,000	65	—	—
1975	44,503,000	70	—	—
1976	49,494,000	75	—	—
1977	54,970,000	80	5,000,000	7.2
1978	59,934,000	87	5,000,000	7.2
1979	56,995,000	82	5,000,000	7.2
1980	60,686,000	87†	5,000,000	7.2
1981	62,672,000	90	7,500,000 (47 MMB)	10.5
1982	65,415,000	90		
1983	67,302,000	90	annual increases	
1984	68,964,000	90		
1985			30,000,000 (189 MMB)	43

*The figures for 1981–1985 are projected. When all eleven JNOC sites are in place, government reserves will stand at 55 million kiloliters (346 million barrels).

†Nearly half of this consisted of operating stocks.

(namely, the IEA), Tokyo has given first priority to reducing vulnerability through stockpiling. Coal and LPG stockpiling is also now under serious consideration.

Under present arrangements, in a major supply interruption the major powers could turn to the International Energy Agency. But because the IEA system has never been tested in a crisis, there is little confidence among policymakers that existing IEA mechanisms for sharing limited supplies would prove effective. A fallback position would be to use strategic stocks, but, at least for the United States, stocks are less than fifteen days of imports at current levels. Privately held stocks in the United States are considerably higher, approximately twenty-five to thirty days of imports, but no policy exists to integrate private and government stockpiling efforts. Japan's stocks are considerably higher: approximately 9.7 days in government storage and about 103 days in government-financed private storage. In both the United States and Japan, no plan or policy exists for the emergency drawdown of stocks. In a different context, the IEA is currently considering a joint consuming nation strategic stockpile that would have from four to ten days' supply for IEA member countries as a hedge against price increases or supply shortfalls.

PUBLIC ATTITUDES ON AN ENERGY CRISIS

The absence of adequate official preparedness for an energy crisis does not mean that there is a lack of popular concern over the issue or a dearth of popular crisis literature on the subject. In a recent survey of one hundred Japanese business executives, seventy-five responded that their current major concern was that of a serious oil crisis. In the same survey in 1980, energy costs placed second as a major cause of concern.[9]

While we know a great deal about Japanese behavior in the international oil market and about the strategies of Japan's trading companies, very little has been written about energy crisis management. One of the most popular treatments of the subject is the 1975 novel *Yudan* (Oil Disruption) by Sakaiya Taichi, which sketches out the ad hoc bureaucratic decision-making process demonstrated during the 1973 crisis. The novel portrays an imagined 200-day cutoff that leads to the economic collapse of Japan and overall national chaos. The author, until recently an employee of MITI, was personally involved in managing the 1973 crisis and had access to confidential data while writing his book.

In response to *Yudan* and similar books about massive electric failures and violent earthquakes, the Japanese government contracted with energy think tanks to examine disruption scenarios, crisis management procedures, and allocation systems. In 1978, the National Institute for Research Advancement (NIRA) produced an exhaustive study on energy crisis management.[10] Under contract, NIRA is currently investigating the IEA sharing mechanism, short-term shortfall scenarios, and the problems of information management during an energy crisis.

Japanese journalists have also done their share to formulate an open and effective crisis emergency strategy. According to the *Yomiuri* newspaper of July 5, 1980, MITI has its own, still secret, updated and refined program for handling any future oil crisis. The document examines two oil-disruption scenarios: 10 and 30 percent cutoffs. In the first case, when voluntary demand proves inadequate to compensate for supply reductions, the more stringent Petroleum Supply and Demand Adjustment law and the Emergency Measures Stabilization law are invoked by cabinet decision. For the larger disruption, severe economic controls are required, with allocation coupons being issued through 3,255 regional and local government offices. These procedures are consistent with the data examined earlier.

---

[9] *Nihon Keizai Shimbun*, Tokyo, January 27, 1981.
[10] *Sekiyu Koyokyu no Chudan*, March 1979.

The Japanese government has been criticized for its failure to prepare the public adequately for the possibility of an energy crisis that would be along the lines treated in the novel *Yudan*. A media-oriented society, Japan responds quickly to news reports. MITI officials have been unresponsive on the issue and are reported to fear the possibility of having to resort to supply allocations or rationing. Research shows that in 1973 the public distrusted official statements about the severity of the oil crisis. Government officials have probably kept their plans secret for the wrong bureaucratic reasons; the real fear involves the Japanese national psychology. Contrary to the popular image, in Japan, where "public" interest receives a much lower priority than private or corporate interest in a conflict situation, an allocation or quota system may not work. The Japanese are used to preparing for national disasters like earthquakes, in which the source of the disaster is impersonal. They may not respond in a cooperative way to an energy shortage for which it is possible to identify the source of the problem. The Japanese people perceive the energy situation as a zero-sum game in which a gain by one person necessarily means a loss by someone else. There is always the fear that someone else is going to get your share.[11] There is also the fact that oil-disruption costs may be borne without regard to income classes or geographical needs; the high concentration of the population in a few areas presents special problems.

DEPENDENCY: AN OUTMODED FOCUS?

Dependency is a supply-oriented concept and does not adequately deal with price issues. Dependency is central to Japanese interpersonal relations, Japan's foreign policy strategy, and its energy supply relationships. In the energy area, serious reservations can be made regarding the long-run effectiveness of a dependence strategy. For historical and economic reasons, the Japanese have paid a great deal of attention to locating, acquiring, and transporting the oil and other resources required to fuel their rapid economic growth policy. As a resource-poor nation, with half of its imports consisting of energy, the Japanese have also been concerned with their high "dependence" on foreign supply sources. Petroleum imports have been of special concern with world demand for OPEC oil likely to remain in the range of 20 to 30 million barrels per day during the 1980s. Japan will have to compete actively for this dwindling commodity. While the diversification of sources is a national objective, Japan is not likely to decrease its dependence on Middle East oil. As indicated in Table 1, the Japanese will actually increase their percentage of reliance on OPEC oil in the decade ahead.

---

[11] Michael Crabtree, "Psychological Response to an Energy Emergency," *The Energy Consumer*, December 1980–January 1981, p. 21.

Every day approximately 14 million barrels of crude oil from the Persian Gulf states pass through the Strait of Hormuz. An additional 1 to 2 million barrels of Persian Gulf production are shipped into the world oil market through other routes. The oil exports of the Persian Gulf represent over 50 percent of the crude oil traded on the world oil market. Needless to say, this is an area of unstable regimes and is subject to Soviet threats.

Should there be a halt in the flow of oil through the Strait of Hormuz for a sustained period of time, the price of oil would rise precipitously. A large and rapid increase in oil prices would cause the United States and Japan to suffer direct economic losses of a magnitude that would rival the Great Depression. Even relatively small supply disruptions can generate large economic losses. The national security implications of a disruption are made evident in a recent U.S. Department of Energy study which calculates that, for Japan, a 6-million-barrel-a-day Persian Gulf cutoff would reduce Japan's gross national product (GNP) by 5.8 percent. The price of a barrel of oil would go from $36 per barrel to $76 per barrel. For a 12-million B/D cutoff, the GNP loss would be three times larger and the cost of a barrel of oil would shoot up to $100.

VULNERABILITY AS A CONCEPT

Current analysis suggests that the chances for long-run increases in the availability of oil are not favorable, prices will remain high, dependence will continue, and the transition to alternate sources will be slow and costly. In such a situation, energy supply becomes a national security issue. The linkage between supply and national security is made clearer when the distinction between "vulnerability" and dependence is made clear. Then we see that "vulnerability," the possible damage resulting from a sudden oil supply interruption, must be dealt with in its own way. There are at least two types of "vulnerability" associated with a dependence on imported oil:

Political-Military Vulnerability to gradual but persistent increases in oil-exporting countries' market power and increased Soviet political influence in the Persian Gulf.

Economic Vulnerability to sudden disruptions in supply and price increases due to accidents, crises, or embargoes in the producing nations.

Japanese usage of the concept of "energy security" has been too focused on dependence. While Japan has developed an elaborate structure to handle dependence, it has not come up with an effective strategy for reducing price vulnerability. The difficult problem, and the one that has not yet been fully addressed by the United States or Japan, is how to minimize the various kinds of damage done by a serious oil supply shortfall. The costs of vulnerability are serious, involving:

1. The direct transfer of wealth to producing nations for high-priced oil.

2. Indirect macroeconomic costs associated with lower growth, unemployment, and inflation.

3. Political and military concessions to oil-exporting states.

The basic problem caused by an oil disruption is the sudden and very large increase in the world oil price. Ways of coping multilaterally with these problems are difficult to identify because they involve the complexities of domestic energy policy and require significant consuming nation cooperation. A bilateral approach may have the best chance of success. One concern is that if this cooperation were handled wrongly, it could lead to producer nation (OPEC) retaliation. Another reason that individual consuming countries have failed thus far to insulate themselves from OPEC's market power and instability has been that the United States and its allies (the major oil-consuming countries) are part of a large integrated oil market. Individual consuming countries can take unilateral action in the form of demand restraint measures, petroleum stockpiling, and/or development of alternative energy sources, but other consuming nations benefit or are harmed when such actions have an effect on the world oil price. As a result, unilateral actions can be counterproductive and create dissension among the allies. This may occur, for example, if the actions of a few countries to develop strategic stockpiles cause world oil prices to rise, or if some countries see themselves bearing all of the costs of actions that will benefit other importing countries during disruptions.

It might be argued that the long-run key to reducing vulnerability might be the implementation of government programs such as those for synthetic fuels or subsidies for conservation, but it can also be argued that these programs are often too expensive and have only limited effectiveness in reducing vulnerability. Also, since these long-range kinds of cooperation are relatively free of short-run political considerations, they have been easier to arrange. More importantly, these programs have dominated the political debate over energy policy and diverted attention from strategies that truly reduce oil vulnerability. Coordinated contingency planning for sudden oil disruptions and shared long-term strategies for reducing instability in the Persian Gulf should now be given a higher "near-term" priority.

THE STRATEGIC PERCEPTION GAP

The American taxpayer has been paying unconscionably for the defense of Japan. We provide the nuclear umbrella, we provide the high seas capability, we're defending their oil. They need it a hell of a lot more than we do.

Robert Komer, *The Washington Post*
February 16, 1981

51

Japan's willingness to do more in the area of international cooperation on energy security depends upon two factors: whether it perceives a threat to its energy supply lines, and whether it is willing to allocate economic resources for the defense of these supply lines. Thus far, Tokyo has been reluctant to use its economic strength to improve its defense capabilities. In part, this is because the Japanese feel no real outside military threat. More importantly, Tokyo believes that the U.S. will protect it for now, and that Japan can best ensure its economic future by not diverting resources into defense expenditures.

Prime Minister Suzuki's decision in December 1980 to restrict Japan's defense expenditures because of budgetary constraints, despite pressures from the United States and certain domestic Japanese quarters to expand the defense budget, was a $200–$400 million gamble that illustrates the considerable gap that exists between American and Japanese strategic perceptions of the international order and the potential ways to most effectively deal with global energy problems. The situation did not change following U.S.-Japan consultations in May 1981, when Prime Minister Suzuki fired his foreign minister for approving a joint communiqué that suggested a U.S.-Japan alliance.

There is no way to discuss Japan's posture on energy matters and the Middle East without examining some of the assumptions and positions taken by Japan's leadership when it comes to the question of "national security." A number of writers have already pointed out how the United States and Japan have been in conflict before (over trade with China in the 1950s, over Japan's diplomatic pro-Arab tilt in 1973, and over nuclear reprocessing in 1977) on issues that reflect differing political-strategic policies and interests.

The energy question—Japan's energy policies and preparation for an energy cutoff—must again be examined within the context of Tokyo's single-minded preoccupation with economic growth during the last thirty-five years. The cost and benefits of such a narrow approach must be reexamined in the light of changes both within Japan and in the broader international context of such policies. Good economic theory, as the Japanese often fail to perceive, does not necessarily make good foreign policy.[12]

As was pointed out earlier, Japan has been fortunate that the postwar context for economic expansion has been peaceful and supportive. While Japanese industriousness was essential to Japan's remarkable economic growth, few Japanese would deny that it was the dynamism and opportunity of the post–World War II era that made the significant dif-

---

[12] The United States' trade deficit with Japan is about $10 billion, which is roughly equivalent to Japan's defense expenditure. This figure is the same as the cost of one aircraft carrier, or nearly the same as the annual liquid fuel bill of the U.S. Department of Defense.

ference. Tokyo's pride in Japan's success is appropriate, but it should be tempered by the realization that the world has changed and Japan's responsibilities have been transformed in the process.

It is within the context of Japan's economic success and increasing political independence that we shall examine how Tokyo's bilateral and multilateral relationships have changed. We ask whether Japan should assume more and different responsibilities if it wishes to continue to benefit from the economic, political, and military security that it has taken for granted and used so freely in its sustained march to economic success.

No one seeks to fault Japan for its success. Quite the contrary, Japan's allies *wish Tokyo to reformulate its strategic vision of the world to allow for better and more systematic cooperation in areas where we have the most mutual interests.* Such an approach will better ensure Japan's economic aims and allow it to maximize its assets. The failure to do so will hurt us all.

Japan's postwar leaders are men who identify the nation's defeat in 1945 with military expansionism. The lessons of prewar Japan have forced them to take every precaution to ensure that Japan's course not be again diverted from the economic prosperity of its people. The Japanese leadership today has made every effort to ensure that a stable, free economy is Japan's lifeline to the world. In recognition of the primacy of economics, they have never created an independent government energy agency as the U.S. has done.

Thinking about energy in strategic terms has not been current in the United States all that long either. While it was no accident that the past two Secretaries of the Department of Energy (James Schlesinger and Charles Duncan) previously held positions in the Defense Department, the linking up of economic, political, and security (defense) issues has been more a response to recent Middle East developments than a clear articulation of an energy security policy. United States Senate hearings on the *Geopolitics of Oil* and subsequent congressional debate on the Persian Gulf have motivated a review of U.S. thinking on energy security. A General Accounting Office report on U.S. international energy policy formulation has criticized the ad hoc nature of U.S. policies. Only recently has the Department of Energy given serious consideration to a government-wide review of the elements in U.S. energy security.

TOKYO'S NEW APPROACH

While the Japanese use the concept of "energy security," they do not use it in a way that reflects the American understanding of the words, nor is the concept something that the Japanese seem to fully understand themselves. This lack of appreciation for the link between "energy" and "security" is reflected in the fact that the subject has not been adequately handled in the broad, vague framework of the new Japanese "comprehensive security" strategy.[13] Traditional, vertically structured bureaucratic alliances in Japan have made it very difficult for the relatively weak Japan Defense Agency (JDA) to have an impact on foreign and domestic policy issues. MITI has tried to secure energy policy for itself, while the Ministry of Finance has attempted to regulate economic policy. The JDA is concerned with defense issues. Energy supply, which cuts across these bureaucracies, cannot be easily managed in the Japanese system. To accommodate the energy security "policy" concern, the cabinet has created the Comprehensive National Security Research Council, the brainchild of the moderate conservatives in control of Japanese policy. This new body is intended to accommodate, through a new policy issue nexus, three very different groups seeking to have an input into Japanese defense and security policy:

1. *Japan's hawks:* The message to them is that, within the security framework, they will get *some* of the defense increases they want.

2. *Japan's "moderate" liberals:* By emphasizing "peaceful diplomacy" and economic assistance, the comprehensive security policy can enlist the acquiescence, if not the support, of many former critics of Japan's defense policy.

3. *The U.S.:* By providing a broader context for the increased security contribution requested by the U.S., the concept of comprehensive national security also furnishes an excuse for holding actual defense spending to a minimum while making it difficult to pin Japan down on what it is doing.

"Comprehensive security" is not an effort to cloak increased defense expenditures in respectability, but, rather, is an effort to hold them to a minimum. Japan's present leaders have no wish to divert resources to defense or anything else that might spoil their success or hamper further economic gains. Fundamentally, these leaders do not share the United States' perception of an immediate Soviet or Persian Gulf threat, and they believe that, by and large, they can manage problems in the next decade much as they have done in the past. The Japanese limit their security concern to the internal stability of certain key oil-producing nations.

The young political and academic leaders who compiled the Com-

---

[13] The Comprehensive National Security Research Group report (commissioned by the late Prime Minister Ohira in April 1979) recommended the creation of a cabinet-level Comprehensive Security Council. This council, a government group comprised of the Prime Minister, his cabinet, and senior-ranking Liberal Democratic Party officials, was formed and has met several times to consider energy and security issues. While the original intention was to form a group similar to the U.S. National Security Council, a bureaucratic struggle prevented this from happening.

prehensive Security Report consider themselves "sensible pragmatists." No uniformed military people were included. It is probably fair to say that the proposals are not "comprehensive" in terms of Japanese domestic politics, fail to really examine "energy security," and do not reflect the strategy so much as the ideology of the ruling economic elite. The comprehensive security approach also reflects the effort to downgrade the bilateral relationship with the United States in order to give Tokyo greater independence.

Behind this "security strategy" is the conventional goal of Japan's present leaders to make Japan the preeminent economic power by the 1990s. There are two major elements to their strategy as it relates to energy:

1. *Economic:* High oil costs will work to Japan's advantage. With its technology and know-how, Japan is in a good position to cash in on the recycling of Arab oil funds. The net effect will be the transfer of wealth from Western Europe and the United States, in particular, through the oil producers, to Japan. In addition, the high cost of oil will make the development of other sources of energy more profitable; Japan has targeted this field for its own technological superiority. This was reflected in Japan's response to the OPEC Long-Term Strategy Report and was demonstrated in the very high budget increases given for "energy-related expenses" in the 1980 budget by the Ministry of Finance.

2. *Defense:* Japan's leaders want to convince the United States that they are serious about defense but want the U.S. to look out for Japan's security interests through the 1980s while Japan develops a high-technology infrastructure that would enable it to rapidly boost its defense capabilities whenever it wishes.

The philosophy of the Comprehensive National Security Research Group is revealed by the conclusions of their report of July 2, 1980:

> It is our hope that the issues raised in this report will serve as a catalyst for widespread national debate and that this will lead to productive results. It is the formation of a national consensus through wide-ranging discussions that will lead to united national efforts for Japan's security.
>
> Looking back on the past national security debate in Japan, we have to admit that no national environment has been fostered to take up this question in a realistic manner. The debate has been split in two extremes, one in favor of a military buildup aimed at autonomous defense, and the other in favor of complete disarmament based on "pacifism". . . . Inasmuch as Japan's security depends on comprehensive efforts in many fields and at different levels, it is not a task that can be left solely in the hands of the Defense Agency. The issue of national security concerns not only the Ministry of Foreign Affairs, which is responsible for Japan's foreign policy, and the Ministry of Finance, which is in charge of its fiscal policy, but also

various other ministries and agencies, such as the Ministry of International Trade and Industry, and the National Land Agency. It is necessary for all the ministries and agencies of the Government to bear comprehensive national security considerations in mind in implementing various policy measures.

This effort at comprehensive security (not a total defense framework) is sometimes explained as a partial accommodation by the government to the changing popular mood. Businessmen in Japan favor increased defense spending, and recent opinion polls indicate that the Japanese people do not think Japan is doing enough for its own defense. On October 23, 1980, the *Yomiuri* newspaper echoed common criticisms of the Japanese government's failure to give adequate attention to the importance of the Persian Gulf and Japan's role in defending the Strait of Hormuz. As indicated earlier, Hormuz, a major trade route since before the time of Alexander the Great, is today the gateway through which 60 percent of all oil traded in international commerce must pass. Some 70 percent of Japan's oil comes from the Persian Gulf, and 80 percent of Japan's oil transits Hormuz and either the Straits of Malacca or other straits in the Indonesian archipelago.

SOME IMPORTANT DISTINCTIONS

A major shortcoming of the Comprehensive Security Report is that it does not adequately differentiate between the concepts of national interest, national security, and energy security. One possible approach at definition might be the following:

1. *National Interest:* A broad notion of normative considerations such as representative government, human rights, and basic principles of society.
2. *National Defense:* Defense of territory, political independence, well-being of citizens, and a role for a military force.
3. *Energy Security:* Reliability of supply and a strategy to prevent oil interruptions, reduce vulnerability, and alleviate economic damage. The protection and development of reliable sources of energy (oil) at prices that do not threaten the social, economic, or political viability of the nation.

The Japanese prefer to avoid these distinctions. This is in part a conscious choice, but it also reflects the fact that Japan today lacks a perspective of global military balance. This is most evident in Tokyo's statements that it intends to be *equal* friends with the United States and the Soviet Union. Another example of this lack of vision came when, during the recent Iran hostage situation, Japan tried to explain its position as being caught between two "friends"—the implication being that the United States and Iran were equally important to Japan. By any standard—trade, defense agreements, or historical ties—Japan's relations with Iran are no match for its relations with the United States. Still, the Japanese perceptions persists.

A recent opinion survey of Japanese leaders concerning the superpower military balance revealed the limited sense of danger that the Japanese have toward the Soviet Union. When "threat" was perceived, it was only in psychological and political terms. The gap between Japanese and American perceptions of the Soviet threat and the nature of the energy crisis is reflected in the nearly inverse ordering of energy security priorities as presented below. While one can question the wisdom of the ordering of U.S. priorities, given the present world situation, the fact that the two sets of priorities are different cannot be ignored.

U.S.	JAPAN
1. Contain Soviet expansionism	1. Diversify supply
2. Stimulate energy production	2. Stockpile crude
3. Foster international cooperation on energy security	3. Give capital and technical aid to suppliers
4. Build strategic reserves	4. Promote conservation and alternative energy
5. Promote conservation and alternative energy	5. Foster international cooperation on energy security

The reasons for these differences are evident. Japan's post–World War II foreign policy has been aimed at achieving economic recovery, convincing its former enemies of its peaceful intentions, and protecting its national interest by being as cooperative as possible with international arrangements for a stable world order. To accomplish these objectives, its policies have been reactive, overly pragmatic, lacking in charity, and overly concerned with short-term, low-risk, and long-gain options. This fits in well with the image of the quiet, cooperative, but generally uncertain ambiguity that one associates with Japanese foreign policy. Japan's situational ethic and tendency to substitute rhetoric for principles is also important.

Tokyo's leadership is made up of moderate internationalists who believe that industrial growth can persist indefinitely. They do not examine structural problems in their foreign relations, preferring to muddle through as long as possible. Their vision, however, is now out of line with world developments and the domestic Japanese consensus on the defense issue.

REASSESSING ALLIANCE POLITICS

The strategic vision in the United States is based on different factors, and Japan's failure to be supportive of American objectives in the world has created bilateral tensions. In the energy area, the Japanese think of the oil market in economic terms and do not view the Middle East strategically. Prime Minister Zenko Suzuki's defense "budget austerity" decision and lack of support for an allied Middle East security force during the Iran-Iraq war have had great implications for the bilateral relationship. Additional vague reassurances on defense issues during his visit to the U.S. in May 1981 were viewed with doubt and skepticism. These developments will have implications for Suzuki's future in managing defense issues in Japan. On November 4, 1980, the Prime Minister acknowledged for the first time that the Soviet buildup in the Pacific was a "potential threat" to Japan. The next day, his Chief Cabinet Secretary pointed out that this remark should not be misinterpreted to mean that Japan regards the U.S.S.R. as an "enemy." Tokyo's leadership clearly does not wish to recognize a new strategic reality: the Soviet Union's enhanced capacity to project its power into the Pacific Ocean and the Persian Gulf region. The meaning of the improved Soviet sea and air capabilities in the Pacific, while recognized in Japan, has not been sufficient to force Tokyo to reorder its priorities.

The magnitude of the problem as seen by the United States does not seem to have convinced Tokyo of the importance of linking economic, political, and military security. The Japanese have not always thought in these terms. They were willing to go to war in the late 1930s, when only 9 percent of their total energy needs were based on oil, mainly from the United States (80 percent) and the Dutch East Indies (10 percent). In 1935, Japan consumed 26 million barrels of oil per year, a one-week supply at current levels.

While it may be an overstatement, it seems that the leadership in Tokyo believes it can get the United States to fall in line. It has made every effort to avoid linking its comprehensive security framework to a strategic concept—a concept of how the Fukuda doctrine (now the Tanaka doctrine), omnidirectional diplomacy, aid-doubling plans, and a variety of other diplomatic plans and promises can be deployed to complement and enhance the military, strategic, and economic objectives of Japan's free-world allies. Tokyo tends to want to go it alone at some point.

Prospects for change are not good. In his 1981 New Year's press conference, the Prime Minister defended Japan's low increase in the defense budget, reiterating the well-known position that Japan does not plan to play a significant role through military power. As outlined in Japan's new Comprehensive Security Report, Tokyo will be satisfied to secure its objectives through economic cooperation, technical assistance, and undefined "political efforts." The security of the Persian Gulf, the high cost of U.S. defense expenditures, and the economic costs to the West for world peace seem to have escaped Japanese logic.

PROSPECTS FOR ENERGY COOPERATION

Differences in security perceptions and in economic policies are not the only issues in the way of energy cooperation. Any attempt to arrange collective strategies in the energy security area must take into consideration relationships existing bilaterally, multilaterally, and between regional groupings. Present energy agreements are handled through a maze of relationships—the Organization of Economic Cooperation and Development (OECD), the Economic Community (EC), the IEA, NATO, and Economic Summits—and between the consuming nations themselves. In addition, the fragmentation of traditional international arrangements during the past two decades has further created a state of international disorder that only benefits producing nations.

While cooperative efforts have been difficult in the energy area, largely because of the diverse domestic energy needs of the various consuming nations, there does appear to be emerging a common recognition that independent strategies have been very expensive and have not succeeded. While the IEA system has never been activated during an emergency, there has been a recognition that high worldwide crude inventories and adequate stockpile inventories can serve to restrain price increases when the market functions. Other, more complex, coordinated actions by the consuming nations, such as a coordinated stock drawdown, emergency import tariffs,[14] and demand restraint measures, are now under consideration in many countries.

A more elaborate global agreement between the oil-producing and the consuming nations, while not an impossibility, is not likely, because it would require joint offer withdrawals if agreement terms were not met, would assume mutual responsibilities, and would demand some form of enforcement for the violation of an agreement.

The options and institutions currently available to the consuming nations have been far from adequate. Since 1973, sporadic attempts have been made to develop concerted responses to disruption—the idea of a common IEA strategic oil stock pool being the most recent in a long line of proposals. The International Energy Agreement (which came into being in November 1974) has fostered consumer country cooperation in a variety of areas, and is the only international forum, to date, to address important

[14]A disruption tariff, as an emergency measure, would be imposed by oil-consuming countries to raise domestic prices, suppress demand, and, in principle, reduce the transfer of wealth to the producing nations.

petroleum matters. Nevertheless, it operates under considerable constraints, relies on voluntary cooperation, and is not equipped to handle the key issue of reducing the transfer of wealth and the macroeconomic impact of an oil price increase.

The annual Economic Summit mechanism,[15] or possible new sub-summit energy bodies, can continue to seek commitments to reduce oil dependence, but thus far they have not addressed the problem of price increases in a supply disruption. Neither the IEA nor the Economic Summits have dealt directly with Third World dependency and the economic impact of loan defaults by less-developed countries (LDCs). While OPEC made special arrangements for the LDCs during the Iran-Iraq war and has suggested that its long-term strategy will give special consideration to oil-importing LDCs,[16] the economic impact of continued oil price increases has already changed the global economic order.

The use of a tariff strategy, unilaterally or collectively, would create a different set of problems; while it would address the wealth transfer issue, it would also induce OPEC retaliation, dampen economic activity, and require a domestic (and cooperatively equitable) rebate scheme. Arriving at a cooperative tariff scheme would be difficult, given the diverse tax and regulatory systems operating in each nation. Internal economic conditions make a disruption tariff unattractive to the EC for the present. In Japan, it would require a complicated legal process, though certain emergency regulations would permit partial cooperation.

As indicated earlier, past and present strategies to implement regulatory and allocation quotas also do not address the transfer of wealth and macroeconomic dislocation costs. Allocations also create cumbersome bureaucratic structures that interfere with market forces.

Furthermore, as was noted earlier, there are significant differences between the U.S. and Japan over energy and security (defense) issues. Considerable coordination and consultation would be required between the U.S. and Japan to arrive at even the rudiments of a collective strategy. Japan should consider this problem as it seeks Alaskan oil or assured U.S. coal supplies.

The bilateral approach might, however, be a good way to begin. The foundations of a unified U.S.-Japan policy are largely in place. While Japan would have its own requirements in such a scheme, it could make a significant economic and strategic contribution, seen from the U.S. side, by:

1. Increasing its defense expenditure.

---

[15] The nations of the Economic Summit include Canada, France, the Federal Republic of Germany, Italy, the United Kingdom, the United States, and Japan.
[16] The oil-consuming developing countries imported 5.3 million B/D for energy use in 1980.

2. Increasing its operational, logistical, and financial cooperation with U.S. forces.

3. Seeking to coordinate, in broad strategic terms, its technical and economic assistance programs throughout the world.

These are not new requests, and they are not out of line with Japan's intentions, capabilities, and interests. If, as Tokyo appears to believe, they are not appropriate requests, given the decreasing value that the leadership places on the long-term prospects for the U.S.-Japan relationship, then the relationship should be reexamined from the U.S. side as well. Japan's trade policies, as they are now, create problems for the advanced nations; its Middle East strategy does not resolve regional issues or strengthen consuming nations' economic interests; and its defense policy does not adequately reflect the realities of Soviet intentions or the instabilities in the Persian Gulf.

Appendix

Adjustment of Trade Results

The trade and exchange rate estimates reported in Table 1, above, represent adjusted variants of the "high oil price" scenario of Napier and Petri.[1] That study developed general equilibrium estimates of trade based on a detailed model of trade relations among Japan, the United States, and a "rest-of-the-world" sector. No new simulations were run for this chapter; rather, the trade flows obtained in the old study were adjusted by using plausible price and income elasticity estimates and other judgmental estimates of the global output effects of further increases in the price of oil.

In general, the foreign exchange *value* of each trade flow was assumed to be given by the relationship:

$$v_i = v_i^* \, r^{\alpha} \, p_{oil}^{\beta} \, y_{row}^{\gamma} \, y_{Japan}^{\delta}$$

where
$\begin{aligned}
v_i &= \text{value of trade flow type i} \\
v_i^* &= \text{value of trade flow in base (\$33) case} \\
r &= \text{exchange rate: yen/SDR} \\
p_{oil} &= \text{price of oil in SDRs} \\
y_{row} &= \text{index of world GNP} \\
y_{Japan} &= \text{index of Japanese GNP}
\end{aligned}$

In the standard case, the following parameter values were used:

Type of flow	α	β	γ	δ
Exports to OPEC	1.00	0.60	0.75	.00
Other Exports	1.00	.00	1.50	−.25
Imports of Oil	−.10	.80	.00	1.00
Other Imports	−1.00	.20	.00	1.25
Invisibles	−1.00	.00	.00	1.50

---

[1] Ron W. Napier and Peter A. Petri, "U.S.-Japan Trade Conflict: The Prospects Ahead," Report to the Department of State, October 1979.

These judgmental values reflect the following considerations: a 1% change in the exchange rate is assumed to increase the foreign exchange value of both types of exports by 1% (the net result of a volume increase of 2% and a value decline 1%); and to decrease the volume, and hence the foreign exchange value, of oil-imports, other imports, and net invisible imports by 0.1%, 1.0%, and 1.0%, respectively. A 1% increase in the price of oil is assumed to increase Japanese exports to OPEC by 0.6% (OPEC revenues would grow by 0.8%, given a global import elasticity of 0.2, and the elasticity of Japanese exports to OPEC with respect to OPEC revenues is taken as 0.75); to increase the Japanese oil import bill by 0.8% (reflecting a 0.1% drop in imported energy demand, and a 0.1% substitution of other energy imports for oil imports); and to increase the value of non-oil imports (mainly through the values and quantities of oil substitutes) by 0.2%. A 1% increase in world GNP is assumed to increase OPEC revenues by 1%, and Japanese exports by 0.75 times that; and to directly increase imports from Japan by 1.5%. A 1% increase in Japanese GNP is assumed to decrease exports to sources other than OPEC by 0.25% (simulating the cyclical component of Japanese export behavior); and to decrease imports of oil, other goods, and invisibles by 1.0%, 1.25%, and 1.5%, respectively.

The main results of these adjustments were presented in Table 1. Some additional sensitivity results follow:

- If Japanese exports to the U.S. are held constant in value terms, and the full adjustment burden of $66 oil is projected onto third markets, the yen exchange rate index would be 87 instead of 89 in 1985.

- If all Japanese trade elasticities are cut to two-thirds of their standard value (export elasticities to 1.33, non-oil import elasticities to 0.67), the $66 exchange-oriented adjustment would require a yen rate of 75 instead of 89.

- If Japan somehow reaches its $33 GNP level (143) despite the fact that oil prices are raised to $66, while the slowdown continues to take its standard toll on other economies, the yen rate for exchange-oriented adjustment would have to be 83 instead of 89.

- If Japan performs according to standard $66 assumptions (GNP 7% below the $33 scenario level), but the rest of the world stops growing altogether between 1980 and 1985, the yen rate for exchange-oriented adjustment would have to be 80 instead of 89.

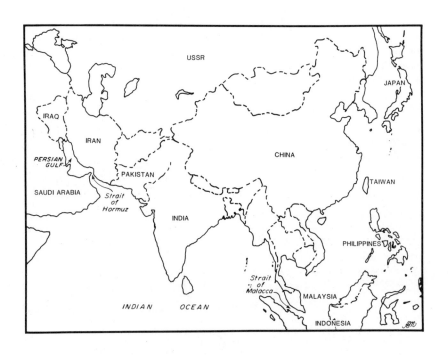

The Dilemmas of Japan's Oil Dependency

Martha Caldwell

INTRODUCTION

During the postwar period, Japan's conservative leadership pursued a low-profile foreign policy, relying on the U.S. security alliance as its central feature. Concentrating on economics rather than politics, the leadership made little systematic effort to establish an independent Japanese foreign policy. It is not surprising, then, that opinions differ about Japan's self-conscious attempt to initiate a more active and independent foreign energy diplomacy during the last decade.

Critics call Japan's oil diplomacy a case of opportunistic "oil grabbing," stimulated by a narrow nationalism.[1] In its most extreme formulation, the argument made by the critics is that Japan has actually continued to separate economics and politics by placing first priority on secure energy supplies, even at the risk of giving in to unreasonable demands made by oil producers. According to this most pessimistic interpretation, Japan's oil diplomacy may ultimately render the nation inextricably dependent on the oil-rich nations.

A second and more widely popular perspective on Japanese oil diplomacy sees in it the reflection of deep-rooted problems within the Organization for Economic Cooperation and Development (OECD). All members of the OECD have at times been charged with pursuing "sauve qui peut" competition for resources and energy supplies. Differing levels of energy self-sufficiency among various OECD nations have made it difficult to develop a joint approach to international energy problems.

---

[1] Hajime Fujiwara, *Nihon Maru wa Chinbotsu Suru* (Tokyo: Jiyu Tsushinsha, 1977), pp. 76 ff.; Ichiro Noguchi, *Nihon no Keizai Nashonarizumu* (Tokyo: Daiyonmondosha, 1976).

According to this line of reasoning, Japanese oil diplomacy is nothing unique. Those who analyze the energy problem from the perspective of the OECD tend to indicate that while progress has been made since the first oil shock, more cooperation is necessary lest lack of coordination reduce the joint bargaining power of all alliance partners.[2]

A third but much less popular interpretation outside Japan is that oil diplomacy reflects the evolution of a more mature Japanese foreign policy. Attempting to develop a more independent foreign policy appropriate for a nation with considerable economic power, Japanese leaders will necessarily make choices which at times diverge from those of the United States or other Western nations. Advocates argue that such an approach is not incompatible with coordination of energy policy among Western nations. By playing the role of a "middleman" sensitive to perspectives of both consumer and producer nations, Japan may be able to contribute significantly to the development of viable joint policies.[3]

None of these differing perspectives on Japanese oil diplomacy has been carefully studied, but they nevertheless permeate the literature. It may be too soon at this point to make a conclusive case for any one perspective or to predict the future, but review and reconsideration are certainly appropriate after a decade of policy development. The primary purpose of this chapter is to explore the origin and evolution of Japanese oil diplomacy in the 1970s, contrasting the abstract theory of resource diplomacy with the concrete trade-offs which Japanese policy makers confront as they attempt to put theory into practice. This analysis investigates Japanese perspectives on the costs and benefits of oil diplomacy and evaluates the mechanisms they developed to manage crisis. Here the focus is on the view from Japan.   .

The Middle East presents a critical test for Japanese oil diplomacy. Supplying more than 75 percent of Japan's imported crude oil, which constitutes about 30 percent of total Japanese imports, the region is a key target of Japanese efforts to secure stable energy supplies. The complex and volatile politics of the region, moreover, set a particularly troublesome context for Japanese oil diplomacy.

The Iran-Japan Petrochemical Project (IJPC), Japan's single largest overseas investment to date, illustrates vividly the dilemmas of Japanese resource diplomacy. The first oil shock and Iranian industrialization programs stimulated the development of the project. With almost 40 percent of Japan's crude oil imports coming from Iran in the early 1970s, Japanese

---

[2] Hisahi Oawada, "Trilateralism: A Japanese Perspective," *International Security*, 5:3 (Winter 1980–81), 24. See also *Report of the U.S.-Japan Economic Relations Group* (Washington, D.C., January 1981), pp. 30 ff.

[3] See "Iran-Iraku Funso o Meguru Shomondai," *Boeki Seisaku*, December 1980, p. 29.

leaders were anxious to step up cooperation with that country. But as the international political and economic context changed at the end of the decade, the costly project was jeopardized by factors not amenable to Japanese control. Attempts made by Japanese leaders to manage the crisis—by spreading the risk among many Japanese participants and by expanding government support—illustrate ongoing problems in Japan's experiment with oil diplomacy.

THE ORIGIN AND EVOLUTION OF JAPANESE OIL DIPLOMACY

The origins of a more active Japanese oil diplomacy can be traced back to the years immediately preceding the first oil shock. The gradually evolving philosophy which capsulized Japanese reevaluation of foreign energy policy in the light of the energy crisis was referred to by Japanese business and government leaders as "resource diplomacy" (*shigen gaiko*). More a compelling perspective than an integrated and coherent policy framework, it represented a reconsideration of Japan's energy vulnerability and a commitment to a new style of foreign oil diplomacy.

In public statements, Japanese energy policymakers stressed major themes of resource diplomacy. The new approach signaled the rising salience of energy problems; former MITI Minister Nakasone, for example, argued that energy had become as important as defense.[4] Aimed at promoting good relations with oil-producing nations, resource diplomacy heralded a new and more active and independent style of Japanese foreign energy policy. The new style of diplomacy had as its goal increasing not only the quantity but also the quality of ties with producer nations; in exchange for oil supplies, Japan would offer technical and financial assistance in a variety of economic development projects. Japan's first energy white paper, published in 1973, emphasized the theme of cooperation with producer nations:

> Oil foreign policy must be developed on the basis of international cooperation. What is particularly needed at this point is positive, many-sided international action.... It will be necessary for Japan to actively cooperate in the economic development of the oil-producing countries, beginning with industrialization, and to take on large-scale development projects as "national projects" involving both government and the private sector. Growing out of this approach, in the future it will be necessary to establish both comprehensive and concrete policies in response to the specific situation in each producing country, beginning with the promotion of

---

[4] Yomiuri Shimbunsha Keizaibuhen, *Enerugi Kiki* (Tokyo: Yomiuri Newspaper, 1973), p. 155.

direct deals, or even further, joint management and investment enterprises in a mutually profitable form.[5]

Resource diplomacy, furthermore, required the establishment of a delicate balance: cooperation with the U.S. and other Western oil consumer nations was to be continued, while ties with the producer countries were to be strengthened. Finally, resource diplomacy was predicated on business-government cooperation. Advocates recognized that special efforts would be necessary to coordinate public and private policy, but they viewed such coordination as essential for the success of the new style of Japanese foreign energy policy.

In the conception and implementation of Japan's emerging oil diplomacy, businessmen popularly referred to as the "resource faction" (*shigen ha*) played central roles. As prominent individuals accustomed to consulting informally with government leaders, they were in a good position to develop support for the new philosophy. While eventually many Japanese businessmen became involved in resource diplomacy, in the early years leadership was taken by three individuals: Soichi Matsune, chairman of *Keidanren*'s energy committee; Sohei Nakayama, counselor to the Industrial Bank of Japan; and Hiraki Imazato, organizer of a number of overseas petroleum development projects.[6]

By the end of the 1970s, so many of Japan's leaders had become committed to a more active resource diplomacy that the term "resource faction" had lost its popularity. Before the first oil shock, however, a small but influential group led the way in advocating a new foreign policy style, in investigating potential overseas oil development and economic assistance projects, and in setting up a number of new organizations to facilitate private as well as public oil diplomacy. More than a year before the oil shock of October 1973, the *Keidanren* energy committee, under the leadership of Shoichi Matsune, called for a comprehensive revision of Japan's energy policy. The "Matsune Plan" called for a more independent foreign oil policy, including expanded participation in Middle Eastern economic development projects.[7] As chairman of the Resources Subcommittee of MITI's Economic Advisory Council (*Keizai Shingikai*), Sohei Nakayama advocated a "resources alliance" with oil-producing nations which would feature Japanese corporate participation in a number of new overseas projects.[8]

---

[5] The first official summary of Japan's foreign energy diplomacy is contained in the Energy White Paper published by MITI's Natural Resources and Energy Agency in 1973. For an English translation, see *Japan Petroleum Yearbook* (Tokyo, 1978), p. C-28.

[6] For a discussion of the resource faction, see Yanagita, "Okami ga Yatte Kita Hi," *Bungei Shunju*, August 1978, p. 109.

[7] *Keidanren Shuppo*, July 19, 1973.

[8] Hisaya Shirai, *Kiki no Naka no Zaikai* (Tokyo: Simul Press, 1973), p. 111.

Japan's business leaders were particularly concerned about the delays that had developed in some of the projects already under way. In 1971, for example, Japanese businessmen began talks with Iranian officials; and in 1972, agreement was reached on the principle of overall economic and technical cooperation between Japan and Iran. The Mitsui group set up a joint venture with Iran (IJPC) in 1973 to build a huge petrochemical complex, but Iranian officials repeatedly criticized the Japanese for long delays and vacillation. Japanese resource faction leaders aimed to moderate such criticism by better coordinating such business efforts, which would, they hoped, also receive stronger government support.

In order to facilitate such coordination, a number of new organizations were established, including the private-sector Committee for the Promotion of Energy Policy and the Middle East Cooperation Center. These organizations provide technical and policy assistance to businessmen in formulating plans and in carrying them out. Resource faction leaders traveled widely, making contacts with officials in oil-producing nations and investigating potential projects. Inspired by growing apprehension that the political and economic balance of power had shifted to the advantage of the producer nations, the resource faction viewed interdependence as a fact of life, a trend to be guided and pursued. Stimulated by fears about resource scarcity, Japanese resource faction leaders nevertheless emphasized the positive aspects of the new approach. Oil diplomacy, they hoped, would provide the vehicle for a completely new style of Japanese foreign policy that would be more active and independent.

The concerns that motivated businessmen in the resource faction were shared by a number of government officials. Former MITI Minister Nakasone made oil diplomacy a centerpiece of MITI's energy policy. In the late spring of 1973, Nakasone toured the Middle East, promising that Japan would never join a "consumer alliance"—a controversial remark which contradicted American calls for a new Atlantic alliance. Nakasone strongly advocated a more independent Japanese oil policy:

> The fact that Japan has no strong commitments to the existing order is both a weakness and a strength. Since Japan is embarking on a journey without a compass or a sense of direction, Japan must promote leadership that sometimes cooperates with the producers in their plans for development and sometimes cooperates with the consumer nations. But at all times it is inevitable that Japan will competitively follow its own independent direction. The era of blindly following has come to an end.[9]

Arguing that Japan could no longer refrain from developing a foreign oil

---

[9] Yasuhiro Nakasone, *Kaito no nai Kokai* (Tokyo: Nihon Keizai Shimbun, 1975), pp. 12–13 (translation by Martha Caldwell).

policy, Nakasone contended that the time had come to develop a policy "standing on the side of the oil producers."

In contrast to MITI officials, Foreign Ministry leaders traditionally oriented toward the U.S. were more cautious about calls to completely redirect foreign policy. There were, to be sure, some young officials who pointed to the growing importance of the Middle East as a region and cautioned against assuming that the weak and hesitating approach taken in the past would be appropriate in the years ahead.[10] While the ministry did establish an International Resources Division within its Economic Affairs Bureau and eventually increased the numbers of staff stationed in the Middle East, the ministry generally took a cautious but interested view toward arguments for oil diplomacy.

Support for a new oil diplomacy grew in the early 1970s first among a number of key businessmen and government leaders, spreading to include Prime Minister Tanaka himself, who called for "multidirectional resource diplomacy." It was, however, easier to talk about oil diplomacy in the abstract than it was to implement it in practice. The initial test came during the oil crisis of 1973–74. Japanese leaders improvised[11] a response to contradictory pressures from the oil producers and the U.S., eventually issuing a strong but belated pro-Arab policy statement. Perceiving themselves to be "walking a tightrope" between consumers and producers, Japan's leaders avoided clarifying the meaning of the statement. The oil crisis provided a difficult context in which to carry out Japan's experiment with oil diplomacy.

Another source of difficulty was the fact that, even in the abstract, the philosophy of resource diplomacy embodied underlying tensions and ambiguities. Those tensions became increasingly clear as the philosophy was put into practice. Based on the premise that it was necessary to maintain a delicate balance between cooperation with consumer nations and cooperation with producer nations, the philosophy provided no simple formula that could be applied to calculate a viable equilibrium. While the concept of resource diplomacy implies a high level of coordination between public and private officials, in practice the interests of the two groups tend to diverge when concrete and highly politicized cases are under consideration. Because of the ambiguities inherent in resource diplomacy and the trade-offs involved, it is much easier to mobilize consensus on its general and abstract principles than it is to forge agreement among the various groups involved in concrete efforts to carry it out.

---

[10] "Chunkinto Taishi Kaigo o Furikaette," *Keizai to Gaiko*, September 1973, p. 2.
[11] See Haruhiro Fukui's analysis of Japanese foreign policymaking in *The Foreign Policy of Modern Japan*, ed. Robert A. Scalapino (Berkeley and Los Angeles: University of California Press, 1977), p. 30.

DILEMMAS OF OIL DIPLOMACY IN PRACTICE: THE MITSUI PETROCHEMICAL PROJECT IN IRAN

Almost a decade has passed since a Japanese investment corporation, the Iran Chemical Development Corporation (ICDC), was established to organize Japanese participation in a huge petrochemical project at Bandar-Khomeini on the Persian Gulf. Despite the fact that the effort has been strongly supported by the Japanese government and was reported to be 86 percent complete before the outbreak of the Iran-Iraq war in September 1980, today the future of the project remains in doubt. The largest single Japanese overseas investment to date, the Iranian petrochemical project illustrates the perils and potentials of oil diplomacy. The uneven evolution of the project reveals some of the concrete conflicts which tend to arise among various Japanese participants, and between Japan and the Western nations, when oil diplomacy is put into practice. The focus of this analysis will be on problems not unique to the Mitsui project: management of conflicts or disagreements among Japanese participants and between Japan and other nations. In addition, abundant public statements and analyses of the project in the Japanese-language literature provide a basis for reviewing the Japanese perspective on the costs and benefits of such a project. The history of the Mitsui project reveals the perils of resource diplomacy, but it also demonstrates the capacity of Japan's government and business leaders to manage crisis and spread risk.[12]

Conflicts of Interest Among Japanese Participants

The Iranian petrochemical project began as a purely private Japanese undertaking. In the spring of 1973, a joint venture, the Iran-Japan Petrochemical Company (IJPC), was established with 50 percent participation by the Mitsui-led ICDC, an investment corporation set up in 1971. The five participating firms in the ICDC are all from the Mitsui group: Mitsui and Company, Mitsui Toatsu Chemical Company, Toyo Soda Manufacturing, Mitsui Petrochemical Company, and Japan Synthetic Rubber Company. The petrochemical complex in Iran, which was originally estimated to cost $500 million, includes an olefin plant, desalination equipment, and an electrolysis plant. Petrochemicals, liquified petroleum gas (LPG), and caustic soda will be produced. The project as it was originally conceived promised to benefit both Japan and Iran: Japan is projected to receive 2 million tons of LPG annually, and the project will increase Iran's capacity to produce petrochemical products for export as well as for the local market. The project was viewed not

---

[12] For an analysis of Japanese group strategies overseas, see Terutomo Ozawa, *Multinationalism, Japanese Style* (Princeton: Princeton University Press, 1979), pp. 183–192.

only as a source of expanded energy imports to Japan but also as a centerpiece of Iranian economic development. By early 1981, the Japanese side had contributed more than $1.7 billion in equity and loans. Estimates were running as high as $5 billion for the project, which was still incomplete following suspension of construction at the time of the Iranian Revolution in 1979 and the Iran-Iraq War in 1980.[13]

Viewed from the perspective of the Japanese participants, the first stage of crisis was surmounted in the fall of 1979. Construction had come to a halt following the Iranian revolution in the spring of that year. By the fall, however, Iranian President Bazargan notified Japan's ambassador to Iran that he hoped construction could be resumed on the project as quickly as possible. The Japanese participants were concerned about a number of problems, such as Iranian delay in construction of ancillary facilities, cost overruns requiring an additional billion dollars in financing, and rumors that the Iranian government might nationalize the project.[14]

During the summer and fall of 1979, government officials and businessmen debated about what should be done. Businessmen called for the reorganization of the effort as a "national project" with strong Japanese government support. In May of that year, the private Middle East Cooperation Center held a special meeting to discuss problems relating to the project; and later in August, *Keidanren* officially called for the reorganization of the project. Among those most influential in helping to form consensus within the government was Naohiro Amaya, MITI Vice Minister for International Affairs. Government leaders such as Mr. Amaya felt that since Japan had up until recently received 17 percent of all crude oil imports from Iran, continuation of the project was a kind of quid pro quo for renewed supplies from Iran.[15] In early September 1979, Mr. Amaya led a Japanese delegation to Iran. Receiving assurances from Iranian officials that necessary housing and natural gas supplies would be made available and that the project would not be nationalized, Mr. Amaya returned to Japan to strongly advocate the formation of a "national project." MITI Minister Esaki was impressed by the Amaya mission findings and negotiated with other ministers, such as Finance Minister Kaneko, EPA Director Kosaka, and Chief Cabinet Secretary Tanaka, to build support for the idea of a national project.[16]

On October 12, 1979, the cabinet formally approved the MITI pro-

[13] This information is provided by Mitsui and Company. See also *Asian Wall Street Journal*, December 1, 1980, p. 18.

[14] "Sai Shuppatsu suru Iran Sekiyu Kagaku Keikaku," *Boeki Seisaku*, November 1979, pp. 5–6.

[15] See Naohiro Amaya, "Enerugi Toshi ni Mizeni o Kire," *Chuo Koron*, October 1979, p. 104.

[16] "Japanese Likely to Support Iran Petrochemical Project," *Asian Wall Street Journal*, September 13, 1979.

posal, setting up a national project. The government agreed to provide 20 billion yen (about $83 million) for the project in equity participation through the Overseas Economic Cooperation Fund. In addition, 80 billion yen ($333 million) worth of loans were to be set up through the Export-Import Bank. In an attempt to further spread the financial risk, participation in the project was opened up to about twenty Japanese companies outside the Mitsui group, thereby expanding financing.

While it appeared, for the moment at least, that the project had been saved by a joint Japanese government and business effort, strong criticisms were raised. The *Nihon Keizai Shimbun* warned in a September 12, 1979 editorial against quick expansion of government involvement, pointing to a lack of firm agreement among various government ministers. Some critics were disturbed by the fact that Mr. Emei Yamashita, president of the Iran Chemical Development Corporation (ICDC), is a former MITI Vice Minister with obvious contacts in the agency.[17] (Mr. Yamashita was later promoted to the position of Vice President of Mitsui Bussan, in May 1980.[18]) The critics argued that it was a bad precedent for the government to bail out private companies simply because they face unexpected difficulty. Mr. Amaya and other government officials, however, contended that it was both necessary and appropriate for the Japanese government to act—not to "save Mitsui," but to assure good relations with Japan's second largest oil supplier.[19] Soon after the project was reorganized, MITI Minister Esaki requested a 30 percent increase in oil supplies from Iran. In the end, despite criticism, the Mitsui project was revitalized with strong Japanese government support.

In the fall of 1979, it thus appeared that the project had been salvaged through these efforts. Soon thereafter, however, a second-stage dilemma developed. Despite optimistic reports in the spring of 1980 stating that construction would soon resume on the project, progress was delayed by the worsening state of U.S.-Iranian relations due to the hostage crisis and by the war with Iraq which began in the fall of 1980. As events developed, the Mitsui project became, in a sense, Iran's Japanese hostage. In May 1980, oil supplies from Iran ended and Iran threatened Mitsui by suggesting that the project could easily be turned over to Hungary for completion. In September and October, the project was repeatedly bombed by the Iraqi air force, leading to growing concern about the fate of Japanese engineers and technicians at the site. Factors outside the control of the Japanese participants once again jeopardized the project, stimulating intensified conflicts of interest.

---

[17] See, for example, *Shukan Shincho*, May 15, 1980, pp. 140–143.

[18] *Nihon Keizai*, May 13, 1980. Mr. Yamashita retired in June 1981 from his position as ICDC president. See *Nihon Keizai*, May 27, 1981.

[19] Naohiro Amaya, "Chonin Kuni Nihon Tetsudai no Kurigoto," *Bungei Shunju*, March 1980, p. 227.

On October 13, 1980, after the third Iraqi bombing and almost a year after the establishment of the national project, Toshikuni Yahiro, head of Mitsui and Company, stated in a Tokyo press conference that unless the Japanese government could provide additional support for the project, it would be impossible for the private sector to continue under the circumstances. Supplies of materials and natural gas had been disrupted, while the interest on loans for the project was said to amount to about 100 million yen (about $500,000) per day. Pressed with demands from the Iranian government for additional financing, Mr. Yahiro stated that the private sector had reached a threshold of maximum feasible risk—that unless further government assistance was forthcoming, Mitsui might be forced simply to withdraw.

A year earlier, MITI officials had been criticized for publicly favoring Mitsui, but now MITI Minister Rokusuke Tanaka turned to criticize Mitsui. In an interview published in the November 11, 1980 *Ekonomisto* magazine, Tanaka called the statements by Mr. Yahiro excessively "self-interested."[20] Since more than one hundred firms were now involved in the project, its fate, said Tanaka, should not be dictated by Mitsui alone.[21] MITI officials said that a decision about the project must await the end of the Iran-Iraq war and a survey of damages to the site. At the heart of the controvery which divided business and government leaders was the question of financing.

Since it was not clear that the Mitsui group would be eligible for full coverage under the government's export insurance if it simply withdrew from a project which was not terminated by Iran, there were strong incentives for the private sector to continue to participate. With losses due to delays mounting and with few alternatives available, Mitsui leaders have hoped to enlist expanded government support. Mitsui officials requested that the Japanese Export-Import Bank and other private creditors allow a moratorium on repayment of loans for six to twelve months.[22] Japanese financial institutions responded that Mitsui should first get Iran to agree to delay repayment on loans to the joint venture, but the government of Iran refused to do so.[23] With time running out on loan repayment schedules, Mitsui requested additional financing amounting to 9 billion yen from Iran.[24] After such requests failed to produce success, the five ICDC firms discussed the possibility of making the ¥3 billion (about

---

[20] Interview with MITI Minister Rokusuke Tanaka, *Ekonomisto*, November 11, 1980, p. 20.

[21] Ibid. Minister Tanaka states in the interview that ICDC head Yamashita had not been consulted about Mr. Yahiro's remarks and was not ready to withdraw from the project.

[22] "Kohi Saikai, Shusen ga Zentei," *Nihon Keizai*, January 19, 1981.

[23] "Mitsui, ICDC Lon ni Shiboru," *Nihon Keizai*, February 8, 1981.

[24] "Iran 90 oku en no Zoshi Yojo," *Nihon Keizai*, February 6, 1981, p. 1.

$15 million) payment themselves. In late April 1981—after some disagreement among the firms involved—the Japanese side decided to suspend payment to the IJPC.

While Mitsui spokesmen said that suspension of payments by the ICDC did not mean that the project had been completely abandoned, they privately admitted that it would take years to determine the fate of the effort. It was decided that a negotiating team from Mitsui would visit Iran to explain the Japanese position; but in May 1981, scheduled discussions between the two sides were postponed. The Japanese government had previously opposed termination of the project, but now there was tacit official support for private sector moves to suspend payments.

The Iranian petrochemical project illustrates complex problems in financing that arise in conjunction with large overseas efforts sponsored by a number of Japanese firms. As the project evolved, its financial structure became more and more complicated. When more corporate participants were added in order to spread the risk, it became difficult to determine who was responsible for making decisions—especially since the Japanese government increased its support for the project (see Figure 1 and Table 1).

The project has been a real test—for the Japanese government as well as for the firms involved. All participants have incurred high sunk costs. But government and private officials have tended to view the project differently. From the perspective of the businessmen involved, particularly Mitsui representatives, the private sector should not be expected to bear huge financial burdens when unexpected difficulties arise. Government officials, on the other hand, tend to view such projects as part of Japan's overall energy security and foreign policy, and therefore feel that commitments to oil-producing nations should not be broken.

A variety of measures were developed by Japanese government and business leaders to manage the problem of spreading financial risk, but it has not been easy to build consensus among the participants. Acrimonious public exchanges between government and business officials reflect growing conflicts of interest between the two sectors over short-term options. The Mitsui project thus illustrates limits to the ability of Japanese business and government leaders to manage the complicated financial and political problems associated with such a mammoth overseas project.

Iranian Oil and Japan's Relations with Western Nations

A second type of dilemma of oil diplomacy has involved tension between the Japanese desire for secure oil supplies and the need to coordinate policies with Western nations. In 1979, after the Iranian revolution, major international oil companies announced that supplies to Japan would be reduced. As a result, Japanese oil refiners and trading companies in-

FIGURE 1

FINANCIAL STRUCTURE OF IJPC

1. Mitsui Group 5
2. Loans from ExIm Bank
3. Overseas Economic
   Cooperation Fund financing
4. 20 additional Japanese companies

ICDC → | IJPC (joint venture) | ← National Iranian Petrochemical Company

creased their purchases of "direct deal" oil.[25] Direct deal oil imports thus reached record highs as a portion of Japan's total oil supplies in late 1979 and early 1980. Just as prices on the spot market rose, the situation in the oil market was complicated by the seizure of the U.S. embassy in Teheran.

Initially, the Japanese government, under the leadership of Prime Minister Ohira and Foreign Minister Okita, continued to emphasize oil diplomacy. When the National Iranian Oil Company pressed Japanese firms to buy 20–30 million barrels of oil on a spot market basis as a kind of quid pro quo for long-term direct deal contracts, government officials in Japan did not at first attempt systematically to restrain Japanese companies from making the purchases. Furthermore, on December 9, 1979, press reports stated that talks would be scheduled between Japanese officials and PLO representatives. Japan's United Nations representative was reported to have met with a PLO official in late November 1979. These moves were popularly interpreted as signs that the Ohira administration had committed itself to an increasingly independent oil diplomacy featuring a "more positive" attitude toward the PLO.[26]

The American response to these Japanese actions was swift and decisive. In talks with Japanese Foreign Minister Okita on December 10, 1979, Secretary of State Vance expressed his dissatisfaction with Japan's uncooperative attitude. In the American view, Japan had failed to show support for the U.S. on the hostage issue; particularly troublesome was the fact that Japanese companies were buying Iranian oil after the U.S. ceased importing it. Japan, in the U.S. view, had shown great insensitivity toward the American position.

To many Japanese, however, Vance's public rebuke seemed unnecessary and inappropriate, a sign of growing American frustration.[27] Tokyo nevertheless responded by quickly dispatching MITI Minister for

---

[25] In late 1979, direct deals rose to over 30 percent of the total. See *Asahi*, February 10, 1980.

[26] *Nihon Keizai*, December 9, 1979; *Asahi*, December 9, 1979.

[27] Naohiro Amaya, "Chonin Kuni Nihon Tetsudai no Kurigoto," *Bungei Shunju*, March 1980, p. 219.

Table 1

IJPC FUNDS
(*millions of dollars*)

		Original Budget	Additional Funds	Total
Equity	Japanese	200	200	400
	Iranian	200	200	400
	(subtotal)	(400)	(400)	(800)
Loans	Japanese	1,040	330	1,370
	Iranian	830		830
	(subtotal)	(1,870)	(330)	(2,200)
TOTAL		2,270	730	3,000*

SOURCES: Mitsui and Company; *Nihon Keizai*, May 8, 1980 and February 2, 1981; *Asian Wall Street Journal*, October 15, 1979.

*Total as of May 1980. These figures represent commitments rather than actual expenditures. Out of the total Japanese investment as of May 1980, about $413 million, or about 23 percent of the total of $1.77 billion, were committed by the Japanese government. It should be noted that many of the recently published higher-cost estimates for the project reflect the appreciation of the yen. In addition, the five Japanese Mitsui group firms have recently decided to provide additional funding not reflected in these figures.

International Affairs Amaya on a "fire fighting" mission to the United States. In a press conference on December 14, Mr. Amaya admitted that the United States' complaint was "proper," and he pledged that the Japanese government would attempt to guide Japanese companies to limit purchases of Iranian oil in view of the hostage crisis. Japan's representative further agreed to hold imports of oil from Iran to the level that prevailed before the hostage crisis, a promise which evidently later made it necessary for some Japanese companies to sell Iranian oil to third parties.[28]

Japanese companies continued to import Iranian oil in early 1980; and in February, former Foreign Minister Sonoda was sent on a tour of the Middle East in an attempt to show Japanese support for Islamic states in the region. During his trip, Sonoda was scheduled to meet with PLO leader Arafat, a move evidently supported by MITI officials. However, the plan for a meeting was abandoned after strong opposition arose from Foreign Ministry and U.S. officials.[29] Japan's foreign policy toward the Middle East remained unclear in the early months of 1980, revealing disagreement within the government.

[28] *Asian Wall Street Journal*, December 7, 1979.
[29] *Asahi*, February 15, 1980; *New York Times*, February 28, 1980.

In April, however, the Japanese position was clarified. As Iran began to press Japan to buy oil at a price of $35 a barrel, Japanese resistance grew. Following lengthy talks between Prime Minister Ohira and U.S. Ambassador Mansfield, promises were made that if Japan supported U.S. sanctions against Iran, the United States would assist Japan in securing oil supplies to the extent possible. Japanese officials decided to use Iran's demands for a price hike as a chance to show support for the U.S. position.[30] Calculating that Japan could withstand a complete cut in supplies from Iran, Japanese officials refused the Iranian offer to sell oil—a move publicly welcomed by U.S. officials.

At the end of April, Japanese leaders moved ahead with plans to bring their policy into alignment with Western Europe. Determined to avoid a situation in which Japan might become internationally isolated over the embargo issue, Japanese leaders energetically consulted with European leaders. To some participants, the process of building a joint strategy between Japan and Western Europe was as important as the outcome. In late April, the Japanese and European Economic Community nations agreed to participate in economic sanctions against Iran until the American hostages were released. A joint Western approach to the Iranian crisis had at last been developed.

After months of hesitation and friction, a common position was solidified. Japanese leaders emphasized their commitment to coordinating policy with Western nations.[31] While some observers criticized the sanctions as "unlikely to produce the desired results,"[32] Japanese leaders stated that good relations with the U.S. were more important than oil. It must be noted, however, that it had taken months for Japan to develop this position. Only after long negotiations with European leaders, and only after Japanese leaders had assured themselves that Japan would not suffer from a cutoff in oil supplies from Iran, did the policy take shape. Japan's participation in the sanctions against Iran thus represents less a dramatic switch in Japanese foreign policy than a careful calculation of the trade-offs involved. As Iran became more and more isolated internationally, Japan moved to develop a joint policy with the U.S. and Western Europe. The Mitsui project was excluded from the sanctions.

Patterns of Interdependence between Japan and the Middle East

The Mitsui project illustrates how the practice of oil diplomacy has led to the rise of internal controversies among Japanese participants and to international tensions between Japan and the Western nations. Another

---

[30] Interview with Takao Tomitate of the Energy Economic Research Institute, in *Asahi Janaru*, May 16, 1980.
[31] "Nihon Dokuji no Taiyo mo," *Asahi*, April 13, 1980.
[32] *Asahi*, editorial, April 11, 1980, p. 5.

facet of oil diplomacy is Japan's relationship with the Middle East by virtue of energy, trade, and financial ties. Many observers have worried that oil diplomacy may make Japan more dependent on the oil-rich nations and thereby increase Japanese vulnerability to pressure from them. Patterns of energy, trade, and financial interdependence illustrate the nature of Japan's relationship with the Middle East.

1. Japanese Exports—Japan's total exports to the Middle East have risen in value from $1.7 billion in 1973 (4.4 percent of all Japan's exports) to $10.6 billion in 1979 (9.8 percent of the total). A slight decrease in levels of exports in 1979 as compared to 1978 reflected in large part a substantial decrease in exports to Iran during that year. Exports to Iran previously amounted to more than 26 percent of all Japanese exports to the region. (In the early months of 1980, Japanese exports to Iran fell to less than 3 percent of the total.[33]) Japan's trade balance with Iran and the Middle East region as a whole has been unfavorable in recent years.

Japanese exports to Iran and other Middle Eastern nations have been heavily concentrated, with more than half of the total in machinery and equipment. In 1979, 31 percent of all Japan's plant exports went to the Middle East; the value of these shipments was $3.6 billion. Japan ranks third behind the U.S. and West Germany in plant exports to the Middle East.[34] Concerned about political instability in the region, plant exporters and MITI officials have called for expanded government insurance coverage for investors in large-scale efforts (such as the Mitsui project) and for additional assistance to plant exporters.[35] As the target of more than 10 percent of Japanese overseas investment in recent years,[36] the Middle East is an important export market for Japan.

2. Middle East Investment in Japan—With the growth of the oil-producing nations' current account surplus, Japan has become, particularly in recent months, an increasingly important capital market for Middle Eastern investors. Oil-rich nations eager to diversify portfolios have looked to Japanese equity and bond investment. Such trends are not new—the Japanese government received $1 billion from Saudi Arabia's central bank in the early 1970s to help deal with foreign exchange difficulties. However, the extent and diversity of investments in recent months are noteworthy.

By March 1980, foreign investors from oil-producing nations had acquired stocks totaling 156 million shares in the Japanese market, an

---

[33] *Digest of Japanese Industry and Technology*, No. 151 (1980), pp. 1, 100–101.
[34] Ibid.
[35] *Asian Wall Street Journal*, February 26, 1981. Keidanren leader Yoshiyama called for a broadened program of assistance, including expanded export insurance and Export-Import Bank loans in non-yen currencies.
[36] *Industrial Review of Japan*, 1980, p. 38.

increase of 2.6 times over the number owned a year earlier. Between January and September 1980, total foreign holdings (not exclusively Arab) increased dramatically, rising from 13 to 20 percent of all stocks purchased. In the month of August 1980 alone, $1.1 billion worth of stocks was purchased by foreign investors. It is not easy to calculate precise levels of Arab equity investment in Japan, since Middle East investors often operate through European banks. Financial analysts, however, estimate that total Arab stockholdings probably far exceed the nominal figure of $454 million.[37] Petrodollar investors have preferred electrical machinery, steel, and electronics stocks. The Swiss Credit Bank, said to be primarily engaged in recycling petrodollars, now ranks among the largest shareholders of Hitachi stock. Kuwaiti investors have been among the leaders in Japanese equity investments. One analyst has calculated that if London and Swiss channels for Arab purchases of Japanese stock are included, such investments are worth $1 billion, or about 220 billion yen.[38]

It is especially difficult to find accurate information on the value of foreign investments in Japanese bonds. Middle East investors may have purchased close to a fourth of all bonds sold in the Japanese market in 1980; these bonds were estimated to be worth $3 billion.[39] Saudi Arabia, in particular, has been a major bond purchaser and is now reported to be buying Japanese government bonds on a regular basis. The Ministry of Finance has, moreover, recently decided to provide guarantees for overseas issues of yen-denominated bonds by Japanese public corporations. Japan Air Lines, for example, may raise 10 billion yen through bond sales to Saudi Arabia.[40] In 1980, the Japanese government offered Arab investors $1 billion worth of yen-denominated "Ohira bonds," a step aimed to alleviate balance-of-payments problems. Foreign deposits in Japanese banks have also increased in recent months, much of the deposits evidently made by Middle Eastern investors.

These investment trends are significant, but it must be remembered that Middle East investments in Japan still represent only a small portion—perhaps 10 percent—of all OPEC investments. More important than overall levels of investment have been signs in recent months that Japan, because of its strong economy, has become a prime target for Middle Eastern investors seeking to diversify investment portfolios. Japanese businessmen appear to be generally unconcerned about these investment trends; instead, most financial analysts and business leaders regard the

[37] *Nihon Keizai*, December 12, 1980; *Far Eastern Economic Review*, July 18, 1980, p. 38; "Oiru Mane," *Ekonomisto*, November 25, 1980, p. 16.
[38] Akio Wada, "New Steps for Strengthening Financial Tie-Ups with Middle East Countries," *Digest of Japanese Industry and Technology*, No. 151 (1980), p. 27.
[39] Ibid.; *Asian Wall Street Journal*, March 30, 1980.
[40] *Asian Wall Street Journal*, January 26, 1981.

Table 2

CRUDE OIL IMPORTS

(% of total)

	1978	1979	1980
Iran	12.9	13.0	5.8
Iraq	3.8	6.1	7.4
Middle East Total	77.8	75.9	73.0

SOURCE: Sekiyu Renmei, *Sekiyu Shiryo Geppo*, January 1981, p. 13.

influx of foreign capital as a sign of worldwide confidence in Japanese firms.[41]

3. *Oil Supplies.*—Prior to the first oil crisis, Japan relied on Iran for 30–40 percent of all crude oil imports. In 1978 and 1979, about 13 percent of all crude oil and about 7 percent of all naphtha imports came from Iran. In 1980, however, imports from Iran almost completely disappeared in the second half of the year (see Table 2). During 1979, Japan's crude oil imports from Iran alone were valued at more than $5 billion.[42]

While the cutback in oil supplies from Iran was certainly a cause for concern among Japanese policymakers, Japan was able to weather the crisis fairly smoothly by increasing imports from nations such as Saudi Arabia and the U.A.E. and by taking effective domestic energy conservation measures. MITI reported that between April and June 1980, energy consumption declined 3.7 percent compared to the previous year.

After the release of the American hostages in January 1981, Japan ended economic sanctions against Iran, and Japanese companies were among the first to negotiate for renewed oil contracts. By mid-February, Japanese traders had negotiated to purchase 170,000–180,000 barrels of Iranian oil per day, or about 4 percent of crude oil imports, from the National Iranian Oil Company. Observers suggested that the renewed oil imports might pave the way for resumption of the Mitsui project.[43] New contracts with Iran presented a delicate problem; Japanese policymakers had to avoid antagonizing either Iraq or Saudi Arabia.

These patterns of energy, trade, and financial interdependence between Japan and the Middle East ensure the continued importance of

---

[41] Keiji Ikeda, "Oiru Mane," *Ekonomisto*, November 25, 1980, p. 17.
[42] Based on Sekiyu Renmei, *Sekiyu Shiryo Geppo*, January 1981, pp. 13 and 29.
[43] "Ni-Iran Sekiyu Kosho Goi," *Nihon Keizai*, February 16, 1981.

Japanese oil diplomacy in the region. Links between Japan and the Middle East are being strengthened, particularly in the area of foreign investment in Japan. Like the Mitsui project, these patterns of interdependence reflect Japan's growing ties to the region.

DILEMMAS OF JAPANESE OIL DIPLOMACY

The evolution of the Mitsui project dramatically illustrates the dilemmas of Japanese oil diplomacy. Growing conflicts of interest among Japanese partners stemmed from unresolved tensions within the theory of resource diplomacy. Japan's attempt to develop a more active and independent foreign energy policy dates back to the years preceding the first oil shock. A self-conscious attempt on the part of Japanese public and private leaders to devise a new overseas strategy, oil diplomacy was aimed to achieve a delicate balance: orienting Japan more toward the producer nations while at the same time maintaining good relations with the West. But, as the Mitsui project shows, it is much more difficult to achieve such a balance in practice than it is to talk about it in the abstract. Over the past decade, Japanese policymakers have repeatedly faced conflicts of interest at home and abroad in their attempt to put oil diplomacy into practice.

The acrimonious debate between Mitsui President Yahiro and MITI Minister Tanaka reveals the crux of the domestic policy problem: *government-business cooperation tends to diminish as levels of risk increase.* To be sure, a number of methods have been developed to spread risk and build consensus, but such arrangements have not emerged easily or automatically. Furthermore, as financial risk is spread further and further, it becomes increasingly difficult to determine who is ultimately responsible. Under such conditions it is easy to pass the buck—from public to private sector, and back again. Such conflicts and disagreements are not unique to the Mitsui project.

National projects, an important vehicle for Japanese participation in overseas energy development, involve a complex and delicate mix of private and public concerns. Japan's experience with the Mitsui project in Iran suggests the need for careful clarification of commitments, with special consideration given to potential political difficulties which might jeopardize such projects. The Saudi Petrochemical Development Company (SPDC) is an example of a slightly different approach. This huge petrochemical project, in which firms from the Mitsubishi group have taken the lead, was designated as a national project from the very beginning. Substantial financial backing was provided by the government; the Japanese government owns 45 percent of the equity in the Japanese investment corporation analogous to the ICDC. Unlike the Mitsui project in Iran, the Saudi petrochemical project also involves participation by Dow Chemical Europe. The participation of non-Japanese firms, some argue, may lend strength to the Japan-Saudi effort.[44]

Another type of oil diplomacy dilemma has involved *friction between Japan and the Western nations*. Japanese leaders have found it difficult, particularly in crisis, to balance initiatives directed at oil-producing nations with policy coordination among Western nations. Japan's response to the Iranian crisis has been erratic: initiatives were taken, only to be followed by retrenchment. Patterns of interdependence between Japan and Middle Eastern nations help to explain such vacillation in Japanese foreign policy. These patterns of energy, trade, and financial links ensure that Japan will continue to pursue a unique path of oil diplomacy in the region, and that the benefits will outweigh the costs. The differing relationships which each OECD nation has formed with the Middle East, furthermore, present obstacles to the formation of a clear and consistent joint Western strategy. Contradictory impulses at the heart of the theory of Japanese oil diplomacy guarantee that such international conflicts will continue in the years ahead.

Some observers suggest that Japan's oil diplomacy is nothing more than "oil grabbing"—opportunistic economic nationalism. Others suggest that it represents the evolution of a more mature and independent Japanese foreign policy. But Japanese oil diplomacy in theory and practice is, in the last analysis, neither a simple continuation of the pure commercial strategy of years past nor the fruition of a full-blown new style of Japanese foreign policy. The historical evolution of Japan's oil diplomacy shows that it has been a serious and self-conscious attempt on the part of Japanese leaders to create a new balance, even if sacrifice of short-term interests to long-term national goals is sometimes necessary. The development of the Mitsui project, for example, was largely determined by the fact that government leaders viewed it as an effort in the national interest which should be preserved even if it is costly. On the other hand, there is nothing in the evolution of oil diplomacy which would justify calling it a new grand strategy. Japanese policymakers—public and private—have responded in an ad hoc fashion to the Iranian crisis, attempting to achieve a balance but moving ahead uneasily. Neither a simple continuation of the pure commercial approach taken in the past nor a totally new and integrated strategy, Japanese oil diplomacy is nevertheless an experiment which Japanese leaders view as necessary.

From the Japanese perspective, oil diplomacy is a difficult but absolutely essential undertaking. Japanese leaders have repeatedly described oil diplomacy as a precarious enterprise, like walking a tightrope,

---

[44] "Sauji Kagaku Shido," *Nihon Keizai Shimbun*, series, May 26 and 27, 1981.

for which they view themselves as ill-equipped. MITI leader Mr. Amaya explains the dilemma in this way:

> If Japan chooses to follow the path of a merchant nation in international society, we must understand the way of the merchant. When necessary we have to beg for oil from the oil-producing nations, and at times bow and beg the forgiveness of the military powers. We must consider the strengths and weaknesses of both sets of nations, discern the real trends of the time, and be careful not to act improperly.[45]

In the context of continuing Middle Eastern political instability, Japanese leaders will find it necessary—but increasingly difficult—to strike the delicate balance which oil diplomacy requires.

---

[45] Naohiro Amaya, "Chonin Kuni Nihon Tetsudai no Kurigoto," *Bungei Shunju*, March 1980, p. 232.

Tokyo Electric Power Company: Its Role in Shaping Japan's Coal and LNG Policy

Roger W. Gale

Tokyo Electric Power Company (TEPCO) is the world's largest privately-owned utility. It has more generating capacity, customers, and assets than any of its American cousins. And, most important, it is far more influential than any of them in the formulation of national energy policy. The suzerainty that TEPCO (actually known as *Tokyo Denryoku K.K.*) exercises over the eight other private electric companies[1] enhances its power and makes it one of the key actors in Japan's energy firmament.

Yet, in comparison to the efforts that have been devoted in recent years to the study of the Ministry of International Trade and Industry's energy policymaking role, TEPCO and the other utilities in Japan have gone virtually unnoticed by foreign scholars. While MITI's influence has grown at the expense of the Foreign Ministry and the Science and Technology Agency, the power of the electric companies has also grown vis-à-vis MITI.

In recent years, the incrementally expanding influence of the utilities has been infused with TEPCO's enterprising aggressiveness. Through the Federation of Electric Power Companies (*Denki Gigyo Rengokai*), TEPCO's influence over MITI, the trading companies, and other actors in the energy arena has become increasingly institutionalized.

MITI is by no means obeisant to TEPCO and the other utilities. But—unlike the domestic oil companies, over which MITI wields consid-

---

[1] See Table 1, below.

85

erable legislative and extralegal clout—the ministry is more of an arbiter between the utilities and the contending interests of other industries and the consumer, rather than a regulator. Its principle interest is to stem the use of oil by utilities and to promote the use of electricity, especially the variety produced by the atom.

With the share of energy supplied to end-users by electricity growing relative to that supplied directly from oil, gas, and other forms of energy, the electric power companies (as is the case in most industrialized countries) can be expected to play an even more crucial role in the future in both supplying energy and formulating the energy policies that go along with that enterprise.

The voracious appetite for new capital in the utility industry dwarfs the demands of any other industry in Japan. And the utilities, rather than the oil companies, are becoming the primary purchasers of energy from abroad.

TEPCO relies on the trading companies to manage its foreign business affairs, but, like its rival for influence, Kansai Electric Power Company (which controls the Osaka-Kyoto area), TEPCO is in the market for such large amounts of uranium, liquefied natural gas (LNG), coal, and oil—all of which are politically contentious commodities—that the trading companies' overseas offices tend to spend a disproportionate amount of time attending to the utilities' affairs.

Japan's gas companies (unable to grow because of an historic opposition to the construction of pipelines that could add new customers in the suburbs) have been reluctantly forced into partnership with the electric utilities' ambitious programs for cornering the world market in LNG.

The paucity of research in English on Japan's utilities has prompted me to write this chapter. Oil and nuclear issues are discussed in other chapters in this volume. I look at two other fuels, which, besides not being systematically studied by foreigners, also happen to be good case studies to highlight the power of the utilities.

In the case of LNG, which TEPCO began importing in 1969, we have an example of a utility initiating a risky, capital-intensive international venture on its own volition. In the case of coal, on the other hand, we have an elegant (still unfinished) study of the reluctance of the private utilities to return once again to the use of coal after a 20-year marriage to oil and the atom.

This chapter has three themes, two of which should already be obvious. One is to introduce the preeminent role of the utilities. The second, really the obverse of the first, is to offer a corrective to the widely-held view that it is sufficient to study MITI in order to comprehend the mechanics of Japanese energy. MITI, I argue, is a majordomo that carries out a broad constellation of tasks. The utilities are superincumbents in their own domestic landscape and are of increasing notoriety internationally as well.

Finally, running through the chapter is a theme that is left implicit and awaits conceptual elaboration by some other essayist. It is that one of the wisdoms of Japan's energy policy is its medium-term perspective. Not coincidentally, the span is measured at around thirty years, the expected lifetime of large electric power plants. In contrast to the United States, where a workable distinction between the purportedly imminently achievable and the possible is not rigidly drawn, Japan has been able to avoid the discordant shifts in energy policy that are so common in the U.S. Both countries have trouble contemplating the future, but Japan's goals have remained stable. Those goals include a diversification of energy sources by type and by geography, a lid on oil consumption, increased reliance on nuclear power, and the medium-term use of LNG and coal.

The U.S., on the other hand, has just shifted from an administration that opposed nuclear power to one that supports it; from one that subsidized certain projects to one that is abandoning them; from one that forced utilities (and everyone else) to shift away from the use of gas to one that is shortly going to begin encouraging the use of gas.

The constancy of policy in Japan and the ample room for autonomous action granted the utilities have enabled them to shift rapidly to LNG—for which the economic infrastructure is comparable to that of nuclear power plants—in order to cope with the lag in the construction timetable for new nuclear reactors. LNG now supplies as much electrical power as TEPCO's six nuclear reactors, even though the decision to import LNG was made fifteen to twenty years after the company made the commitment to "go nuclear."

The discussion that follows is divided into four parts. The first section focuses on TEPCO and its place in Japanese energy policy. That is followed by a brief review of Japan's medium- and long-term energy goals. The third section focuses on LNG policy. The fourth section focuses on coal.

To a very large extent, statistical data being the main exception, my sources of information have been utility, government, and trading company officials whom I interviewed between 1975 and 1980, a period of immense change in Japan's thinking on energy.

THE ELECTRIC POWER INDUSTRY

Since its establishment in 1887 as the Tokyo Electric Light Company, TEPCO has been the dominant utility in Japan. It was usually the leader in the introduction of foreign technology, and it had the closest relations with the national government because of its location in Shinbashi, close to the government center. As in most capitalist countries, there was in Japan a proliferation of small electric light companies in the early part of the twentieth century as entrepreneurs extended the benefits of electricity to new areas.

That period was followed by a period of consolidation of control in

Jurisdictions of Nine Regional
Electric Power Corporations

SOURCE: Overseas Electrical Industry Survey Institute, Inc.

the hands of a relatively small number of large urban companies; but until World War II, there were still more than four hundred electric companies in Japan. In 1939, in line with the government's wartime industrial policies, the generating and transmission facilities belonging to the private companies were seized and turned over to a new government-controlled entity, the Japan Electric Power Generation and Transmission Company. Three years later, the remaining distribution companies were consolidated into nine quasi-private distribution monopolies. After that, the geographical allocation of territories remained essentially the same as that now in existence (see map).

In 1951, the Tokyo government divested itself of its holdings in the electric industry and sold its generating facilities to nine public stock companies that succeeded the distribution monopolies established in

1942. TEPCO maintained the continuity of its history during the turbulence of the war, but the histories of some of the other companies go back only to the postwar period.

Only a year after the end of the Occupation, the government moved back into the power generation business on a limited basis through the creation of the Electric Power Development Company (*Dengen Kaihatsu Gaisha*). EPDC has more autonomy than the ordinary government-spawned corporation (*kodan*) in Japan, but the government exercises control over it through stockholdings, budgetary arrangements, secunding of personnel, and the placement of retired MITI officials in top positions (*amakudari*). EPDC's president, for example, Yoshihiko Moruzumi, is a former MITI vice-minister. The government owns 72.4 percent of EPDC's stock.

From its beginnings, EPDC has been closely affiliated with MITI, although it is probably an exaggeration to claim, as a MITI publication does, that it "gives directions to and supervises" EPDC.[2]

EPDC's original charge was to undertake large-scale hydroelectric construction projects (which were at that time the main source of new generating capacity) that were, in that capital-strapped period, beyond the financial resources of private companies. During this same period, Japan's oil companies, also without capital to build new refineries, were forced to sell majority control to American oil companies in order to secure money.

EPDC also built coal-fired plants which it continues to operate, and, to the chagrin of most of the private companies, it has been the pioneer in the development of air quality control equipment and innovative technologies for burning coal. Its success has encouraged MITI to pressure TEPCO and the other large utilities in central Japan to exert similar efforts.

To foreclose EPDC's entry into the nuclear power generation business (as well as to spread the risk of introducing nuclear reactors), the utilities prevailed upon the government in 1957 to allow the creation of JAPCO, the Japan Atomic Power Company (*Nippon Genshiroku Hatsuden K.K.*). It is a utility-controlled entity (the nine utilities own 74.6 percent; EPDC, 9.8 percent; and the rest is scattered), whose job it has been to introduce first-of-a-kind reactors.

EPDC secunds staff to JAPCO and owns shares in it, but its institutional dream of owning its own reactors has not died. With MITI's blessings, EPDC has sought to purchase two Canadian CANDU reactors. Because of the opposition of the Science and Technology Agency, which wants funds to build an indigenous reactor, EPDC has been embroiled in a very heated intrabureaucratic battle.

---

[2] *MITI Handbook, 1977–78,* (Tokyo: Ministry of International Trade and Industry, 1977), p. 69.

The private companies want to see neither EPDC nor the Science and Technology Agency win, since the companies would be asked to finance a large part of the cost of developing a new reactor.

Heavily dependent on American technology even before the Second World War, the utilities remain wedded to imports. TEPCO, through Toshiba and Hitachi, has customarily bought or licensed General Electric technology; Kansai, through Mitsubishi, has been a devotee of Westinghouse. Their conservative attitude toward technology has long been a sore point with the Science and Technology Agency, which wants to promote indigenous technology.

The declining enthusiasm for nuclear power in the United States and the consequent delay in the construction of reprocessing plants and fast-breeder reactors—the technologies that create a "closed cycle" to complement the light water reactor—have forced Japan to depend on its own technological abilities to a much greater extent than ever before. The private companies, while philosophically supportive of an ambitious advanced nuclear program, are reluctant either to finance the development of new fuel-cycle technologies or to see them owned and managed by the government.

The controversy around nuclear power has forced the utilities to develop their own "in-house" expertise in international affairs. TEPCO and Kansai both have offices in the United States, and, in concert with the Japanese government, are acting far more assertively than in the past. That assertiveness can be measured by the number of delegations that visit Washington and other capitals, by the size of consulting contracts with foreign experts, and by the extent to which the utilities have become known among government and industry officials in the United States and Europe.

During the last few years, as MITI has tried to encourage the diversification of energy sources, the utilities have exhibited their affinity for relying on the United States and other capitalist countries by their reluctance to buy oil and gas in large quantities from either China or the Soviet Union. The 1979 trade agreement with China (which is now in considerable disarray) was predicated on TEPCO and other Japanese utilities buying Chinese crude oil. The Japanese government has also encouraged the utilities to purchase Soviet gas. Recent discoveries of natural gas in the ocean bottom off Sakhalin Island are to be commercialized; but the Tyumen gas project, in which the Soviet Union has attempted to enlist Japanese (and American) support, is now a dead letter, in large part because of the reluctance of the electric companies to join with Tokyo Gas Company in promoting the project.

As of September 30, 1980, Japan's electrical generating capacity totaled 140,000 megawatts, the third largest system in the world after those of the United States and the Soviet Union. TEPCO's capacity was 32,000

Table 1

ELECTRIC POWER COMPANY STATISTICS
(*as of March 1980*)

Company	Capital (*million ¥*)	Customers (*thousands*)	Capacity (*thousand megawatts*)
Hokkaido	73.5	2.5	3.3
Tohoku	179	5.4	6.4
Tokyo	510	17.3	30.6
Chubu	288	12.4	15.2
Hokuriku	77	1.4	2.7
Kansai	352	9.0	23.1
Chugoku	130	3.9	7.3
Shikoku	80	2.1	4.1
Kyushu	170	5.7	8.8
Total for nine private companies	1,859.5	59.7	101.5
Electric Power Development Company	70	wholesale only	7.8
Japan Atomic Power Company	62	wholesale only	1.6
Other, including industrial generation			27.1
TOTAL			138.0

SOURCE: Overseas Electrical Industry Survey Institute, Inc.

MW, or about 22 percent of the national total; Kansai's capacity was 22,000 MW. Aside from Chubu, the other utilities are all much smaller. Figures for capital, assets, customers, and revenue are reflected in the size of their generating capacity (see Table 1).

Within TEPCO's territory live 31 percent of the country's population and 35 percent of its industry, a far higher concentration than is the case for any utility in the more dispersely populated United States. Along with the extraordinary centralization of political and economic power in Tokyo, this concentration accounts for TEPCO's political influence.[3]

Its economic influence stems more directly from its enormous capital budget. During the fiscal year that ended in March 1981, TEPCO had a capital spending plan of ¥1 trillion (about $5 billion), the largest capital

---

[3] Tokyo Electric Power Company, *Annual Report*, 1978 and 1980 editions.

Table 2

a) PROJECTED GROWTH RATE IN DEMAND (%)

1978–1983	1983–1988	1978–1988	
5.9	5.5	5.7	(base load)
7.3	5.7	6.5	(peak)

b) POWER SUPPLY AND MARGIN

	1978	1979	1980	1981	1982	1985	1988
Supply	95	102	108	115	122	148	174
Demand	85	91	99	105	112	135	158
Margin	10	11	9	10	10	13	16
Margin %	11.8	11.1	9.8	9.7	8.8	9.3	9.7

SOURCE: Chuo Denryoku Kyogikai, preliminary draft of a 10-year forecast, 1979.

spending budget for any company in Japan and the largest for any private utility in the world.[4] If the company's projected increase in demand for electricity is borne out, its spending for new power plants and transmission lines will remain at a similar level, adjusted for inflation, for at least a decade.

Whereas American utilities are now projecting very modest growth in demand of only 2–3 percent a year over the next two decades (compared to 7–8 percent during the 1960s), Japanese utilities expect growth rates in excess of 5 percent. Generating capacity is expected to be added at a somewhat slower rate, according to the utilities, resulting in a declining reserve margin during the August peak (see Table 2).

These forecasts have been thrown into question, however, by the absolute decline in the demand for electricity experienced by TEPCO during the summer of 1980. During the six-month period ending on September 30, 1980, there was a 1.1 percent decline in demand. Even during the August peak (during which the use of electricity for air conditioning and for radio and television by the vast audience for the annual high school baseball tournament usually breaks records), there was a slight decline in 1980. It is not clear whether the decline in demand is related largely to unseasonably cold weather or indicates a much greater

---

[4] Ibid., 1980 edition.

elasticity in demand than was previously thought. The effect was to reduce TEPCO's revenue so greatly that it was unable to pay an interim dividend to its stockholders.[5] TEPCO recouped, however, by the end of the fiscal year ending on March 31, 1981. The company ended with a net profit of ¥ 129.8 billion (about $590 million), compared to the ¥33.5 billion deficit of the previous year.

TEPCO's superincumbency is not a new phenomenon, but as energy has become a pathological concern for Japan, the visibility of TEPCO's political and economic power has risen higher on the national horizon.

Through the Federation of Electric Power Companies, headquartered in the Keidanren Kaikan, TEPCO exercises its might at the monthly president's meetings and through the federation's staff, the senior members of which tend to be from TEPCO.

The company's sheer size accounts for most of its influence, but TEPCO has also used its purchasing power to great advantage. It has, for example, secured large quantities of very low sulfur (hence, very clean) crude oil from Indonesia and elsewhere that other utilities are not able to secure regularly or in sufficient amounts. Despite its cost, it has been cost-effective for TEPCO because it obviates the need to invest in sophisticated air pollution control devices that smaller utilities like Kyushu Electric have had to spend $100–$200 million on per plant.

Critics of TEPCO complain that its style is "feudalistic" and that in recent years the company's executives have become overly protective of the other utilities. Consumer organizations protest rate increases, and antinuclear groups demonstrate against the company's ardent backing for that technology; but in comparison to the defensiveness that most American utilities have come to assume in recent years, TEPCO is not feeling beleaguered.

Whatever resentment may be borne by other utilities against TEPCO manifests itself largely in the rivalry (not to be confused with competition) that has long characterized relations between Tokyo and Osaka.

There are no obvious indications of any fundamental change in the relationship between TEPCO and the other utilities except in TEPCO's ties with Tohoku Electric Power Company, whose territory borders TEPCO's to the north and northwest. Population density around Tokyo and the consequent lack of acceptable sites for nuclear power plants have led TEPCO to build all of its reactors in either Fukushima Prefecture, where there are now six reactors operating and four more under construction or in planning, or in Kashiwazaki-Kashiwa in Niigata, where the first

---

[5] Tokyo Electric Power Company, *Semi-Annual Report for the Six Months Ending September 30, 1980.*

of a series of plants is now under construction. A third site has also been selected in northern Honshu, should nuclear power remain a viable option for Japan beyond the 1980s.

More recently, after the collapse of an arrangement under which Tohoku was to have imported LNG from Iran, TEPCO stepped in to arrange an alternative contract to purchase LNG from Indonesia. TEPCO managed the negotiations (with the assistance of Mitsubishi Corporation), which culminated in the signing of a contract in April 1981 between TEPCO and Pertamina, the Indonesian state oil and gas company.

While TEPCO is *primus inter pares*, it is not famous for the introduction of new technology. The company has made only a minimal commitment (compared to some American utilities) to funding the development of alternative forms of renewable energy and to co-generation. TEPCO has a conservation campaign, and it no longer spends money on advertising that promotes the use of more electricity; but, lacking a legislative mandate or effective regulatory pressure (something most American utilities do have), TEPCO has not been compelled to initiate new programs. Nor, therefore, have the other Japanese utilities.

Curiously, though, there are indications that TEPCO is becoming more adventurous while still shying away from relying on Japanese technology. TEPCO was the first company in Japan to use LNG, and is now the world's largest importer of that fuel. However, that is probably less technologically important (since LNG requires no special technology to be used in boilers) than two other recent decisions. Last year, TEPCO ventured $25 million to buy a 4.5 MW fuel cell plant from an American company, and it is close to consummating a contract with General Electric for a 1,000 MW combined cycle gas turbine plant. The fuel cell plant is seen by its manufacturer, United Technologies Corporation, as the first realistic test of its technology. The combined cycle plant will be the largest of its kind ever ordered. Both will use LNG fuel.

What most distinguishes TEPCO from its American cousins—besides its size—is its relative autonomy and freedom from regulation. MITI does not give TEPCO the freedom to do as it pleases, but it does guarantee it a broad freedom *from* unwanted regulatory controls.

Political scientists trained in institutional approaches would be wont to emphasize MITI's legislatively mandated *de jure* powers to, among other things, approve the construction of new plants, establish rates, and regulate safety and certain environmental standards. MITI shares these powers with the Science and Technology Agency and the Environment Agency. With both agencies, MITI's relations are endemically strained. While these powers are superficially akin to those which government agencies in the United States exercise, the relationship between the utilities and the government in the two countries is distinctly different.

For one thing, issues are settled privately in Japan. Public hearings, interventions, and court actions are rarities. MITI and the utilities do not always agree at the start, but by the time the decision-making process reaches the formal stage where the media and the public are involved, the issues usually have already been resolved.

A graphic illustration of the essentially nonconfrontational relationship between MITI and the utilities is the 50 percent rate increase granted to most of the utilities in 1979. Because of the inflationary impact of the increase, the Prime Minister's office became involved. But when the decision was reached, the utilities came within a few percentage points of securing the increases they requested.

Rate increases in the United States have become in most states the *bête noire* of the utilities, which are often under suspicion of making false claims, are scapegoats for other economic ailments, and, in the end, are rarely able to secure the whole increase they requested. There is also normally a one- to two-year lag in granting an increase in the U.S.; whereas in Japan it takes a few months, and the increase goes into effect immediately.

A second difference is that in Japan's centralized regime, MITI is the only body through which TEPCO and the other utilities work (except, of course, via Liberal Democratic Party channels). MITI oversees national construction plans, rates, and other issues. There is no American equivalent. In comparison, the Department of Energy has little power.

Besides regulating the utilities, MITI also promotes them, especially their nuclear power plant programs. It and the Science and Technology Agency are avowed partisans of nuclear power. The U.S. Atomic Energy Commission used to promote nuclear power in the U.S.; since its abolition in 1974, however, there has been no official advocate for nuclear power in Washington. MITI's Agency of Natural Resources and Energy has a Nuclear Energy Industry Division, whose role is described as "promoting" and "cultivating" nuclear power. (MITI has three other divisions that also deal with nuclear power.)[6]

In addition, the energy agency administers laws by which ratepayers are taxed in order to compensate local governments for allowing construction of power plants within or adjacent to their jurisdictions. (See Richard Suttmeier's chapter in this volume.)

MITI's Industrial Location and Environmental Protection Bureau helps utilities secure sites for new plants, mediates disputes, and represents industry in the internecine battles that rage with the Environment Agency.

MITI is also an ally of the oil companies' interests in siting, in environmental regulations, and in protecting the companies from international

---

[6] *MITI Handbook, 1977–78*, p. 65.

calamities. At the same time, however, there are significant differences in MITI's relations with the oil companies that highlight its special role vis-à-vis the utilities.

A very cogent difference, of course, is that the oil industry has been dominated by foreign oil companies since the end of the Second World War, and MITI and the general populace have suspected these companies of harboring notions of expansionism and of attempting to garner exorbitant profits.

MITI has tried to counter the power of these companies by fostering (some would say organizing) the creation of the Kyodo group, a consortium of domestic oil companies that was to be the embryo of a fully integrated indigenous company. When that experiment failed (Kyodo has had serious financial problems since its inception, and two companies left the group in 1979), MITI turned to bolstering the power of the Japan National Oil Company (JNOC), a *kodan* which is now empowered to purchase oil for strategic storage. MITI has threatened to put JNOC into the refining business if the domestic companies do not upgrade their facilities to handle the inferior grades of crude that MITI wants them to buy.

In contrast, since the creation of EPDC in 1952, there have been no serious attempts by MITI to reorganize the electric industry.

It is curious, too, that while MITI officials often retire to take senior positions in oil companies, few are hired by the electric companies (except EPDC).

Since the early 1970s, when oil prices began their vertiginous rise, MITI has resorted to a variety of unpublicized tactics, subsumed under the rubric of "administrative guidance" (*gyoseishido*), to control prices. MITI has attempted to moderate electricity prices, but the antagonisms that have arisen between the oil companies and MITI have been more confrontational.

Another important difference is that MITI, through JNOC, provides loans and guarantees for offshore exploration. The utilities rely entirely on the private capital market, are pressured into financing the Science and Technology Agency's fuel cycle facilities, and are to be solely responsible for the next generation of facilities.

THE ROLE OF ELECTRICITY IN JAPAN'S ENERGY STRATEGY

Electricity provides about 30 percent of Japan's primary energy supply. As in most industrialized countries, electricity's role will grow during the next two decades as nuclear power and other alternatives replace oil as the primary motive force. TEPCO estimates that electricity will provide about 37 percent of Japan's primary energy by 1995. Besides the shift away from oil, other reasons for the growth in the demand for electricity include the greater use of electronics and the continued urbanization of the population.

It is important to note that, except for the 11 percent (15,000 MW) of electricity generated by nuclear power plants and the 21 percent generated by hydroelectric plants, the other 68 percent of Japan's electricity is generated by fossil fuels. Almost exactly half of the total generation is oil-fired.

LNG is not included in the International Energy Agency's ceiling for oil imports, established at the Tokyo Summit in 1979; but it is a hydrocarbon, and it is a diminishing resource that by the turn of the century will probably have surpassed its peak level of availability. Thus, Japan's attempt to wean itself from oil is, in fact, being accomplished largely through the substitution of another scarce commodity, LNG (see Table 3).

According to the most recent projection for electricity demand, there will be, between fiscal years 1980 and 1987, a 5.4 percent annual growth in demand, with an August peak of 6.7 percent growth per year.[7]

Between now and 1987, the utilities estimate they will have to add 74,000 MW worth of new capacity, including 33,000 MW worth that is not already either under construction or approved. As of the end of 1980, the following capacities were under construction: nuclear, 18,000 MW; hydro, 14,000 MW; and thermal (including LNG, coal, and oil), 32,000 MW.[8]

In TEPCO's case, the goal is to reduce oil-fired generation from 50 percent of capacity to between 19 and 26 percent by 1990. Nuclear power and LNG will provide nearly an equal share of the new capacity until 1990, when coal will probably start being used again.[9]

LNG STRATEGY

Questions abound about the future of nuclear power and about the acceptability of burning coal in a densely populated country. LNG, on the other hand, despite its volatility and the ensuing opposition to its importation into the United States, in not a "problem fuel" for the Japanese. Public hearings on the construction of new storage terminals around Tokyo Bay and in the Inland Sea provoke only minor protests; and the siting of power plants for LNG (originally, LNG was used mostly in converted plants that used to burn oil), all of which are in congested areas, is not subject to the long delays that utilities routinely face in building hydroelectric, nuclear, or coal-fired plants in rural areas.

A good hypothesis is that it is the well-organized fishermen's coop-

---

[7] *Electric Power Industry in Japan, 1980* (Tokyo: Overseas Electric Industry Survey Institute, n.d.)

[8] Chuo Denryoku Kyogikai, preliminary draft of a 10-year forecast, 1979.

[9] Tokyo Electric Power Company, *Annual Report, 1980.*

Table 3

a) FUEL CONSUMPTION BY ELECTRIC UTILITIES, 1955–1979

Year	Oil (*thousand kl.*)	Coal (*thousand metric tons*)	LNG (*thousand metric tons*)
1955	307	7,211	—
1965	11,865	20,073	—
1975	61,104	7,179	3,326
1976	64,532	7,771	3,920
1977	68,464	8,136	5,703
1978	64,294	7,729	8,936
1979	60,556	8,385	11,708

b) FUEL CONSUMPTION BY TOKYO ELECTRIC POWER COMPANY, 1951–1979

Year	Oil (*thousand kl.*)	Coal (*thousand metric tons*)	LNG* (*thousand metric tons*)
1951	20	790	—
1955	80	1,530	—
1965	4,230	5,000	—
1975	14,670	—	3,270
1976	15,090	—	3,860
1977	16,230	—	4,940
1978	14,550	—	5,580
1979	13,110	—	

SOURCES: Overseas Electric Industrial Survey Institute, Inc.; and Tokyo Electric Power Company, *Annual Report, 1980*, Japanese edition.

*Also includes LPG.

eratives, farm organizations, and local towns that are the main barrier to the construction of new power plants, not the urban elites who in the United States customarily lead the barrage against utilities. Because LNG-fired plants are all in urban areas, they have been built on much tighter schedules than most other plants; hence the rapid increase in the use of LNG compared to nuclear power. In Tokyo Electric's case, they both supply about the same amount of power, despite the fact that TEPCO only decided to start importing LNG in 1969.

While the United States has dithered, Japan has been pursuing a no-holds-barred LNG import policy that has turned it into the world's

Table 4

JAPANESE UTILITY IMPORTS OF LIQUEFIED NATURAL GAS

From	Metric tons/year	Consumer
Alaska	960,000	Tokyo Electric; Tokyo Gas
Brunei	5,140,000	Tokyo Electric; Tokyo Gas; Osaka Gas
Abu Dhabi	2,060,000	Tokyo Electric
Indonesia	7,500,000	Kansai Electric; Chubu Electric; Kyushu Electric; Osaka Gas; Nippon Steel
Malaysia	6,000,000	Tokyo Electric; Tokyo Gas
Indonesia	3,200,000 (starting 1983)	Chubu Electric; Kansai Electric; Osaka Gas
Indonesia	3,300,000 (starting 1983)	Tohoku Electric; Tokyo Electric
Australia	6,000,000 (starting 1986)	Tokyo Electric; Kansai Electric; Chubu Electric; Kyushu Electric; Tokyo Gas; Osaka Gas; Toho Gas under negotiation
U.S.S.R.	7,500,000 (starting mid-decade)	
Canada	two separate projects to start mid-decade	

SOURCES: Tokyo Electric Power Company; and Institute for Energy Economics.

largest consumer of the frigid stuff. Japanese utilities now have contracts with eight countries for about 34 million metric tons per year of LNG. By 1984 or thereabouts, actual imports will reach about 20 million metric tons, compared to 12 million metric tons in 1979 (see Table 4).

It would be too simplistic to claim that the surge in LNG imports has come about purely by accident. But when TEPCO began importing Alaskan LNG in 1969, it did so not as part of a long-term energy strategy, but simply because it was there and at the time seemed the quickest, cheapest way to cut air pollution in a country that was in the midst of a severe environmental crisis. Unlike other fossil fuels, LNG contains virtually no sulfur or nitrogen oxides, the two pollutants that are controlled by statute.

TEPCO's experiment was a success; and despite the huge capital costs for liquefaction terminals at the points of origin, cryogenic tankers, and regasification terminals in Japan, LNG remains a viable economic alternative that not only fills the gap caused by delays in the nuclear program but also is nearly environmentally benign.

The price of LNG has climbed from the early 1970s, when it was often flared, to today, when new and rewritten contracts peg it at the price of crude oil. Some experts have accused Japan of driving up the price of LNG, with the consequence that Algeria has cut off its supplies of LNG to the United States because of a price dispute.

LNG has been one fuel for which Japan has not had to compete directly with the United States and other importers. For a time, it appeared that the United States and Japan would share Indonesian and Australian LNG. Now, however, with the Indonesia project delayed indefinitely because of terminal siting problems in California and an unexpected increase in American domestic reserves of natural gas, Japan is likely to monopolize the Asian LNG business. (Japan also imports LNG from North America: from Alaska and, starting after the mid-1980s, from Canada.)

The cost of LNG projects put a damper on new projects; but in the last year, optimism has been restored, and TEPCO has signed contracts with four new partners: Indonesia, the Soviet Union, Canada, and Austrialia.

About 65 percent of Japan's LNG is used for electric power generation, a thermally inefficient end-use but the only practical one in Japan.

By the middle of the decade, according to the Central Power Council, 82 percent of the LNG will be used for power generation, amounting to about 15 percent of total electric generation.[10]

Japan is the only country to use LNG for power generation; but because of the fuel's environmental advantages, its availability under 20-year contracts, and the lack of a need for sophisticated technologies for burning it, it has provided an ideal medium-term way to diversify energy sources. As a TEPCO spokesman said to me: "If we quantify the social costs, the inordinate delays, the remote and extra-large sites, and the ensuing transmission losses with which we have had to contend with nuclear power, then LNG is far less expensive. And in comparison to coal, the environmental problems are in an entirely different category."

Coal, as we shall see, is readily available, but there are fears that the world coal market will be dominated by American companies. In the case of LNG, there is little prospect of a cartel or a preponderance by one country emerging.

Another reason that Japan burns LNG somewhat unconventionally is the perennial public protest against pipelines. City gas companies, which store most of the LNG used (although TEPCO is now building its

---

[10] Chuo Denryoku Kyogikai, preliminary draft of a 10-year forecast, 1979.

own terminals), have not been able to build the infrastructure needed to distribute gas once it arrives at the large centralized regasification terminals around Tokyo, Osaka, Nagoya, and other cities. Japan has only 311 miles of long-distance pipelines, and, as a result, has to transship more than 60 percent of its petroleum products on coastal tankers. The controversial Narita Airport is still not operating at full capacity because sufficient fuel is not available: towns along the projected pipeline route in Chiba Prefecture continue to block its completion.

MITI is talking about encouraging the construction of a fleet of coastal LNG tankers to distribute gas more widely for more diversified usage, but most experts think the cost of such vessels makes them uneconomical.

Because boil-off rates are high and the increase in imports has outpaced the schedules for construction of storage terminals, there is only about a seven-day supply of LNG kept at Tokyo Gas Company's two terminals in Tokyo Bay. In contrast, the supply of oil stockpiled by private companies and the government now exceeds one hundred days. Clearly, the regularity of supply is the key to successful dependence on LNG, and so far there have been few problems.

While Californians continue to debate the prudence of building a terminal on their shores to receive LNG, Japanese utilities have had a relatively free hand, in sharp contrast to the usual situation in both countries. Since Japan is nearly the same size as California in area, but with six times the population, the difference in perception of the dangers of LNG is quite interesting.

TEPCO was required to hold a public hearing in 1979 in Kawasaki City, the first municipality in Japan to require hearings and the filing of environmental impact statements for large projects. A year later, TEPCO held a hearing in Futtsu, in Chiba Prefecture, the site of another terminal. In neither case was there appreciable opposition.

COAL STRATEGY

The alacrity with which TEPCO and other utilities have been pursuing LNG has not been matched in intensity by their quest for sources of imported coal. Available in far larger quantities, for a span of at least the next two centuries, from politically stable countries, coal is nevertheless a fuel to which TEPCO is only reluctantly returning. It is MITI, using the successful example of EPDC's pioneering development of new technologies for burning coal, that is in the vanguard of the movement to use coal, not the utilities.

Until the Second World War, domestically mined coal was the primary source of thermal power generation in Japan. Cheap oil, endemic labor disputes with the Socialist-related *Sohyo* unions, accidents, and the

Table 5

COAL USE BY TOKYO
ELECTRIC POWER COMPANY

Year	Metric Tons
1951	790,000
1955	1,530,000
1965	5,000,000
1972	1,120,000
1973	140,000
1974–	0

SOURCE: Tokyo Electric Power Company, *Annual Report, 1978*, Japanese edition.

exhaustion of the most efficient mines conspired to force Japan away from the use of coal, even before it became an environmentally suspect fuel. Domestic production declined steadily, bottoming out at around 20 million metric tons, a level that MITI has maintained through a complexity of subsidies and incentives.

In TEPCO's case, the use of coal peaked in 1965, in which year 5 million metric tons were burned; seven years later, TEPCO used only about one million metric tons. In 1973, the last year that coal was burned, TEPCO burned only 140,000 metric tons (see Table 5).

By the mid-1970s, only two utilities—Kyushu Electric Power Company and Hokkaido Electric Power Company—continued to burn coal. Both relied almost entirely on domestic coal that was mined on those two islands.

MITI's projection in August 1979 for energy supplies in 1985 set as a goal the importation of 22 million metric tons of steam coal (the kind used for power generation). In 1979, for the first time, imports of steam coal (including a significant amount bought by the cement industry) surpassed the million metric ton mark; in 1981, imports will probably reach about two million metric tons.

TEPCO will probably convert one oil-fired plant in Yokosuka to burn coal, and it is discussing the possibility of joining with EPDC to build a huge coal-fired generating complex on the Pacific coast near Mito, about 125 miles northeast of Tokyo. The 5,000 MW complex would be the largest ever built. But TEPCO does not project that coal will be burned in significant quantities until around 1990, by which point MITI estimates that Japan's demand will have reached 53.5 million metric tons.

Kansai and other utilities are also pledged to construct new coal-fired plants, or to convert existing plants to coal, but there is no enthusiastic program aside from EPDC's.

While MITI's figures may be difficult to attain on schedule, they are not the most optimistic. According to a compilation of projects by the U.S. Department of Energy, the amount of steam coal that Japan is predicted to be importing by 1985 varies from a low figure of 6–7 million metric tons (World Coal Study) to the Central Intelligence Agency's estimate, published in September 1980, of 30.3 million metric tons.[11]

Eventually, Japan's imports of steam coal will probably far exceed any of these projections, particularly if coal gasification and liquefaction technologies now being developed in the U.S. and Japan are commercialized; but unless the utilities become more enthusiastic about coal, the 1985 imports will probably exceed the modest estimate of the World Coal Study but fall short of MITI's goal.

There are a number of reasons for the utilities' reluctance (or inability) to switch more quickly to coal in accordance with MITI's wishes.

First, there are a number of technical constraints. Coal is dirty. It is expensive to ship, blend, and store. Sites for coal-fired plants must be about two-and-a-half times as large as those for conventional plants; in a land-scarce country, that has economic consequences. Ash disposal is problematic because of the growing opposition to landfill projects along the coast. And, since coal-fired plants cannot be easily built near Tokyo or Osaka, expensive transmission lines would have to be built.

So far, the idea of returning to burning coal has not become a highly charged political issue, because the utilities themselves are conscious of the many disadvantages to using coal. EPDC's experience in the construction of new plants near Hiroshima (in Takehara) and in Kyushu suggests that coal-fired power plants can meet Japan's rigid clean-air standards, and that, unlike nuclear power, coal is not opposed by a large portion of the population.

Nevertheless, the high population density around nearly every power plant site in Japan makes coal far less attractive an option for Japanese utilities than it is in many sections of the U.S. Ocean freight charges and the cost of port infrastructures, blending facilities, and ships all make coal much more expensive than it is in the U.S. As a result, despite the economic competitiveness between coal and nuclear power in the U.S., TEPCO and other Japanese utilities remain convinced that nuclear power, despite its escalating cost, is cheaper than coal.

A second reason for the utilities' lack of spontaneous excitement about coal is that the private companies have sensed that they are being pushed into the coal importing business by MITI. Only when MITI hinted

---

[11] "Prospects for Steam Coal Imports to Japan," Department on Energy memorandum, n.d. [ca. 1980].

that it would help EPDC finance the acquisition of large reserves of coal in Australia and encourage it to secure minority shareholdings in a number of companies did the utilities band together in 1979, through the Federation of Electric Power Companies, to establish the Japan Coal Development Company, a coordinating body that is preparing to secure long-term contracts for coal for the utilities. EPDC reluctantly joined the new company, giving up its ambition to coordinate Japan's coal development strategy. Armed with control of the situation, the utilities need not be in a hurry to exercise their power.

This intranational stumbling block to the rapid shift to coal is accompanied by an international factor that is rooted in Japan's historical experience in buying energy from the United States. During the past three or four years, MITI and the utilities have succeeded—after many years of effort—in convincing a majority of the population that, despite the dangers inherent in its use, nuclear power is essential to Japan's security, since it reduces the nation's dependence on foreign oil and other raw materials. While it is still an inchoate issue in the popular mind, many Japanese decision-makers question whether the importation of large amounts of American and Australian coal will strengthen Japan's security or only exacerbate economic antagonisms.

Some Japanese understand that their country's potential dependence on American coal could, like the United States' excessive dependence on Japan for automobiles, strain bilateral relations. Although the purchase of coal from the U.S. would improve the perennial balance-of-payments deficit that the U.S. suffers vis-à-vis Japan, it might not offset the impact of high-value electronics that will probably increasingly penetrate the American market.

Many Japanese also look askance at the American investment in Australia's coal industry. On a number of occasions, high-ranking Japanese officials have attempted to elicit the White House's view of the expansion of American oil companies into new markets, but one of these officials told me privately that the U.S. claimed to be unable to involve itself in regulating investment in other countries.

Japan is already the world's largest importer of coal. Virtually all 60 million metric tons that she has purchased annually in recent years have been metallurgical-grade coal used by the steel industry. The utilities have learned from the steel companies that the U.S. coal industry is inefficient and prone to extended strikes, and that the development of western mines (the most economically logical for the utilities to buy from) may be delayed because of the cost of building an infrastructure to move coal, especially to the West Coast, from which it would be convenient to ship it to Japan.

A more thorough analysis of the efficacy of importing coal is in order. The important point in this discussion is that while Japanese utilities are capable of moving with great haste, as exemplified by their aggressive LNG acquisitions, they are also capable of moving with glacial slowness when they are not attuned to MITI's desires.

CONCLUSION

I have tried in this chapter to convince the reader that the Japanese utilities are important actors in the shaping of the country's energy policy, much more important than would be assumed from reading the English-language literature on Japan's energy conundrums. I have also tried to convince the reader that TEPCO and some of the other Japanese utilities are more important within Japan than American utilities are singularly (or it might even be argued, collectively) within the United States. Obviously, I have barely skimmed the surface; yet, because my discussion is based largely on interviews, it does, I hope, transmit to the reader some of the drama involved in the making of decisions that will affect the whole future of a country. The Japanese utilities, I think, recognize the responsibility they have; yet, like American utilities, they find it impossible to be confident of their ability to forecast the future. In LNG and nuclear power, they think they have found a rational road to the future; in coal, they are not yet sure if they have a source of light or of heat.

The Japanese Nuclear Power Option: Technological Promise and Social Limitations*

Richard P. Suttmeier

One of the leading students of Japan's energy problems put the case for nuclear power recently as follows: "While we cannot solve the energy problems of Japan only with the utilization of nuclear power, it is apparent that we can never solve the problems without such a useful energy [source] as nuclear power."[1]

While not all energy-concerned Japanese would agree, the statement does represent what might be considered a "centrist" position on energy strategy. In this centrist view, Japan must pursue a mixed strategy of energy development, relying on a variety of energy sources to achieve the basic objective of markedly reducing dependence on imported oil. In the centrist view, the desirability of pursuing the nuclear power option is less at issue than is the extent to which energy policy can rely upon nuclear development. Thus, a "battle of megawatt estimates" rages among energy planners and analysts. While it does so, many of the protagonists are fighting on a second front to control domestic and international forces which increasingly threaten the viability of the nuclear option.

* This chapter was written while I was a National Fellow at The Hoover Institution. I am grateful to Hoover for its support during that period. My thanks also go to Mr. S. Hayden Lesbirel of the Australian National University for sharing an unpublished study of Japanese nuclear siting problems with me, and for his helpful comments on an earlier draft of this chapter.
[1] Toyoaki Ikuta, "The Energy Issue and the Role of Nuclear Power in Japan," in *Australia and Japan: Nuclear Energy Issues in the Pacific*, ed. Stuart Harris and Keichi Oshima (Canberra and Tokyo: Australia–Japan Economic Relations Research Project, 1980), p. 28.

106

THE APPEALS OF NUCLEAR POWER

Among free-world countries, Japan's installed nuclear capacity has until recently been second only to that of the United States. By the end of 1980, Japan had twenty-two operating reactors with an installed capacity of approximately 15,000 MW. Approximately 12 percent of Japan's electricity, or about 3.6 percent of Japan's primary energy, was generated at nuclear plants, as Figure 1 illustrates. In addition to its occupying a leading position in nuclear-generating capacity, Japan has also developed over the years, at great expense, an accomplished nuclear industry and research and development capability. But as with other industrialized nations with nuclear power capabilities, the uncertainties surrounding nuclear technology have slowed the pace of this development and have created doubts about what was once thought to be a bright nuclear future.

The appeals of nuclear power for Japan in a world of energy uncertainty are fairly straightforward. With the successful development of its own nuclear industry, Japan can regard nuclear power as a "semi-indigenous" energy source. Although Japan still relies on foreign supplies for natural uranium, enrichment services, reprocessing services, and some reactor technology, continued technological progress in Japanese research and development on enrichment and reprocessing is intended to further reduce foreign dependence in these areas. Although Japan's uranium suppliers (the U.S., Canada, Australia, and others) are seen to be somewhat more reliable over the long run than OPEC oil producers, Japan continues to seek diversification of its supplies of this raw material. In addition, ongoing R&D on plutonium-burning advanced thermal reactors and fast breeder reactors offer the possibility, in the Japanese view, of reducing fuel dependence as well.

The nuclear option is also appealing because nuclear materials are more conveniently stockpiled than fossil fuels. Per unit of contained energy, nuclear fuels are also considerably cheaper than imported fossil fuels. Nuclear fuels therefore promise to ease pressures on Japan's import bill (50 percent of which is now committed to petroleum) and to offer the possibility of lower electricity-generating costs. According to one nuclear proponent, the economic and energy security advantages of nuclear can be summarized as follows:

> As of September 1980, the comparative generating cost of one KWh of electricity was roughly ¥18.00 in the case of an oil-burning thermal power plant, while it was almost half, or about ¥9.00, in the case of nuclear power, and ¥13.00 in the case of a coal-fired plant. In terms of foreign exchange outlays to procure fuel, nuclear power generation needs only about one-eighth that of oil-burning thermal power generation. In addition, the fuel requirement of a nuclear power plant is a mere one ten-thousandth of an oil-burning thermal power plant. Moreover, a nuclear power plant can be

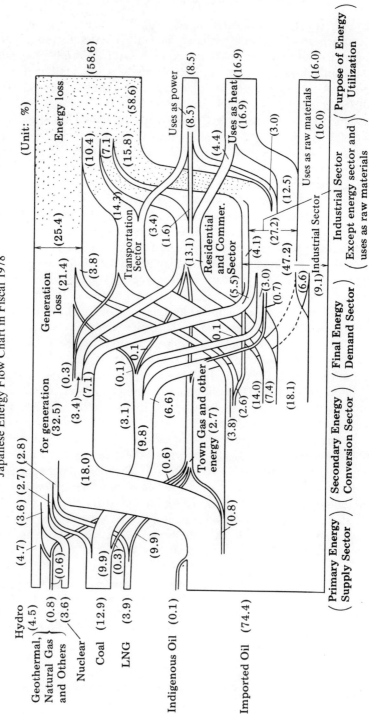

FIGURE 1

Japanese Energy Flow Chart in Fiscal 1978

(Unit: %)

SOURCE: *Atoms in Japan*, December 1980, p. 29.

run for almost a year with a single fuel charge, showing that nuclear power is outstanding from the point of view of energy security.[2]

Thus, for a resource-poor but technology-rich nation, the nuclear option would appear to make considerable sense. Indeed, the nuclear calculus would seem to be uniquely favorable to Japan among the industrialized nations. It is not surprising, therefore, that government and industry have been actively seeking to promote nuclear power with what appears to be considerable determination. The long-term policy guiding these actions has been to first import and bring into commercial operation American light water reactors (LWRs) while laying the foundation for an independent indigenous nuclear "fuel cycle." While the major theme of the policy has been to develop another option for meeting domestic energy needs, a second and largely understated theme has been to develop the technological capability for a high value-added export industry. An analysis of the export potential of the Japanese nuclear industry is beyond the scope of this chapter, but it should be noted that, as with the advocates of "new energy technology," discussed by Prof. Samuels elsewhere in this volume, the energy crisis is seen by Japanese nuclear proponents as providing international commercial opportunities as well as domestic challenges to the nuclear community.[3]

THE LOGIC OF JAPAN'S NUCLEAR DEVELOPMENT

Surprisingly, it was less than a decade after the horrors of Hiroshima and Nagasaki that government and industry leaders began to lay plans for the "peaceful atom" in Japan. After an initial flirtation with British technology, Japan, along with most of the rest of the world, succumbed to the appeals of American light water reactor technology. Japanese utilities and equipment manufacturers had long had technical ties to American industry, and these, coupled with a vigorous U.S. government execution of its "atoms for peace" policy, facilitated the conversion.[4]

Although the pace of indigenous R&D picked up during the course

---

[2] Hiromi Arisawa (Chairman, Japan Atomic Industrial Forum), "Keynote Address at the 14th JAIF Annual Conference," Tokyo, March 10, 1981 (unpublished draft translation from the Japanese text).

[3] Discussions are now under way between MITI and Hitachi regarding the development of 200–300 MW reactors for export to countries without large power grids. See *Atoms in Japan*, February 1981, p. 32. Also see John Marcom, Jr., "Japan Has High Hopes for Reactor Exports," *Asian Wall Street Journal*, March 13, 1981.

[4] For a useful discussion of the early years of the Japanese program, see Hideo Sato, "The Politics of Technology Importation in Japan: The Case of Atomic Power Reactors," a paper presented at the Social Science Research Council Workshop on Japanese Technology Transfer, Kona, Hawaii, February 7–11, 1978.

of the 1960s, the main thrust of policy until the late 1960s was to pursue a technology transfer strategy designed to bring commercially operable reactors on line as quickly as possible. The Japan Atomic Power Company (JAPCO) was established by government and industry to facilitate this transfer, first by bringing into operation the British gas-graphite reactor (Tokai 1, which started operation in July 1966), and then by introducing the first LWR, a boiling water reactor (BWR) which started operations at Tsuruga in March 1970.[5] Tokyo Electric and Kansai Electric, however, were not far behind JAPCO. The former started up its Fukushima I-1 unit (General Electric BWR technology) in March 1971, while Kansai had already begun operations at its first Mihama unit (Westinghouse pressurized water reactor technology) four months before.

The commitment to light water technology has influenced Japan's nuclear history in two important ways. First, the vigor with which LWRs were commercialized has been an enduring point of criticism from anti-government critics in the scientific community.[6] Underlying the policy for peaceful uses of atomic energy in Japan are the so-called "three principles" of nuclear development: that it be autonomous, under democratic control, and not secret. Reliance on the U.S. has seriously compromised the first of these principles, according to the critics. The critics have also argued that light water technology is still "unproven," even in the United States, and that the decision to import and employ it prior to the establishment of a strong, indigenous nuclear R&D capability was irresponsible. To support both of these points, the critics note that LWRs have had their share of problems, and that when these have developed in Japan, American engineers too often have had to be called upon in order to solve them.

The second consequence has been that in committing itself to light water technology, Japan also committed itself to what was until the mid-1970s the dominant American view of nuclear progress. According to this view, uranium supplies and enrichment services were expected to be scarce relative to anticipated future demand. Since LWRs used fissile material inefficiently, spent fuel from reactors had to be reprocessed in order to recover unused uranium and the plutonium created in the course of reactor operation. This material could then be recycled in LWRs or, for the longer run, be used in follow-on fast breeder reactors (FBRs). In addition, reprocessing would facilitate waste management in this view.

This recycling logic of light water technology seemed eminently sensible to nuclear proponents in resource-poor Japan. They therefore set

---

[5] Twenty percent of the investment in JAPCO came from government, 40 percent came from the utilities, and 40 percent came from Japanese heavy electrical machinery manufacturers (Sato, "Politics," p. 33).
[6] For the origins of this criticism, see Sato, "Politics."

about devising a long-term strategy to create Japanese capabilities for as much of an indigenous fuel cycle as possible. By the beginning of the 1980s, considerable progress toward this goal was evident. At Ningyo Toge, a pilot enrichment plant using centrifuge technology had trial-produced enriched uranium even as more centrifuges were being added. Industry had established a preparatory group to make final plans for a follow-on commercial-scale enrichment facility. Most of the complex LWR technology had been mastered, and almost 100 percent of the components for new plants could be manufactured in Japan. A pilot reprocessing plant using French technology was in operation at Tokai-mura, and the institutional foundation had been laid for commercial reprocessing in Japan. A pilot breeder reactor was in operation, and plans were set for a follow-on demonstration-scale unit. Finally, plutonium from the Tokaimura facility had been fabricated into fuel for the Japanese-designed Fugen advanced thermal reactor. The latter was a feat of some symbolic importance to those who have long hoped for the production of indigenous fuels for use in indigenously designed and produced reactors.

Not surprisingly, progress in the development of nuclear technology in Japan has been the result of close government-industry collaboration in the areas of industrial structure, R&D, siting and licensing, and in various international activities ranging from uranium acquisition to nonproliferation. The nuclear industry is composed of some of Japan's largest and most powerful corporations, and can be thought of as having two main pillars. One is composed of the nine regional electric power companies (plus JAPCO), while the other is composed principally of the manufacturers and vendors of electrical equipment and engineering services, who are organized into five major industrial "groups."[7] The peak organization representing both vendors and utilities is the Japan Atomic Industrial Forum.

Government authority for nuclear policy is formally concentrated in the Prime Minister's office. The Japan Atomic Energy Commission (JAEC) for many years served as an advisory committee to the Prime Minister on both promotional and regulatory matters. In 1978, regulatory authority was vested in a new Nuclear Safety Commission (NSC), which, like its JAEC counterpart, serves as an advisory committee to the Prime Minister. Staff support for both the JAEC and the NSC is provided by the Science and Technology Agency (STA). The STA also has had the main responsibility for managing the nation's nuclear R&D effort. Actual performance of R&D, however, is conducted by the Japan Atomic Energy

---

[7] The five groups are: Mitsubishi; The Tokyo Atomic Industrial Consortium (Hitachi); Mitsui (Toshiba); Sumitomo; and The First Atomic Power Industry Group (Kawasaki-Fuji).

Research Institute (JAERI) and by the Power Reactor and Nuclear Fuel Corporation (PNC), both public corporations, in cooperation with industry. Whereas JAERI's work tends to be more in areas of long-range basic research (e.g., the government's Tokamak fusion program), PNC is more engaged in applied research and development (Fugen, the FBR program, enrichment, reprocessing). The underlying philosophy behind PNC is that it serve as a mechanism for undertaking very expensive, high-risk R&D projects which industry is unwilling to undertake. At the same time, it is expected to facilitate the development of the technological capabilities of industry by an extensive use of contracts, let to the major nuclear industrial groups in a judiciously balanced fashion.

As in other industries, the government is willing to intervene if problems of industrial structure impede the utilization of technological capabilities possessed by industry. A recent example is STA and MITI support for the establishment of the FBR Engineering Company (a joint venture of four of the nuclear giants—Mitsubishi Heavy Industries, Hitachi, Toshiba, and Fuji Electric) over the objections of the Fair Trade Commission.[8]

In recent years, the Ministry of International Trade and Industry (MITI) has assumed a more central position in nuclear affairs. Although MITI is engaged in some R&D (mainly on safety and on direct industrial applications of nuclear power), its most important responsibilities are in licensing, safety regulation, and plant inspection, in site selection and promoting public acceptance of nuclear power, and in utility rate setting. Since these are the areas of great current public concern, MITI is very much on the front line in nuclear affairs at present.

In spite of an increasingly difficult financial situation, government budgetary support for nuclear power in recent years has been generous. The 1980 nuclear budget was 24.6 percent above that of 1979, including a 10.3 percent increase in the general account.[9] Although the budget for 1981 shows only a single-digit increase for the first time in twenty-two years, it still manages a 9.6 percent increase.[10] Expenditures for nuclear R&D represented approximately 18 percent of the government's expenditures for science and technology, by far the largest single item in the science-related budget.

It is also helpful to view expenditures on nuclear power as part of the government's energy-related budget. Figure 2 relates sources of revenue, budget accounts used, and the projects on which funds were expended in Fiscal Year 1980. The bulk of nuclear R&D funds comes out of the general account and goes to the STA (¥157,888 million). In addition, however, half of the ¥82,710 million (¥41,355 million) destined for the "New En-

[8] Atoms in Japan, April 1980, p. 20.
[9] Atoms in Japan, June 1980, p. 15.
[10] Atoms in Japan, January 1981, p. 4.

FIGURE 2

Energy-Related Budget for Fiscal 1980
(in millions of yen)

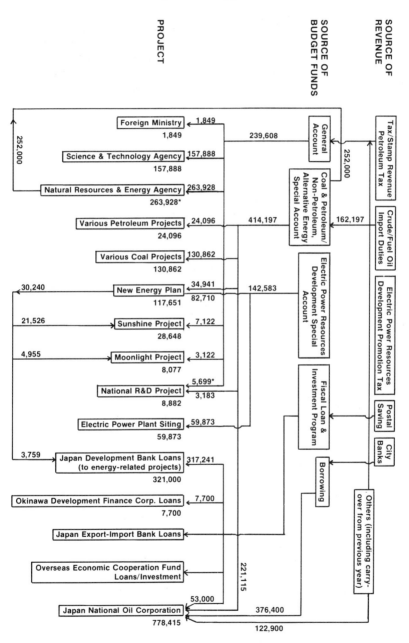

SOURCE: *Japan Petroleum and Energy Weekly*, 15:4–6 (January 28, February 4, and February 11, 1980).

(*) Includes budget for projects not directly related to energy

ergy Plan" is for nuclear R&D as well.[11] These funds come out of the Electric Power Resources Development Special Account (EPRDSA), the revenues for which come mainly from the Electric Power Resources Development Promotion Tax. The latter is a levy on electric power generation, which was increased by a whopping 353 percent in 1980 from ¥ 85/1000 kwh in 1979 to ¥300/1000 kwh.[12]

While over 50 percent of the new revenues going into the EPRDSA are mainly intended for R&D projects under the New Energy Plan, in the past the account served primarily as a source of liquid assets, administered primarily by MITI, to give it flexibility in dealing with localities identified as sites for power plants. As Figure 2 indicates, some ¥59,873 million ($253 million) were budgeted for this purpose in 1980. Approximately two-thirds of this fund went to localities cooperating with power plant construction in the form of grants, as is shown in Figure 3.

As the discussion below indicates, these sums may not be enough to deal with what may be an increasingly intractable siting problem.

NUCLEAR POWER IN JAPAN'S ENERGY FUTURE

On November 28, 1980, the Cabinet approved the targets prepared by MITI for "oil-alternative energy supplies" for the year 1990. In doing so, the government committed itself to reduce Japan's dependence on imported oil as a source of primary energy from the current 75 percent to 50 percent.[13] To achieve this goal, the plan calls for increasing reliance on coal (from 12.9 percent to 17.7 percent of primary energy), natural gas (from approximately 4 percent to 10.2 percent), and nuclear power (from 3.6 percent to 10.9 percent).[14]

The requirements for achieving the nuclear target are so staggering that energy policy projections that employ it strain credulity. For the target to be reached, Japan would need an installed nuclear capacity in 1990 of 51,000–53,000 MW. While these figures are quite consistent with the official targets the government has used during the last few years, it is worth pondering what such a growth in capacity would entail.

As we have seen, current installed capacity is approximately 15,000 MW. There are currently under construction an additional seven units totaling 5,613 MW. It would be necessary, therefore, to complete by 1990 slightly more than thirty additional units, each in the 1,000 MW range, including seven which have received preliminary approval. Lead times for construction, however, have now stretched out to about fifteen years, and,

---

[11] *Japan Petroleum and Energy Weekly*, 15:4–6 (January 28, February 4, and February 11, 1980), 21–22.
[12] Ibid., p. 6.
[13] *Atoms in Japan*, December 1980, pp. 6–7.
[14] Ibid.

FIGURE 3

Electric Power Plant Siting Account
(*in millions of yen*)

A. *Under jurisdiction of MITI*		FY 1980	FY 1979
(1)	Grants to localities cooperating with power plant construction	39,974	37,514
(2)	Studies on environmental impact of nuclear power plants	6,301	9,219
(3)	Subsidies to improvement of nuclear power plant safety	4,440	3,345
(4)	Grants to improvement of nuclear power plant safety	1,025	360
(5)	Miscellaneous	1,164	1,089
	Subtotal (A)	52,904	51,527
B. *Under jurisdiction of the Science and Technology Agency*			
(1)	Grants to localities cooperating with power plant construction	1,440	1,405
(2)	Studies on environmental impact of nuclear power plants	4,123	3,991
(3)	Grants to improvement of nuclear power plant safety	1,392	563
(4)	Miscellaneous	14	11
	Subtotal (B)	6,969	5,970
	Total (A + B)	59,873	57,497

SOURCE: *Japan Petroleum and Energy Weekly*, 15:4–6 (January 28, February 4, and February 11, 1980).

in addition, such a building program would be enormously expensive. It is estimated that costs would run in the neighborhood of ¥10 trillion (at ¥ 300 billion per unit).[15] The enormity of the task has led other informed observers to make far more modest estimates. These range from a still ambitious 40,700 MW estimate issued by the utilities' Central Electric Power Council[16] to what might be a more realistic figure of 30,000–35,000 MW suggested by Toyoaki Ikuta, President of the Institute for Energy Economics.[17]

While the main thrust of government policy to reach the 1990 target will be to build new plants, attention in the last few years has also turned to increasing the average capacity factor of operating plants. The capacity factor is the ratio of power generated to the product of designed power

---

[15] Ibid.
[16] *Atoms in Japan*, September 1980, p. 39.
[17] Ikuta, "Energy Issue," p. 25.

times gross hours. This measure has fluctuated considerably over the last few years, being influenced mainly by the need for periodic inspections. Efforts are now being made to streamline the inspection system, improve the training of operators, and upgrade the quality of plant components. It has been estimated that if the average capacity factor could be increased by 20 percent, six million kiloliters of oil per year (roughly the amount of oil used annually by the Japanese fishing industry) could be saved.[18]

In spite of the government-industry nuclear establishment's efforts over the last few years to build momentum for nuclear power, momentum has clearly been lost. Two main causes can be identified.

NUCLEAR POWER IN THE INTERNATIONAL ENVIRONMENT

Although Japan has made heroic strides towards indigenous capabilities in nuclear power, it is a measure of the elusiveness of self-sufficiency in energy that the nuclear program has been as disrupted as it has been by international events. The most upsetting international development in the last few years was the nonproliferation policy initiatives of the U.S. government. While Japan sought to actualize the elements of the light water reactor fuel cycle throughout the 1970s, the original logic of the fuel cycle came under serious scrutiny in the U.S. during the same period and was officially abandoned in the early years of the Carter administration. In the American view, the nuclear proliferation implications of the original fuel cycle conception began to take on additional significance in the overall nuclear calculus. In light of these implications, the economic justification for reprocessing, recycling of plutonium in LWRs, and the prompt development of FBRs was no longer seen as compelling. The Carter administration upheld the Ford administration's moratorium on U.S. reprocessing, extended it to FBR activity in the U.S., and attempted to use the considerable leverage the U.S. possessed to persuade other nations to follow suit. The administration's initiatives were followed by even stronger Congressional action with the passage of the 1978 Non-Proliferation Act, which required, among other things, that U.S. nuclear cooperation agreements with other nations be renegotiated to ensure that nonproliferation objectives were being met. Since U.S. policy specifically requires U.S. permission for the reprocessing or retransfer of fuels of U.S. origin, and since it is impossible to assume such permissions will be granted, U.S. policy has introduced a major source of uncertainty into Japanese fuel cycle development plans. Although Japan clearly hopes for more favorable treatment from the Reagan administration,[19] U.S.

---

[18] *Atoms in Japan*, March 1980, p. 5.
[19] See the *Washington Post* dispatch from Tokyo in *The Stanford Daily*, February 13, 1981, p. 2.

attitudes toward the future of the Tokaimura plant, and the U.S. stance in renegotiating the U.S.–Japan agreement, remain to be seen.

International opposition to the new U.S. policy was widespread. The U.S. attempted to deal with this opposition by initiating the International Fuel Cycle Evaluation (INFCE). While the findings of INFCE were consistent with Japanese aspirations to move forward with reprocessing and FBR development, the attention that the nuclear proliferation issue received contributed to a worldwide reconsideration of the nuclear power option. While it is difficult to trace cause-and-effect relations between the nonproliferation debate and public support for the Japanese program, it is unlikely that Japanese nuclear proponents regarded the debate as an unmixed blessing in their efforts to build a public consensus for nuclear power. Although there are indications that the Japanese public resented U.S. policy vis-à-vis Tokaimura (and in this sense supported the nuclear proponents),[20] the international debate probably also raised doubts about the wisdom of Japan's commitment to an indigenous fuel cycle. If faith in the wisdom and integrity of the government's policies for nuclear power is crucial for winning public acceptance, U.S. policy and the subsequent nonproliferation discussions may not have helped the pronuclear cause, in spite of the vindication at INFCE of Japan's position.[21]

A second major perturbation in the international environment was the accident at Three Mile Island. The initial Japanese response to TMI was to initiate a thorough safety review of its PWRs, only one of which was in operation at the time of the accident. Subsequently, the NSC stiffened its requirements for periodic plant inspections. The longer-term impacts, however, have been to make the public more wary of nuclear power and to force a delay of at least one year in the start of construction for seven new plants.[22] In addition, the utilities have had to reconsider the financial burdens of the nuclear option as the staggering costs of cleaning up TMI have become evident.[23]

Finally, TMI has prompted the U.S. Nuclear Regulatory Commission to rethink the criteria used for the selection of sites for nuclear plants. Hearings are to be held on the relative importance of accident mitigation through remote siting in relation to hazard prevention through engineering refinements. The additional weight that the NRC could attach

---

[20] See S. Hayden Lesbirel, "Factors Influencing Long Term Uranium Demand in Japan with Special Reference to Nuclear Siting," unpublished Honours Thesis, School of Modern Asian Studies, Griffith University (Australia), November 1980, p. 60.

[21] For an argument in support of the importance of nuclear policy credibility and the impact of U.S. policy on it, see Richard P. Suttmeier, "Japanese Reactions to U.S. Nuclear Policy: The Domestic Origins of an International Negotiating Position," *Orbis*, Fall 1978, pp. 651–680.

[22] *Energy in Japan*, 46 (September 1979), 8; *Atoms in Japan*, February 1981, pp. 6 and 15.

[23] Lesbirel, "Factors," p. 19, note 45.

to remote siting is seen by the Japanese as an expression of a loss of confidence in safety features engineered into the plant. Since "physical distance" is a scarcer good in Japan than in the U.S., Japan's approach to safety must be based on engineering. It is a measure of the influence which U.S. experience still has on Japan that Japanese nuclear proponents have criticized the NRC thinking on this issue with vigor.[24]

The economic conditions of the industrialized world, especially the slowdown in the growth of demand for electric power coupled with escalating interest rates, have also led to a worldwide slowdown in nuclear plant orders. The case for nuclear power in Japan is not helped by the diffuse influence these developments have. The international slowdown in nuclear industrial activities has provided the industrialized world with an opportunity to reconsider the nuclear option. There are signs that this reconsideration has resulted in a diminished appeal of nuclear power, for a variety of reasons, at the public opinion level and at the industrial decision-making level in some countries as well. While Japanese conditions objectively would still seem to make the nuclear option worth pursuing regardless of what other nations do, it is hard to imagine brighter nuclear prospects in Japan without some brightening on the international scene.

In addition to the diffuse influence resulting from an international slowdown, the state of the U.S. nuclear industry specifically troubles Japan's nuclear proponents. Even as U.S. government influence on Japan has waned as a result of the former's nonproliferation policy and the troubled economic relationship more generally, leaders of the Japanese nuclear industry have still looked to the U.S. for leadership. Reports that General Electric is phasing down its nuclear business and is considering closing its Tokyo office are received with some consternation among Japanese nuclear circles.[25]

The credibility of Japanese government policy is of central importance in winning public acceptance of nuclear power. That credibility, however, is not independent of international "reference cases," the most important of which still is the U.S. The implementation of Japanese nuclear policy would have far smoother sailing if the U.S. were proceeding vigorously with its own nuclear development. In spite of major objective differences in the energy supply situations of the two countries, the fact that it is difficult to discern vigor in the U.S. program makes it more difficult for Japanese proponents to explain why Japan should push ahead with the nuclear option.

The international environment will continue to impinge on Japan's

---

[24] *Atoms in Japan*, September 1980, p. 17.

[25] *Mainichi*, July 1, 1980, in U.S. Embassy, Tokyo, *Daily Summary of the Japanese Press* (hereinafter *DSJP*), July 8, 1980, pp. 15–16.

domestic program. This will be particularly notable in the complex interactions of post-INFCE nonproliferation issues, of which there are many, with Japanese international initiatives to achieve energy security. Reprocessing is likely to remain at issue between the U.S. and Japan. In its last year in office, the Carter administration reportedly had already expressed its disapproval of Japanese plans to build a commercial-scale reprocessing plant, on the grounds that even without it there will be too much unneeded plutonium in the world economy by the late 1980s.[26]

Japan has indicated a willingness to explore opportunities for international institutional arrangements for the management of spent fuel and plutonium storage, and has agreed to participate in a U.S. initiative to explore the feasibility of storing spent fuel at a remote site in the South Pacific. Japan is uneasy about this study, however, fearing that if feasibility can be established, the U.S. will pressure Japan to further defer reprocessing. One of the Japanese arguments for reprocessing (in addition to the economic argument) has been that, with the country's limited land area and with the legal requirement that plant licensing be contingent upon provision for the removal of spent fuel, reprocessing is necessary for spent fuel management. Although the U.S. rejects the fuel economies argument for reprocessing, it is sympathetic to Japan's spent fuel management problems. It does not believe, however, that reprocessing is the way to solve them. The Japanese fear that the establishment of a feasible away-from-reactor storage option would thus strengthen the U.S. hand in opposing reprocessing.

Japan may be uneasy about the Pacific island study for another reason. As in other countries, no solutions have yet been found for nuclear waste disposal. Japan is now working more actively in this area, and within the last year has entered into international agreements for controlled experimental ocean dumping of low-level nuclear wastes. A site in the Pacific has been chosen, but strong opposition to the plan has developed from the Pacific island nations. In addition, it is by no means clear that Japanese public opinion is comfortable with the plan, particularly in light of reports that Korea had been secretly dumping wastes into the Sea of Japan and that wastes had also been carelessly dumped in Suruga and Sagami Bays from 1955 to 1969 by the Japan Radioisotope Association under the guidance of the STA.[27] Since the Pacific island nations have also expressed opposition to the U.S. fuel storage idea, Japan's participation in the proposed study may complicate its dealings with those nations on the ocean-dumping scheme, a project it regards as more integral to its nuclear policy than the former.

---

[26] *Nihon Keizai*, May 8, 1980, in *DSJP*, May 13, 1980, p. 16.
[27] See *Tokyo Shimbun*, October 3, 1980, in *DSJP*, October 9, 1980, p. 6; and *Yomiuri*, September 30, 1980, in *DSJP*, October 3, 1980, p. 5.

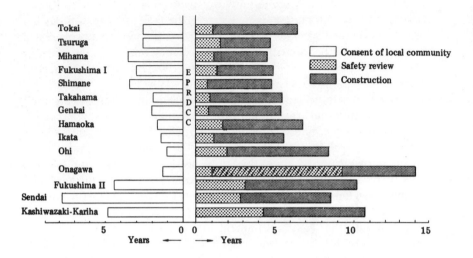

FIGURE 4

Lead Time for Start-up of First Unit at Various Sites

SOURCE: *Atoms in Japan*, June 1980, p. 5.

SITING AND PUBLIC ACCEPTANCE

As in other industrialized countries, public doubts about nuclear safety in Japan have slowed the momentum of nuclear development. As in other countries, one can find expressions of public opinion that are pronuclear; but again as in other countries, individuals who are willing to express support for nuclear power in the abstract are usually unwilling to support nuclear power if a plant is to be constructed near their own homes.

Although there are national organizations opposing nuclear power in Japan, including the Japan Socialist Party, the Democratic Socialist Federation, and the Japan Communist Party,[28] it has been local opposition to particular plants that has been the most intractable problem for nuclear development. For a period in the 1960s and early 1970s, it appeared as though local public opposition would not be a serious obstacle. As Figure 4 indicates, lead times prior to start-up remained relatively constant during this period, and the time required to win consent of the local community prior to a decision by the Electric Power Resources Development Coordinating Council was actually diminishing. The trend, however, has now been reversed.

---

[28] A summary of the positions of Japanese political parties on nuclear power appears below in the Appendix to this chapter.

120

There are a number of constraints on site acquisition in Japan which, when taken together, make the Japanese case unique. First, Japan is one of the most seismically active of the industrialized countries. Second, Japan lacks appropriate fresh-water resources for reactor cooling systems and must therefore choose sites on its coast. However, Japan is also one of the world's great fishing and fish consuming nations. Fishing interests therefore figure prominently in site selection controversies, and questions concerning the protection of fishing rights have taken on additional salience in the age of 200-mile economic zones. Finally, Japan is a densely populated country, particularly in its coastal regions. The identification of seismically stable sites, which would be appropriately distant from population centers and not be a threat to local fishing interests, is thus by no means a simple task. According to a 1976 study, there are only about one hundred such sites in Japan, and these of course are also subject to competition for uses other than nuclear power plants.[29] A more recent study puts the number at seventy-seven.[30]

One consequence of Japan's siting problem is that nuclear expansion is occurring where nuclear plants already exist. In December 1970, there were three plants in operation and ten under construction and/or in preparation, at nine sites in seven prefectures. In December 1979, the number of sites had only increased to fourteen, and only three additional prefectures had agreed to the location of plants within their boundaries, in spite of the fact that thirty-six units were in operation, under construction, or in preparation.[31] As shown in Figure 5, the most heavily concentrated area at present is Tokyo Electric's Fukushima I and II sites with six units totaling 4,700 MW in operation, and with four additional units (4,400 MW) under construction or in planning. The concentration at Fukushima I will be topped, however, if Tepco's plans for a single site at Kashiwazaki-Kariwa in Niigata (seven units of the 1,000+ MW range) are realized.

During the 1970s, the government attempted to deal with the siting–public acceptance problem through three different approaches. In 1974, by legislation, the Electric Power Resources Development Promotion Tax and the EPRDSA were established. As we have seen, the funds were to be administered by MITI and were to be used for public works expenditures in areas where power plants were to be located. The rationale was to assist local areas in absorbing the costs of additional infrastructure development required by the construction of the plant, and thus to provide an incentive (less generously, these funds have been

---

[29] National Institute for Research Advancement, *Analysis and Evaluation of the Nuclear Power System*, Interim Report of the Research Committee of the Nuclear Power Systems (Tokyo: NIRA NRO-50-2, 1976).
[30] Lesbirel, "Factors," p. 48.
[31] *Atoms in Japan*, June 1980, p. 4.

FIGURE 5
Japan's Nuclear Power Generating Capacity
(As of December 31, 1979)

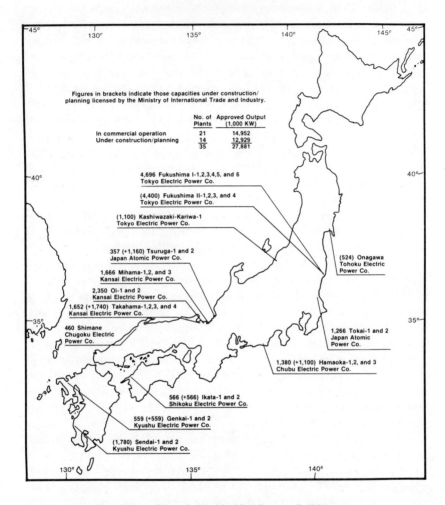

	No. of Plants	Approved Output (1,000 KW)
In commercial operation	21	14,952
Under construction/planning	14	12,929
	35	27,881

Figures in brackets indicate those capacities under construction/planning licensed by the Ministry of International Trade and Industry.

4,696 Fukushima I-1,2,3,4,5, and 6
Tokyo Electric Power Co.

(4,400) Fukushima II-1,2,3, and 4
Tokyo Electric Power Co.

(1,100) Kashiwazaki-Kariwa-1
Tokyo Electric Power Co.

357 (+1,160) Tsuruga-1 and 2
Japan Atomic Power Co.

1,666 Mihama-1,2, and 3
Kansai Electric Power Co.

2,350 Oi-1 and 2
Kansai Electric Power Co.

1,652 (+1,740) Takahama-1,2,3, and 4
Kansai Electric Power Co.

460 Shimane
Chugoku Electric Power Co.

(524) Onagawa
Tohoku Electric Power Co.

1,266 Tokai-1 and 2
Japan Atomic Power Co.

1,380 (+1,100) Hamaoka-1,2, and 3
Chubu Electric Power Co.

566 (+566) Ikata-1 and 2
Shikoku Electric Power Co.

559 (+559) Genkai-1 and 2
Kyushu Electric Power Co.

(1,780) Sendai-1 and 2
Kyushu Electric Power Co.

SOURCE: *Japan Petroleum and Energy Weekly*, 15:1 (January 7, 1980).

referred to as "cooperation money") to localities to adopt a favorable attitude toward having a nuclear neighbor.

Although this program may have eased the siting problem somewhat, by 1980 it was admitted that more had to be done to win the support of the localities, and the adoption of differential utility rates favorable to areas with nuclear plants was discussed. The government's Fiscal Year 1981 draft budget makes provision for subsidies to implement this concept beginning in October 1981. Two plans are being proposed. The first involves grants based on a sliding scale for individuals and enterprises in nuclear power producing areas. For individuals, these grants will range from ¥300 per month in areas with nuclear generating capacity below 1,000 MW to ¥900 per month where installed capacity exceeds 6,000 MW. The range for enterprises is from ¥75 to ¥225 per month. The second program involves grants to prefectures which export power to other prefectures. To qualify, a prefecture must generate 1.5 times the power it consumes, and the amount of the grant will vary according to the amount of power reported.[32]

A second approach used in the 1970s was to create a reserve of sites through land use planning. In 1977, the government established a ministerial Council for Promoting a Comprehensive Energy Policy. One of its tasks was to designate sites to be set aside for power plant construction. Since 1977, twenty-five sites have been so designated, with twelve specifically identified for nuclear units.[33]

Finally, a major overhaul of Japan's licensing and regulatory mechanisms was undertaken during the 1970s. The Japanese initiatives in this area were inspired in part by the reorganization of the U.S. Atomic Energy Commission (AEC), which was designed to separate organizationally promotional and regulatory functions. In addition, the controversy in Japan over who bore responsibility for the radiation leak on the nuclear ship *Mutsu* created pressures for a reexamination of the regulatory authority independent of the U.S. reorganization. Following the *Mutsu* fiasco, a special Council on Nuclear Administration was created to study the structures and procedures used in all areas of nuclear licensing and regulation. On the basis of its findings, it produced a report recommending reform. Because of conflicting bureaucratic interests, change proceeded glacially, but reform legislation finally passed the Diet in 1978. It provided for a new Nuclear Safety Commission having equal status with the JAEC, and placed a large share of the responsibility for licensing commercial nuclear power plants in the hands of MITI. MITI and the NSC working together were to provide a "double check" system for approving new plants, as Figure 6 illustrates. In addition, provision was made for two formal public hearings as part of the procedures.

Although the initial phase of site selection primarily involves negotiations between utilities and the localities, Figure 6 indicates that MITI has a major role in preparing the case for the first major decision in the process, which is made by the Electric Power Resources Development Coordination Council. The EPRDCC is a body which was established before the dawn of the nuclear age to rule on the need and appropriateness of power development projects. It continues to rule on nonnuclear

[32] *Atoms in Japan*, January 1981, p. 5.
[33] *Atoms in Japan*, June 1980, p. 5.

FIGURE 6
Simplified Outline of Licensing Procedures for Nuclear Power Plant

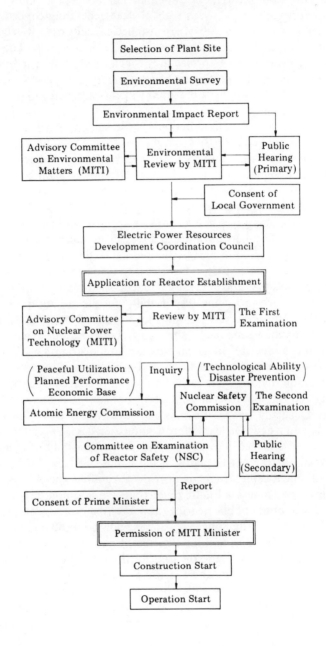

SOURCE: *Atoms in Japan*, December 1980, p. 13.

plants as well. Although there are major nonnuclear technical issues to be considered in the first phase of nuclear site selections (particularly issues related to the environmental suitability of the site), an important objective in this phase is to build local political support.

However, the creation of political support is no easy matter, and it is no longer the case that building consensus can be readily orchestrated by the central government. Local siting problems are often quite complex, and the problems vary from site to site. Studies of siting problems, however, are beginning to shed some light on the issues. The work of S. Hayden Lesbirel, for instance, suggests that the nature of the local economy, rather than the constellation of partisan political forces or the presence of national antinuclear groups, is the most critical variable for predicting the outcome of siting disputes. Lesbirel's findings support three major hypotheses. First, lead times for winning public consensus tend to be shorter at sites where the economic outlook is relatively pessimistic. Second, lead times tend to be longer at sites where the power and influence of groups engaged in primary sector economic activities is increasing. Finally, lead times for approval of additional reactors in areas that already have at least one tend to be shorter, since the local economies have not developed a strong base of secondary industry (indicating a failure of the EPRDSA approach) and thus have come to depend on continuing nuclear construction.[34]

In another recent study, the Japan Atomic Industrial Forum (JAIF) found that the site selection and licensing processes did not enjoy full legitimacy with local residents, and that the local economic benefits of locating a plant in a region did not compensate for potential economic losses.[35] The question of economic loss has been an issue for a number of years and was in part responsible for the establishment of the EPRDSA. However, concerns over economic loss involve much more than the local absorption of the costs of infrastructure development needed for the plant. The JAIF study is consistent with Lesbirel's findings that the establishment of a nuclear plant in itself does little to stimulate long-term economic growth. Furthermore, plants can be amortized over fifteen years, with their value reduced by as much as 50 percent in five years. As a result, substantial tax advantages to the locality from fixed assets taxes on the plant are not realized. Instead, the value of the locality's most valuable resources, its farmlands, coastal area, and fisheries, are compromised by the potential for accidents. While it has been the practice for utilities, in advance of operations, to compensate local fishing interests handsomely[36]

---

[34] Lesbirel, "Factors," pp. 91–92.

[35] *Atoms in Japan*, June 1980, pp. 4–8.

[36] In one recent settlement, reached after ten years of negotiations, Tohoku Electric agreed to pay ¥3.96 billion ($2 million) to fishermen in Maki Town, Niigata, for lost fishing grounds. See *Atoms in Japan*, December 1980, p. 6.

for the right to locate, the localities increasingly feel that this procedure is not adequate to deal with possible contingencies after operations have begun. Fishermen in particular are concerned that even the rumor of inadvertent releases of radioactive materials into local waters would ruin their livelihood.

Questions concerning the legitimacy of the licensing procedures are also not new, but their public recognition by the nuclear establishment is. The essence of the problem is that local government authorities are expected to represent local interests in site selection proceedings but are woefully unprepared for such participation. Local government has neither the expertise nor the resources to acquire the expertise to credibly evaluate the technical environmental issues on which it is expected to make decisions on behalf of its constituents. It also lacks authority, as well as expertise, to insist on an integrated regional development program as a fair return for the area's hosting a nuclear plant. Whereas at one time local officials could have been coopted by the utilities and the central government, local public opinion today makes such a course increasingly unlikely. The result is that both local officials and their constituents are dissatisfied with procedures which they regard as being stacked in favor of the nuclear proponents in distant cities.

The problems of legitimacy and the importance of local leadership are nicely treated in a recent report by Kazuyasu Nemoto of the Central Research Institute of the Electric Power Industry. Nemoto notes that the initial stage of site selection is crucial. The utilities do not have an obligation to publicly announce their interest in a site, and would oppose such an obligation, since it would lead to sharp increases in land prices. Instead, the initial stage of the siting process involves a great deal of informal behind-the-scenes negotiations between the utilities and local "influentials" (elected and administrative officials, officers of agricultural and fisheries cooperatives, union officials, etc.). Nemoto believes that if major conflicts are to be avoided, local government officials must be able to effectively mediate the interactions between the utilities and the local people at this stage. However, their ability to perform this mediation function at present is questionable for the following reasons.

First, local public opinion is somewhat inchoate. While organized interests are part of the informal negotiation process, these interests usually cannot speak for the majority of citizens in the area. There is thus a "silent majority" whose views on the project cannot be readily anticipated.

When the licensing process moves into a more formal stage with the initiation of environmental impact assessments by the utilities, and the review of these assessments by MITI, efforts to involve the local people have been minimal. Furthermore, according to Nemoto, these assessments have been conducted without reference to the need for regional development schemes, and thus are seen as deficient in their neglect of comprehensive assessments of socioeconomic effects. Throughout the assessment process, tasks are largely in the hands of the utilities and MITI, and are perceived as being oriented primarily toward winning EPRDCC approval rather than toward producing proposals which the local population could endorse. The inclusion of a public hearing in the process has not built conviction that local interests are being protected. Access to and rules for the hearings are restrictive. Nuclear opponents consider the hearings a farce and an occasion for public demonstrations. Even some nuclear proponents regard them, in their present form, merely as "ceremony."

Present siting procedures require that the prefectural governor give his approval to the project before EPRDCC approval can be granted. Governors, however, look to recommendations from local officials in this matter. Yet, neither the prefectural level nor the local level have the data and expertise needed to make a sound judgment of the overall environmental effects of the project. Thus, according to Nemoto, "there is no way for the local residents [and officials] to know how their regional environment may be changed by a nuclear power plant and how their everyday lives will be affected."[37]

The most recent siting dispute, which received widespread attention in Japan during the early months of 1981, illustrates some of the points made in the studies cited above. The case involved a vote by the citizens of Kubokawa, Kochi prefecture, to recall their mayor after he took the initiative to invite the Shikoku Electric Power Company to conduct a preliminary site survey.[38] Although the mayor was acting with the support of the town council, his action came after he had entered into an antinuclear agreement with the local Socialist and Communist parties during the election campaign, which pitted him against two other Liberal Democratic Party candidates. The case also involved efforts by the leaders of the LDP to stem the tide of the recall campaign by promising to keep open a line of the Japan National Railroad which had been scheduled for discontinuation. Their efforts, however, were both unsuccessful and apparently resented in some quarters.

The Kubokawa case is not significant as a democratic rejection of nuclear power. It appears that the recall was more a rejection of a man who was not "sincere" in office in relation to his campaign behavior. Whatever the motives of the recalled mayor, his leadership failures in office have now set back the site acquisition process. There is agreement among some nuclear proponents that a better sense of strategy might

---

[37] Kazuyasu Nemoto, "Public Acceptance Issues in Japanese Nuclear Power-Siting Policy," *Atoms in Japan*, February 1981, pp. 18–22.

[38] This discussion is based on conversations in Tokyo on March 30, 1981, with officials from the Japan Atomic Industrial Forum.

have produced a different outcome. Thus, the Kubokawa case supports Nemoto's emphasis on the importance of shrewd leadership at the local level. The case also illustrates the limited effectiveness of old-style pork-barrel-type intervention by the central government.[39]

Perhaps the most interesting aspect of the Kubokawa case, however, is that it may have revealed for the first time a new type of nuclear opposition. Among those who supported the recall because of opposition to nuclear power (nuclear opponents represented about 30 percent of the vote, or slightly more than half of the 51 percent majority) were members of a younger generation of farmers committed to the expansion of the area's dairy industry. These appear to be representative of a new generation of rural youth who see their futures in promoting farming and fishing in rural areas instead of migrating to cities for industrial employment. The existence of such groups with preferences for rural life-styles adds a significant new dimension to the problem, in light of Lesbirel's findings concerning the relationship between the strength of the primary sector and resistance to siting.

The JAIF report on siting problems noted above includes a number of recommendations to remedy the present stalemate. These range from strengthening the authority and capabilities of local government, and greater interministerial cooperation at the center, to the search for new financial mechanisms to foster regional economic development. While the new subsidy programs for Fiscal Year 1981, discussed above, are intended to address some of these problems, one senses that other problems (e.g., center-periphery relations and the prerogatives of local governments) will require changes in highly institutionalized patterns of behavior and may be less responsive to the use of instruments of public policy. Furthermore, a reaffirmation of rural life-styles on the part of the younger rural generation seemingly will require a major rethinking of strategies for winning public acceptance.

CONCLUSION

It is sometimes argued that "technical fixes" offer a convenient approach to the solution of social problems. The appeal of the technical fix is that objectives can be attained without the need to embark on cumbersome and costly programs to change people's attitudes and values. Technical fixes, however, are not without their boundary conditions. In the view of those observers who are skeptical of technical fixes, more often than not it is the boundary conditions that count. Hence, the mere availability of the technology does not guarantee that desired problem solutions are attain-

---

[39] The recalled mayor was reelected in a special election after promising to hold a referendum on the acceptability of a nuclear plant in the township (*Atoms in Japan*, April 1981, pp. 10–13).

able. Instead, some degree of organizational and/or attitudinal change is required if the technology is to be deployed and its benefits realized. Nuclear power in Japan, as well as in other countries, has clearly reached the limits of its promise as a technical fix, as some thoughtful Japanese proponents of nuclear power have long realized.

Japanese nuclear leaders have shown a willingness to incur substantial costs over the long run for technological development, and their efforts have been rewarded with impressive technological progress. Heavy investment in R&D will continue to be required if the objectives of nuclear technology development are to be realized, and a willingness to make this investment is apparent. Increasingly, however, it is not investment in technology that is at issue, but rather the willingness to incur costs to alter the boundary conditions. The latter costs should be understood broadly to include not only money and time, but also a full range of costs associated with altering institutionalized patterns of action.

The account above indicates a willingness among some leaders in Japan to incur these costs of changing values, attitudes, and established ways of doing things. Unfortunately, however, the costs keep mounting as new sources of concern over nuclear power appear in both the domestic and international environments. The willingness and ability to continue to incur costs are finite, however. One can't help wondering whether the costs are approaching the point where enthusiasm for the nuclear option among energy planners will begin to fade rapidly. This point clearly hasn't been reached yet, largely because all available alternatives are themselves exceedingly costly. Indeed, this latter fact is the key to the continued viability of the nuclear option.

The pursuit of the nuclear option is thus coming to resemble the predicament of Sisyphus. The flavor of the times is captured nicely in a recent commentary in the journal of the Japan Atomic Industrial Forum on the JAEC's annual White Paper. Responding to JAEC "appeals for increased public information work and peaceful coexistence between power companies and local fishing interests," *Atoms in Japan* reaches the following somber conclusions on the siting dilemma:

> Nevertheless, one cannot but doubt the effectiveness of formal public information work and the new system created for this purpose. Public hearings tend to become mere formalities, as they are boycotted by opposing groups. There is the possibility also that movements against nuclear power will become more widespread, now that they have been given a new struggle target—opposition to ocean disposal of radioactive waste. The question is, what concrete measures can be taken to solve siting problems? No real agreement will be possible so long as the method of solving all problems with compensation and "cooperation money" is used, and it is recognized that demands made by local residents as the price for approval of siting are tending to be so inordinately high as to comprise a real threat to future

construction plans, and even to stable and sound social development. To promote the siting of new nuclear power plants, it has become necessary to make persistent efforts to win a rational public agreement by *tirelessly* explaining *the absolute need* for nuclear power and its safety, not only to local people but also to political parties, trade unions and local citizens' groups who are now opposed to nuclear power, listening patiently to their opinions and discussing with them measures needed [for] regional development.[40]

The revelation in late April 1981 of a serious mishap at JAPCO's Tsuruga plant is unfortunately consistent with the imagery of the Sisyphus myth. In light of the above discussion of the public acceptance problem, two aspects of the case could make it a serious setback politically.

First, the allegations that JAPCO attempted to "cover up" the facts that contaminated waste water had been released into the plant and that cleanup workers may have been exposed to dangerously high levels of radiation will raise serious public doubts about the social responsibility of the utilities and the effectiveness and legitimacy of the government's regulatory efforts.

Second, the difficulties of securing new sites are likely to increase dramatically. The Tsuruga area had long been considered one of the most favorable for securing new sites. It already had a number of operating plants (see map in Figure 5), which seemingly had not compromised the local fishing industry, and the local leadership had been considered effective, progressive mediators of the concerns of the local population and the interests of the utilities.

The fact that high levels of radioactivity were reported in Tsuruga Bay as a result of the release of contaminated waste water from the plant led to a boycott of seafood from the Tsuruga area. Thus, the worst fear of the nation's fishermen—that the mere rumor of radioactive contamination would have a damaging effect on local fishing industries—has been realized. The incident is also likely to lead to a redefinition of what constitutes good local leadership on nuclear matters, and to make the effective pro-nuclear local politician an endangered species.

It would be premature to refer to Tsuruga as Japan's TMI. However, in light of the public acceptance problems characteristic of the Japanese case, it is likely that the Tsuruga incident will seriously complicate plans to increase the role of nuclear power in order to reduce Japan's energy dependency.

---

[40] *Atoms in Japan*, January 1981, pp. 16–17 (emphasis added).

Appendix

Energy and Nuclear Power Policies of Political Parties*

*From *Atoms in Japan*, June 1980, pp. 12–13.

Party Names and Outlines (in descending order of conservatism)	Policies to Reduce Japan's Dependence on Oil	Attitudes toward Nuclear Power Plants	House of Representatives		House of Councilors	
			New Seats (%)	Former Seats (%)	New Seats (%)	Former Seats (%)
The Liberal Democratic Party The Liberal Democratic Party (LDP) is the largest conservative party in Japan, formed in 1955 by a merger of the Liberal Party and the Japan Democratic Party. The political principle of the party is "the building and protection of a liberal society based on capitalist economy." In the latest simultaneous Diet elections for the House of Representatives and the House of Councilors, the LDP won seats well above the numerical majority in each house.	In order to reduce oil dependence to 50% by 1990 (dependence rate in 1977 was 75%), conservation and alternative energy development should be promoted.	Nuclear energy should receive highest priority in the development of alternative energy sources, and by 1990 nuclear energy should constitute 11% of Japan's primary energy (share in 1977 was 2%).	286 (56.0)	258 (50.5)	135 (53.6)	124 (49.2)
The New Liberal Club The New Liberal Club (NLC) was formed in 1976 by six members from both Houses who seceded from the LDP that year. The party's goal is to win moderate gradual reforms based on true conservatism through an overall reassessment of existing institutions and policies, and to set up a comprehensive security system. To this end, the party aspires to form an open national political organization of citizens.	Energy demand-supply program should be set up and fully implemented. For energy-conservation investment and development of new energy technology, various incentive measures should be provided by way of taxation and finance.	Nuclear energy is the main alternative energy source before new energy sources come into full use. Safety should be assured by technical standardization and domestic production. Construction of nuclear power plants should be promoted with the understanding and cooperation of the people.	12 (2.3)	4 (0.8)	2 (0.8)	2 (0.8)
The Democratic Socialist Party The Democratic Socialist Party (DSP) was organized in 1960 mainly by members who repudiated class-based parties and seceded from the Japan Socialist Party. Under the banner of democratic socialism, the party aims at the establishment of a welfare society. The DSP draws its base support from a labor federation of unions in the electric power, automobile, textile and other industries.	Wile maintaining 5% or more economic growth rate to ensure an adequate employment rate, energy conservation (15% by 1985) and alternative energy development should be promoted in order to reduce oil dependence.	Nuclear energy should be the most important alternative energy source for development. Nuclear power generation should make steady progress on the basis of assured safety. The operating rate of existing plants must be improved.	33 (6.5)	36 (7.0)	12 (4.8)	10 (4.0)
The Komei Party The Komei Party (Clean Government Party) was inaugurated in 1964 as a political organization of Soka Gakkai or Value Creation Society, a lay organization affiliated with the Nichiren Seisoh sect of Buddhism. In 1972 the party proclaimed its adherence to the principle of separation of politics and religion, with a party platform upholding humanist socialism in order to enlist broad support irrespective of religion. In the latest elections, however, the party lost 30% of its former Diet seats.	15% energy conservation should be achieved by 1985. Concurrently, research and development should be vigorously promoted for alternative energy sources other than imported oil.	For construction of nuclear power plants, rigorous safety examination and environmental assessment are necessary, and construction should begin only when a consensus of the local residents is obtained.	34 (6.7)	58 (11.4)	26 (10.3)	28 (11.1)

The United Social Democratic Party

The United Social Democratic Federation (Shaminren) was launched in 1978 by members who withdrew from the Japan Socialist Party, advocating "free socialism." The party repudiates centralized socialism, and its platform is to assure democracy and citizen participation in plitics and to realize social justice in an industrial society. "Free socialism" has also been called "citizens' socialism."

Investment in energy conservation should be promoted. Oil-guzzling economy must now be reformed in order to create a welfare society. Maximum efforts must be devoted to development of soft energy. Coal is simply a temporary stopgap for the next ten years.

About a three-year moratorium (freeze on nuclear power generation) should be put into practice. During this period, construction of new nuclear power plants should be suspended, and defective reactors should be eliminated. Those already operating or under construction would be allowed to operate on condition that safety is assured, but should be dismantled eventually.

The Japan Socialist Party

The Japan Socialist Party (JSP) was organized in 1945 by a merger of proletarian groups as a party to uphold social democracy. However, the JSP is internally split between pro-Soviet and pro-Chinese factions. It is backed by organizations of personal supporters of Socialist members and a labor federation, which influences the nature of the party as being dominated by unions and other leaders. It is called a "front-line" party.

The structure of industries now centering on heavy and chemical industry should be reorganized into a energy-conserving structure. Coal should be the main alternative energy, supplemented by hydropower, solar heat, geothermal heat, wind power and wave power.

Nuclear energy has significant defects as regards safety and reliability, now being only in the phase of research. Therefore, construction of new nuclear power plants or extension of existing facilities should be stopped. Complete overhaul of existing facilities is needed.

The Japan Communist Party

The Japan Communist Party (JCP) was inaugurated in 1922 with a platform for building a communist society. Originally the party followed a pro-Soviet line, but now it pursues its own independent policy, intending to achieve socialism that respects "freedom and democracy," independent of Chinese or Soviet communism. It had about 350,000 party members as of May, 1979.

The industrial structure, transportation and traffic systems should be converted for energy conservation. Active measures should be taken for "democratic recovery and development of domestic coal" and research and development of new energy sources.

The three principles for the peaceful utilization on nuclear energy (augonomy, democratic, and open to the public) must be strictly maintained. Systems should be reformed for research, safety examination, and control, with safety receiving highest priority. All existing programs should be subjected to total reexamination.

About a three-year moratorium...	3 (0.6)	2 (0.4)	2 (0.8)	3 (1.2)
Nuclear energy has significant...	107 (20.9)	107 (20.9)	47 (18.7)	52 (20.6)
The three principles...	29 (5.7)	41 (8.0)	12 (4.8)	16 (6.3)
Others	7	4	15	11
Vacancies		1	1	6
Total	511	511	252	252

The Politics of Alternative Energy Research and Development in Japan*

Richard J. Samuels

JAPANESE ENERGY ALTERNATIVES

Two international oil crises have clearly illuminated Japan's energy dilemma, the contours of which are by now widely familiar (Kaya, 1979; Goodman, 1980; Tsuru, 1980). The Japanese economy, accounting for more than 10 percent of the world's GNP, is precariously dependent upon imported energy. Seven years after the first jolt, imported energy continues to account for almost 90 percent of Japan's primary energy use. Fully three-quarters of this primary energy comes from petroleum, 99.8 percent of which is imported. Moreover, over one-half of Japan's primary energy is put to industrial use, compared to Great Britain's one-quarter and the United States' one-third, further accentuating the degree to which Japan's foreign petroleum fix is a dagger pointed at its own economic heart. Nowhere in the world is there greater incentive for the development of alternative energy resources than in Japan.

But what are the alternatives? There seem to be many, but their

*Support for this project was received from the Japan-MIT Endowment for International Energy Policy Studies.

The author gratefully acknowledges the very capable research assistance of Tanaka Akihiko of MIT, and the generous assistance extended to him by Ogura Shinichi of the Science and Technology Agency of Japan. He would also like to thank Professors Kaya Yoichi of Tokyo University, Sawa Takamitsu of Kyoto University, and Watanuki Joji of Sophia University for their comments and encouragement. The advice and criticism of Dr. Ronald A. Morse and of Professor Richard K. Lester of MIT were also extremely helpful.

identification depends entirely upon how "alternative energy" is defined. To illustrate, we can respond less rhetorically with two corollary questions: Alternatives *to* what? and Alternatives *for* what? Each generates a separate cluster of Japanese energy alternatives: the former evokes petroleum and thereby Japan's energy *dilemma*, while the latter evokes commercial possibilities and thereby Japan's energy *opportunity*. It is the purpose of this chapter to sort through both of these conceptions in order to profile the political as well as the technological choices they present to Japanese leaders. After briefly sketching what is meant by "alternative energy" in this section, I will provide in the following section an overview of Japan's energy R&D apparatus. In the third section, I will explore the politics of Japanese energy R&D by focusing upon the public actors and private interests involved in the recent creation of the New Energy Development Organization (NEDO), which, like the Synthetic Fuels Corporation in the United States, emerged in response to the 1979 oil crisis and promises to become the nation's premier energy R&D organ.

The question, Alternatives *to* what?, frames most discussions of energy alternatives. With petroleum as a common referent, most analyses focus upon energy-specific imperatives for the diversification of Japanese dependencies, both by geographic origin (supplier) and by energy source (supply). This straightforward concern for alternatives to petroleum, particularly Middle Eastern petroleum, shaped Japan's response to both the 1973 and 1979 oil crises. *Supplier* policies have included (a) the seeking of assurances of stable supplies from producer nations, and (b) the acquisition of new foreign petroleum sources. Martha Caldwell and Ronald Morse each explore the diplomatic and national security aspects of these imperatives elsewhere in this collection. Supply policies have included (a) the exploitation of non-oil energy resources, (b) the development of new energy technologies, and (c) conservation. On these pages we are most concerned with the latter two, particularly the Japanese research program for the development of new energy technologies. The two most important non-oil sources of supply, nuclear energy and coal, are examined in more detail elsewhere in this collection by Richard Suttmeier and Roger Gale, respectively.

Virtually all studies identify four generic categories of alternatives to petroleum: (1) nuclear, (2) fossil fuels, (3) "renewable," and (4) conservation.[1] The first category, nuclear (including both fission and fusion technologies), and the second category, fossil fuels (including coal, liquefied natural gas, and synthetic fuels derived from coal, shale, tar sands, and other sources), are the most unambiguous. The third category, how-

[1] The most comprehensive treatment of these alternatives is found in *Energy: The Next Twenty Years*, by Kenneth J. Arrow et al. (Cambridge, Mass.: Ballinger Press, 1979).

ever, is an ill-defined potpourri of alternatives, usually including solar, geothermal, hydroelectric, wind, wave, biomass, and other nonfossil, nonnuclear energy sources. These are variously labeled "nonconventional," "local," "clean," "renewable," or "natural" energy resources. However, nothing could be more "conventional," or more easily linked to a general supply network, than hydroelectric power; few sources are "cleaner" or more "renewable" than nuclear fusion; and none are more "natural" than the direct combustion of fossil fuels. We must rely upon these official designations for analytic purposes, but we do not endorse them. Conservation technologies are subsumed in the fourth category. The Japanese commonly include under this heading magnetohydrodynamic power systems, hydrogen, and gas turbines, as well as waste heat utilization technologies and lightweight materials research. Conservation is clearly a different sort of alternative to petroleum, in that its purpose is the more efficient use, rather than the augmentation, of energy supplies. Although some alternatives to petroleum may be more exotic than others (photovoltaic energy, for example, evokes sunshine and purity, while coal evokes darkness and grime), nearly all are related to evolving technologies that hold great promise for Japan as alternatives to petroleum.

The question, Alternatives *for* what?, however, suggests an even greater range of policy choice. It addresses broader and more fundamental strategic and industrial policy goals, and thereby forms a potentially more significant part of Japan's response. Lacking both significant military capabilities and natural resources, Japan closely coordinates its national security and energy programs with its industrial policy. The latter frequently enjoys preeminence. Thus, in addition to issues of energy *supply* that quite naturally arise when one considers alternatives to petroleum, the question, Alternatives *for* what?, engenders additional *commercial* alternatives. When viewed in the context of Japanese industrial policy more generally, the obvious challenge for the Japanese is the amelioration of energy supply vulnerabilities through the development of commercially viable energy technologies that might at the same time further enhance Japan's international competitiveness.

The significance of the commercial component in national alternative energy strategies is certainly not unique to Japan, but its emphasis in the Japanese case is important for several reasons. First, it is offered as a corrective to those Japanese observers who stress only the vulnerability and the precariousness of their energy dilemma. Although the image of the "emerging superstate" is more pleasant, it is generally suppressed in publications and government documents, while that of the "fragile blossom" enjoys a more widespread public face in Japan. Secondly, the Ministry of International Trade and Industry (MITI) has been assuming an increasingly significant role in energy R&D. At the time of the first oil shock MITI had an energy R&D budget of only ¥400 million. In fiscal 1980, MITI spent over ¥80 billion for energy R&D activities (Kagaku

Gijutsuchō Kenkyū Chōseikyoku, 1979; and Naikaku Soridaijin, 1980). We are reminded that MITI's mandate is commercial, not scientific or technological. The vigor with which MITI has moved into energy R&D is a clear indication of the government's perception of the relationship between Japan's energy security and its national economic health.

The Japanese are understandably concerned about shifting their energy dependence on foreign oil to foreign uranium or foreign synthetic fuel technologies; this energy-cum-national-security concern is entirely consistent with new directions in "knowledge-intensive" industrial development currently being promoted by MITI. Having striven diligently to "catch up with and surpass" the West (and having succeeded at the very least in half of that task), Japanese leaders, both in the energy area and in the broader realm of industrial policy, have begun to stress the need for "domestically developed technologies" (*jishu gijutsu*). Japan's energy R&D programs, especially the growing number of those administered by MITI, are therefore at the cutting edge of Japanese industrial policy, and they continue in the Japanese pattern of placing the commercialization of technologies, whether domestically developed or licensed from abroad, at the forefront of industrial growth. There is no reason to artificially limit Japan's alternative energy R&D effort to Japan's oil vulnerability. The Japanese certainly do not. Energy security, narrowly defined, may be the "push" for an active alternative energy R&D effort, but national security, broadly constituted and inclusive of commercial considerations, acts as the "pull." Alternative energy R&D thus looms large in Japan's energy and industrial future, and it is that to which we now turn.

ALTERNATIVE ENERGY R&D IN JAPAN [2]

The National Science Board (U.S.) recently published an estimate of government-funded energy R&D in several advanced industrial nations. The data seemed to dispel the widespread belief that most technologically advanced nations redoubled their energy R&D after the 1973 supply disruption. They show relative cutbacks in energy R&D in several countries.

---

[2] By research and development, I am referring to a significant part of the process by which (to paraphrase Arrow et al., *Energy*, p. 543) "new facilities are created to supply energy, existing technologies are adapted to changes in costs or regulation, and new processes are introduced that incorporate advances in materials and technology." Of course, R&D, and the larger process of which it is part, is far more complex than budgetary figures can adequately reveal. Insofar as this essay is concerned only with mapping the contours of the Japanese energy R&D effort, it is merely a first cut into that complexity. More detailed examinations of Japanese energy and Japanese energy technology will result from related work being undertaken by this author and his colleague Professor Richard K. Lester at the Center for Energy Policy Research at MIT.

Table 1

ESTIMATED GOVERNMENT-FUNDED ENERGY R&D*
(*as a percent of total government-funded R&D*)†

	1961–1962	1965–1966	1969–1970	1974–1975	1976–1977
Japan	7	3	8	8	n/a
U.K.	15	13	9	6	7
U.S.A.	7	5	5	6	9
West Germany	16	16	16	11	11

SOURCE: National Science Board, *Science Indicators 1978* (Washington, D.C.: Government Printing Office, 1979).

*Energy R&D is defined here as those activities "aimed at the supply, production, conservation, and distribution of all forms of energy except as a means of propulsion for vehicles and societies."

†These figures are based upon available OECD estimates and may not in all cases perfectly correspond to the time period indicated.

But what appears to be a moderate relative increase in U.S. energy R&D between the pre-1973 and post-1973 periods belies a real increase of almost 300 percent. Likewise, Japanese energy R&D budgets have more than quintupled since 1973, despite there being no apparent change in energy's share of Japan's total R&D budget. Nor does this increase disappear when we control for inflation. Japanese government energy R&D expenditures expanded in real terms nearly four times faster than the Japanese Gross Domestic Product (GDP) between 1974 and 1979. Of the five OECD nations that have together accounted for about 90 percent of

Table 2

REAL GROWTH IN
ENERGY R&D BUDGETS
(1974–79)

U.S.A.	228.1%
Japan	98.5%
West Germany	62.3%
Canada	3.0%
U.K.	-3.2%

SOURCE: International Energy Agency, *Energy Research, Development and Demonstration in the IEA Countries* (Paris: OECD, 1980, p. 15.)

Table 3

DISTRIBUTION OF ENERGY R&D IN JAPAN
(1978)

Energy Source	Percent of Total	
Fossil Fuels Total	7.1%	
Petroleum, LNG		4.0%
Coal		2.6%
Other		0.5%
"Renewable" Total	4.5%	
Solar		2.3%
Biomass		1.1%
Other		1.1%
Nuclear Total	65.7%	
Electric Power		16.7%
Nuclear Fuel Cycle		16.8%
Fusion		9.5%
Radiation, Safety		7.9%
Other		14.8%
Conservation	21.6%	
Industrial		8.4%
Transport		5.3%
Electric Power		3.7%
Other		4.2%
Other	1.1%	1.1%
Total	100.0%	100.0%

SOURCE: Sōrifu Tōkeikyoku, *Shōwa 54 Nen Enerugī Kenkyū Chōsa Kekka no Gaiyō* [An Outline of the Results of the 1979 Energy Research Investigation] (Tokyo, February 1980).

all OECD energy R&D throughout that period, Japanese performance was second only to that of the United States (see Table 2). Moreover, a recent survey conducted by the Prime Minister's office of Japan contradicts the National Science Board's suggestion of stasis relative to the broader national R&D effort. The survey found that energy R&D in Japan—including both public and private sectors—was growing at twice the rate of total R&D (Sōrifu Tōkeikyoku, 1980). Energy R&D in Japan is clearly alive and well. The combined public and private sectorial distribution of that effort is displayed in Table 3.

However, this snapshot, as it were, masks the somewhat unconventional relationship between the public and private sectors in Japanese energy R&D. It is widely known that private industry, accounting for over two-thirds of all R&D spending, has a much larger share of national R&D

in Japan than in any other advanced industrial nation (Gerstenfeld and Sumiyoshi, 1980). Energy R&D, however, does not conform to general patterns of research expenditure in Japan. As we see in Table 4, the bulk of the energy R&D effort in Japan is government directed.[3] This finding is confirmed by other studies as well. *Nihon Keizai Shimbun* survey data demonstrate that R&D expenditures are substantially lower in the chemical and energy sectors than elsewhere in private industry (*Japan Economic Journal*, September 16, 1980); and the Institute for Energy Economics has projected that the existing patterns of public sector dominance will increase over the next decade. By the Institute's estimate, the government will be paying for more than two-thirds of all energy R&D by 1990 (Institute for Energy Economics, 1980).

It is not difficult to comprehend why governments come to dominate energy R&D. The lead time to commercialization in some energy areas is particularly long. Moreover, project costs are often extremely high. In addition to the need for sustained and expensive commitments, two other considerations are pertinent. First, there is often much legitimate question about the basic need for many energy technologies. Secondly, the security dimension is more salient in energy than in some other areas. None of these considerations are unique to energy, but as a cluster they do seem to characterize energy R&D. Thus, if we look again at Table 4, we find that the general balance in favor of government dominance also masks important variation. Although the government dominates in nuclear R&D, the area in which this cluster of concerns seems most tightly fused, industrial R&D, accounts for almost 90 percent of all fossil fuel and other energy R&D. In 1978, at least, industry dominated R&D in solar, geothermal, wind, wave, biomass, and energy conservation technologies almost by default. Although it is not reported in Table 4, the only nonnuclear alternative energy area in which the government outspends industry is in coal conversation technologies.

The Japanese government's direct share of energy R&D deserves special attention. In fiscal 1980, the government budget for energy R&D totaled ¥314 billion, an increase of almost ¥100 billion (47 percent) from 1979, reflecting the growing insecurity of Middle Eastern petroleum sup-

---

[3] These figures should be interpreted with caution. As noted, the private sector response rate was 80 percent, whereas 100 percent of public firms and research institutes returned their questionnaires. One might therefore suspect that these distributions are skewed in favor of the public sector. One might reasonably assume that a minimum of between one-fifth and one-quarter of private sector R&D is unaccounted for. However, the aggregate figure of ¥152.3 billion reported for public firms and research institutes is itself about 25 percent less than government-reported budgetary aggregates for 1978. I assume, therefore, that this survey instrument underestimates *both* public sector and private sector energy R&D, and I thus feel some confidence in utilizing these distributions for analytic purposes.

Table 4

DISTRIBUTION OF ENERGY R&D BY SECTOR (1978)*

	Actual Billion Yen / Row % / Column %

	Private Firms and Research Institutes		Public Firms (*Tokushu Hōjin*), Research Institutes, and Public Universities		Total
Fossil Fuels	¥17.0 billion 14%	87.2%	¥2.5 billion 1.7%	12.8%	¥19.5 billion 7.2%
"Renewable" Sources	¥7.2 billion 5.9%	59.5%	¥4.9 billion 3.2%	40.5%	¥12.1 billion 4.4%
Nuclear Energy	¥41.8 billion 34.5%	23.1%	¥139.4 billion 92.1%	76.9%	¥181.2 billion 66.5%
Conservation	¥55.1 billion 45.5%	92.4%	¥4.5 billion 3.0%	7.6%	¥59.6 billion 21.9%
Total	¥121.1 billion (44.5%)		¥151.3 billion (55.5%)		¥272.4 billion

SOURCE: Sōrifu Tōkeikyoku, *Shōwa 54 Nen Enerugī Kenkyū Chōsa Kekka no Gaiyō* [An Outline of the Results of the 1979 Energy Research Investigation] (Tokyo, February 1980).

*This survey was remarkably comprehensive. It included over five thousand firms with capital stocks in excess of ¥100 million, nearly one thousand research institutes, and almost nine hundred universities. The response rate was 100 percent from both the public research institutes and from the universities, and was 80 percent from the private firms. The data reported here are adapted from that survey. We exclude 2 percent of the government's reported total.

plies resulting from the Iranian revolution. The government's energy R&D program, although not strictly centralized, is far from anarchic. The bulk of government funds is budgeted for twenty-eight designated energy "projects." A project is constituted as a collection of R&D activities in energy technologies which are "(1) related to the solution of societal and economic needs, which (2) extend across a large number of scientific and technological fields, which (3) require the involvement of many organizations, and which (4) require the establishment of targets and management by administrative agencies" (Naikaku Sōridaijin, 1980, p. 13). In short, a project is that which is so designated by the government. It follows, then, that "nonprojects" include all government sponsored and/or subsidized energy-related R&D not designated as a "project." The distribution by energy area and by administrative agency of government efforts in 1979 and 1980 is represented in Figure 1. A more detailed breakdown follows in Tables 5 through 8.[4]

As an obvious rule of thumb, we can note that the Science and Technology Agency (STA) is responsible for nuclear energy R&D, clearly the bulk of the total effort, whereas MITI is responsible for virtually all else. This distinction seems to have been institutionalized in the April 1974 introduction of Japan's "Sunshine Project," itself a reaction to the first oil crisis. Sunshine Project activities were restricted to the nonnuclear alternatives to petroleum, and have been administered by MITI's Agency of Industrial Science and Technology.[5] But what appears to be an obvious division of labor between STA and MITI belies the complexity of their relationship. As we shall see in the following section of this chapter, MITI has been expanding the scope of its energy activities—in both the nuclear and the nonnuclear areas.

MITI has moved aggressively to fill a critically important vacuum in nonnuclear energy R&D. As reported earlier, at the time of the first oil shock MITI had an energy R&D budget of only ¥400 million; but with the introduction of the Sunshine Project and other more recent activities, MITI energy R&D stood at over ¥80 billion in fiscal 1980 (Kagaku Gijutsuchō Kenkyū Chōseikyoku, 1979; and Naikaku Sōridaijin, 1980). Perhaps to highlight the narrowness of the STA focus on nuclear energy, MITI insists upon stressing the *comprehensiveness* of its own energy R&D effort. MITI employs the term *sōgō* ("comprehensive") in the Japanese titles of three of its most important energy-related organs: the blue ribbon Advisory Committee for Energy (Sōgō Enerugī Chōsakai), the key policy section within the Agency of Natural Resources and Energy (Sōgō Enerugī Seisakuka), and the recently established semigovernmental New Energy Development Organization (Shin Enerugī Sōgō Kaihatsu Kikō).

The nuclear area is less clear, but has equally borne witness to MITI expansion. While it remains tiny in comparison to the STA's nuclear R&D budget, MITI's own nuclear R&D has doubled in the last year alone. MITI had the prescience to create the Agency of Natural Resources and

---

[4] These government data do *not* seem to include government-funded energy R&D which is channeled as loans through the semigovernmental Japan Development Bank to private industry. Some of these funds may be considered energy R&D expenditures. See *Asahi Shimbun*, September 2, 1980.

[5] This same MITI agency also administers the "Moonlight Project," created in 1978 as the conservation technology complement of the supply-technology-centered Sunshine Project. See the Appendix, below, for Sunshine Project budgets over time.

142

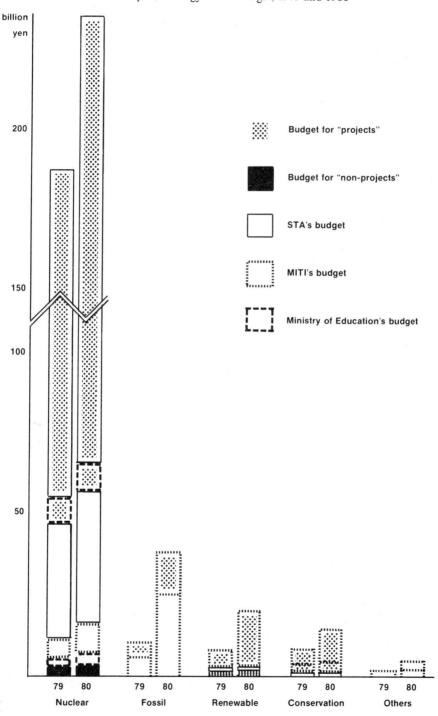

FIGURE 1
Japan's Energy R&D Budget, 1979 and 1980

Budget for "projects"

Budget for "non-projects"

STA's budget

MITI's budget

Ministry of Education's budget

SOURCE: Naikaku Sōridaijin, *Enerugī Kenkyū Kaihatsu Kihon Keikaku* [Basic Plan for Energy R&D] (Tokyo, July 15, 1980).

Table 5

OFFICIAL GOVERNMENT ATOMIC ENERGY PROJECTS AND NONPROJECT RESEARCH

(in millions of yen)

Projects	STA		MITI		Ministry of Education		Ministry of Foreign Affairs	
	1979	1980	1979	1980	1979	1980	1979	1980
1 Uranium manufacture and conversion	3,052	3,672						
2 Uranium enrichment (centrifuge separation)	19,089	23,238						
3 Reprocessing	14,219	18,428						
4 Radioactive waste disposal	10,158	11,538						
5 Plutonium manufacture	2,451	2,411						
6 Light water reactor	6,151	8,542						
7 New style power reactor }	46,974	64,735						
8 Fast breeder reactor }								
9 Multipurpose high temperature gas reactor	3,261	3,921						
10 Nuclear fusion	23,959	29,708			7,852	8,240		
11 Atomic powered ships	4,067	6,451						
Project total	133,381	170,649*	0	0	7,852	8,240	0	0
Nonproject research	36,347	41,268	5,489	10,001	3,408	3,304	1,323	1,849
Total	169,728	211,917	5,489	10,001	11,260	11,544	1,323	1,849

SOURCE: Naikaku Sōridaijin, *Enerugī Kenkyū Kaihatsu Kihon Keikaku* [Basic Plan Energy R&D] (Tokyo, July 15, 1980).

*Since some items are multiply categorized, the project total does not match the actual sum.

Table 6

OFFICIAL GOVERNMENT FOSSIL FUEL PROJECTS
AND NONPROJECT RESEARCH
(*in millions of yen*)

	MITI	
Projects	1979	1980
1 Coal gasification	1,812	4,839
2 Coal liquification	1,089	3,712
3 Seabed oil production system	1,124	3,315
Projects total	4,025	11,867
Nonproject research	5,977	26,908
Total	10,002	38,775

SOURCE: Naikaku Sōridaijin, *Enerugī Kenkyu Kaihatsu Kihon Keikaku* [Basic Plan for Energy R&D] (Tokyo, July 15, 1980).

Table 7

OFFICIAL GOVERNMENT "RENEWABLE" ENERGY PROJECT
AND NONPROJECT RESEARCH
(*in millions of yen*)

		MITI		STA		Ministry of Agriculture, Forestry, and Fishery	
		1979	1980	1979	1980	1979	1980
1 Geothermal	project	3,576	8,607				
	nonproject	0	932				
2 Solar	project	3,709	9,483				
	nonproject	58	70				
3 Ocean	project	82	166	429	96		
	nonproject			8	22		
4 Wind	project	58	123				
	nonproject	15	17				
5 Biomass	project	7	11	63	204	0	5
	nonproject	12	431				
Total		7,517	19,840	500	322	0	5

	1979	1980
Total	8,017*	20,160*

SOURCE: Naikaku Sōridaijin, *Enerugī Kenkyū Kaihatsu Kihon Keikaku* [Basic Plan for Energy R&D] (Tokyo, July 15, 1980).
*The total does not match the actual subtotal because of the multiple categorization of some items.

145

Table 8

OFFICIAL GOVERNMENT ENERGY CONSERVATION PROJECTS AND NONPROJECT RESEARCH

(in millions of yen)

		MITI 1979	MITI 1980	STA 1979	STA 1980	Construction 1979	Construction 1980	MAFF 1979	MAFF 1980	Transportation 1979	Transportation 1980
1 MHD	project	914	1,322								
2 Hydrogen	project	690	951								
	nonproject			0	35						
3 Nuclear steel manufacture	project	1,530	539								
4 Reclamation of resources	project	880	2,543								
5 Energy conserving housing	project					74	88				
6 Waste heat use	project	793	1,023								
7 Efficient use in agriculture, forestry, fishery	project							879	964		
8 Gas turbines	project	604	4,281								
Other nonproject research	project	723	1,536	888	1,701					26	60
Total		6,134	12,195	888	1,736	74	88	879	964	26	60

SOURCE: Naikaku Sōridaijin, *Enerugi Kenkyū Kaihatsu Kihon Keikaku* [Basic Plan for Energy R&D] (Tokyo. July 15. 1980).

Energy in July 1973, just before the oil shock.[6] One of the emphases here was atomic energy, particularly the nuclear generation of electricity. Predictably, this Agency has rapidly expanded its budgets and personnel since the oil crisis. Whereas the STA enjoys special relationships with the Atomic Energy Commission, the Nuclear Safety Commission, the Japan Atomic Energy Research Institute, and the Power Reactor and Nuclear Fuel Development Corporation, MITI's Agency for Natural Resources and Energy has both a Nuclear Industry Division (within its Administrator's Secretariat) and a Nuclear Power Generation Division (within its Public Utilities Department). MITI is charged by the Electric Power Law with the regulation of electric utilities, and because nuclear energy is almost entirely restricted de facto to electric power generation in Japan, MITI has much to say about Japan's nuclear power option.

Figure 2 represents an attempt to be more comprehensive in the attribution of administrative responsibility for the full range of alternative energy R&D in the public sector. Here, in the pairing of government agencies, their subdivisions, and their related external organs, the complexity first becomes obvious. Clearly, generalizations derived from budgetary data about the locus of control in alternative energy R&D are problematic.

In sum, documentation of the collective public sector energy R&D program is easier than attribution of the locus of governmental power. Likewise, in the absence of reliable aggregate data on private sector energy R&D in Japan, we are left with little more than a capacity for general comparison.[7] Nevertheless, these comparisons can help us reconstruct the larger picture. *On the basis of estimates of the distribution between governmental and industrial activities reported earlier in this section, and with the knowledge of current aggregate levels of government energy R&D expenditures, we can estimate Japan's total energy R&D effort to have been between ¥550 billion and ¥600 billion in fiscal 1980. This total of all governmental and nongovernmental spending is approximately half to three-quarters of public sector energy R&D in the United States* (International Energy Agency, 1980b, p. 14). Absolute levels of energy R&D spending must therefore be evaluated in terms of an overall Japanese strategy of plugging into existing R&D efforts worldwide. While this renders cross-national comparisons of R&D figures problematic, it also

---

[6] Takano Takeshi calls it a "fluke"; see his *Tsūsanshō no Yabō* [MITI's Ambitions] (Tokyo: Weekend Books, 1980), p. 47.
[7] This is not unique to Japan. It is true for the United States as well. The International Energy Agency has been unable to gain access to full details of most OECD nations' industrially financed energy research programs. See International Energy Agency, *Energy Research, Development and Demonstration in the IEA Countries* (Paris: OECD, 1980), p. 27.

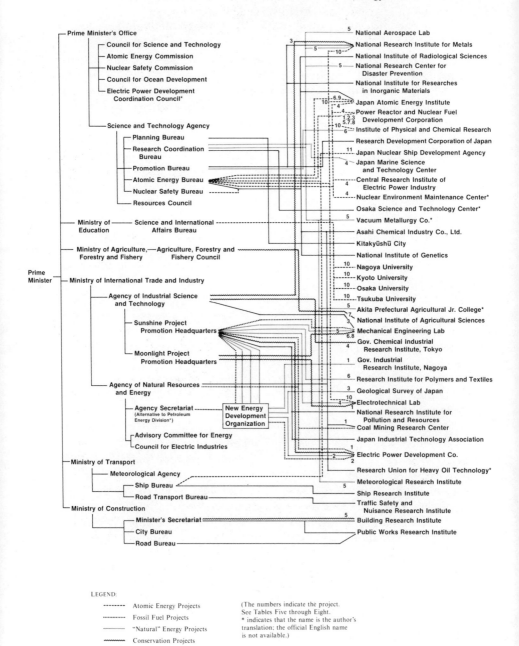

FIGURE 2
Official Administrative Network for Alternative Energy R&D

LEGEND:

-------- Atomic Energy Projects

.... Fossil Fuel Projects

~~~~~~ "Natural" Energy Projects

〜〜〜 Conservation Projects

——— Non-Projects

(The numbers indicate the project.
See Tables Five through Eight.
* indicates that the name is the author's
translation; the official English name
is not available.)

SOURCES: Naikaku Sōridaijin, *Enerugī Kenkyū Kaihatsu Kihon Keikaku* [Basic Plan for Energy R&D] (Tokyo, July 15, 1980); *Sunshine Information Center News*, No. 2 (1979); and Tsūshō Sangyōshō, *Shin Enerugī Kaihatsu Suishin no Chūkakutai ni Tsuite* [Concerning the Central Organ for Promotion of New Energy Development] (Tokyo, June 1980).

suggests an important international dimension of Japanese energy alternatives.[8]

But evaluation of this aspect of Japan's alternative energy strategy is equally perplexing. Given our low (at least when compared to U.S. levels) estimate of Japan's total energy R&D effort, given the obvious imperatives of Japan's energy dilemma, and given Japan's sophisticated technological intelligence apparatus, one might expect to find widespread evidence of the *collaborative* diversification of Japan's energy dependencies. This is, in fact, a part of Japan's response. The most prominent example is the $1 billion "Fukuda Initiative." Former Prime Minister Fukuda Takeo proposed an ambitious program of joint Japanese-American energy research while visiting Washington in May 1978. In November 1978, final agreement was reached. Formally known as the "United States–Japan Agreement in Energy and Related Fields," this project superseded the existing 1974 "Agreement for Cooperation in Energy Research and Development," and emphasizes nuclear fusion and coal conversion technologies. Secondary foci include solar, geothermal, and high-energy physics research. But, in fact, while Japan has invested $60 million in the five-year effort to upgrade the Department of Energy's Doublet III fusion program, the bulk of its commitment (approximately $375 million) has been in the American synthetic fuel program. This initiative notwithstanding, collaborative diversification, at least in multinational forums, does *not* seem to be a very significant part of the Japanese strategy. Japan's official participation rate in International Energy Agency (IEA) collaborative projects in which it has an ongoing domestic program is, at 43 percent, one of the lowest of all IEA member countries. In comparison to the United States and to West Germany, whose contributions together account for nearly three-quarters of all the funds for these IEA projects, Japan contributes 2.4 percent, less than half of the Swedish contribution. Although multinational joint ventures in the *private* sector, such as Japanese corporate participation in Australian coal liquefaction, American synfuel, and Canadian biomass programs, have increased since the Iranian revolution, the bulk of Japan's alternative energy R&D is being pursued at home by Japan on its own.

Analysis of the creation in 1980 of the New Energy Development Organization (NEDO), the subject of the next part of this chapter, is even more revealing of Japan's alternative energy strategy, for we are reminded that "strategies" seem most coherent only in retrospect, and that the policy process is seldom guided by the logic that suggests itself in cross-sectional data. We move, then, away from our snapshot of alternative energy R&D in Japan to an examination of the politics that helped shape it.

---

[8] Cross-national comparisons of R&D budgets are made even more problematic by variation in nations' definitions of "R&D." Despite efforts to coordinate data collection and definition, even the IEA data are suspect in this regard.

THE POLITICS OF ALTERNATIVE
ENERGY R&D IN JAPAN

The year 1980 was a watershed for alternative energy R&D in Japan. The government redefined its effort and provided for the allocation of an unprecedented ¥2.9 trillion over the next decade in the effort to achieve energy security. The keystone of the government program was the Alternative to Petroleum Energy Development and Introduction Promotion Law (hereafter The Alternative Energy Law of 1980), a law hammered out at heavy political cost only after substantial bureaucratic struggle. A look at how this battle was fought offers us a glimpse of governmental decision-making and the role of private industry in the policy process. The battle stands as testimony to how mythical the views are of a monolithic and harmonious Japan Incorporated. Figure 3 provides a referent for the narrative that follows.

What eventually became the Alternative Energy Law of 1980 was first proposed by MITI bureaucrats in the autumn 1978 first draft of their "1980s Vision", but it was not until the spring of 1979, in the midst of the fallout from the Iranian revolution and the nuclear reactor accident at Three Mile Island, that representatives of the MITI Ministerial Secretariat, the Agency for Industrial Science and Technology, and the Agency of Natural Resources and Energy came together for intraministerial discussion of how MITI should proceed in the energy area. At that time, the MITI discussions centered on the creation of an Alternative Energy Public Corporation, a *kōdan* (public corporation) over which MITI would enjoy full supervisory control. MITI officials worked on this and other proposals throughout the summer of 1979, but they withheld any formal announcement of their program until after the general election in October, and until after the Prime Minister publicly issued a pledge to confront Japan's energy dilemma.[9] MITI then revealed a four-point program in late November (see Figure 3). As originally proposed, each of the pillars of this program would have enhanced MITI's power in energy policymaking.

The first pillar was a draft of an "Alternative Energy Introduction and Promotion Special Measures Law" which would allow the Minister of

---

[9] Prime Minister Ohira and the ruling Liberal Democratic Party (LDP) were mildly rebuffed at the polls in the October 1979 general election. Winning 248 seats, only two more than half, the LDP fell far below expectations for a "stable majority." Resisting pressures for resignation from within his own party, Ohira grew feisty. He repackaged several major political irritants, and in November invested his new Cabinet with responsibility for four policy priorities, the first two of which, (1) energy policy and (2) financial reconstruction, represented diametrically opposed governmental imperatives. While the former demanded substantial increases in government spending in the search for alternative energy technologies, the latter demanded restraint and austerity. Each abutted the other in its fiscal underbelly. Each defined an opposing constituency, and this opposition framed the debate over Japanese energy policy in 1979–80.

FIGURE 3

The Alternative Energy Law of 1980

(Sekiyū Daitai Enerugii no Kaihatsu oyobi Dōnyū no Sokushin ni kansuru Horitsu)

MITI's Four-Point Program

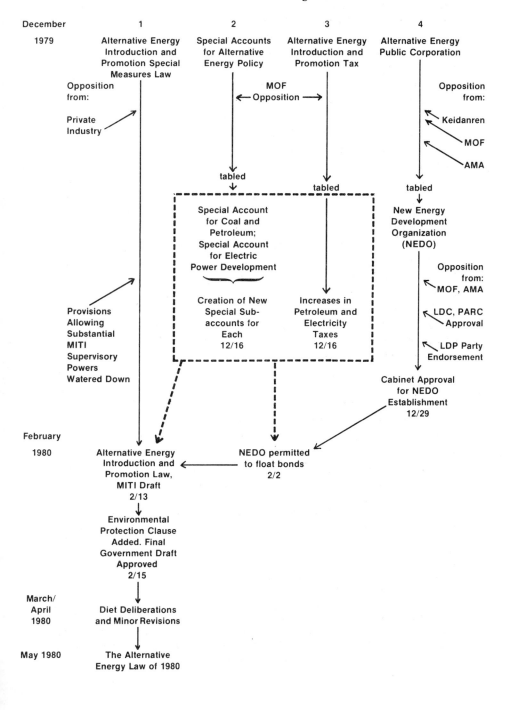

International Trade and Industry to establish legally binding targets for private industry in the conversion from oil to alternative energy resources. It would also give MITI the authority to issue nationwide energy targets and to develop incentive policies for industry and consumers to meet them. In addition, the law as originally drafted would require industrial energy users to report all plans involving energy use in excess of these targets, and the MITI Minister would be empowered to draft plans and provide guidance for energy conversion (*Nihon Keizai Shimbun*, November 24, 1980). The second and third pillars of MITI's alternative energy program both addressed financial matters. MITI proposed to establish new special accounts earmarked for alternative energy R&D which would be funded by revenues raised by the introduction of new taxes on petroleum and electricity consumption. The fourth pillar of the program entailed the creation of an Alternative Energy Public Corporation, the proposed MITI-supervised *kōdan* mentioned above. None of these four proposals survived the December budgetary process intact, and, as we shall see, their transformation has been interpreted both as a victory and as a defeat for MITI.

The first public opposition to the MITI proposal was voiced by former Keidanren chairman Doko Toshio even before MITI formally unveiled it. In anticipation of the MITI announcement, Mr. Doko was first to tie the issue of fiscal reform directly to the energy issue. In speaking to the top policymaking board of Keidanren on November 13, he announced:

> I have doubts about the idea of an Alternative Energy Public Corporation. While we do have to make energy policy a priority in the 1980 budget, the creation of a new tax structure would present many problems. We need first to reconsider the existing energy tax system.
>
> (*Nihon Keizai Shimbun*, November 14, 1979)

The Administrative Management Agency (AMA), the bureaucratic organ most directly charged with administrative reform, joined in opposition several days later. On November 17, AMA officials announced their opposition to the creation of an additional public corporation at a time of fiscal retrenchment. Moreover, they took the offensive and proposed the elimination of the Coal Mine Damage Corporation, the Rationalization of Coal Industry Corporation, and the Electric Power Development Company, the three existing energy-related *tokushu hōjin* supervised by MITI (*Nihon Keizai Shimbun*, November 18, 1979).[10] The Ministry of Finance

---

[10] The English term "public corporation" is an imprecise and narrow one. Like Chalmers Johnson (1978), I prefer the term "public policy company"; but for the sake of consistency with the Japanese formal designations, I refer to all special legal entities wholly or partially engaged in public-sector-directed enterprise as *tokushu hōjin*.

(MOF) later joined in what was becoming a chorus of opposition for essentially the same reasons as the AMA. Acting upon its responsibility for reducing Japan's enormous national debt, the MOF was opposed to any increase in government bureaucracy.[11] It refused to incorporate the MITI plan in the MOF budget proposal submitted later in December. The Keidanren opposition, however, was rather different in kind. Unlike the AMA and MOF, which sought reductions in the bureaucracy for the sake of the public sector, Keidanren interpreted the MITI program as further undesirable governmental encroachment upon the *private* sector. On November 27, both Mr. Doko and Inayama Yoshihiro, his successor as Keidanren chairman, met with Prime Minister Ohira to present the Keidanren position. They insisted that alternative energy development was a matter for the private sector, and they rejected the idea of a new public corporation. Nevertheless, they provided room for compromise by stating that while a reduction of public expenditures was desirable, no reduction should adversely affect the development of energy alternatives. Prime Minister Ohira reportedly expressed his pessimism toward the MITI program:

> Mr. Sasaki [Sasaki Yoshitake, then Minister of International Trade and Industry] has explained his proposal for a new Alternative Energy Public Corporation, but I have to question the wisdom of establishing a new public corporation at a time when we are also trying to reorganize existing ones.
> (*Nihon Keizai Shimbun*, November 28, 1979)

While the proposals for MITI supervision of industrial energy use and for the new public corporation were receiving the most vocal criticism, the two financial proposals were proving to be rather more amenable to compromise solutions. All parties to the debate seemed to agree to the need for reform of the energy tax system. For example, the leading Japanese financial daily pointed out in an editorial that of the almost ¥ 3 trillion generated in fiscal 1979 from energy-related taxes, over three-quarters was spent on the maintenance of roadways and only 13 percent was earmarked for energy R&D (*Nihon Keizai Shimbun*, December 10, 1979). The MOF firmly opposed MITI's two financial proposals, insisting that revision of the current tax system would generate sufficient funds for an aggressive alternative energy R&D effort. On December 16, less than one week before the submission of the final MOF draft budget, represen-

---

[11] Nearly 40 percent of the general account budget in fiscal 1979 was funded by national bonds. Debt financing had been introduced in fiscal 1966, marking Japan's transition from surplus to deficit budgeting. Indications of a gathering fiscal storm appeared as early as 1970; and while the government did tighten its belt at that time, there subsequently occurred an "organizational forgetting" of the potential for crisis, finally thrusting the issue of "financial reconstruction" to the top of the government agenda by mid-1979 (Noguchi, 1980, p. 30).

tatives of MITI and the MOF met to negotiate the funding for this effort. MITI abandoned its proposal for new taxes and new special accounts, and an MOF/MITI compromise was worked out which nevertheless provided MITI with enormous additional revenues from existing taxes. Use of the same taxes which had been funding the Sunshine Project between 1974 and 1980 was dramatically altered; whereas they had provided a total of ¥ 38 billion for the Sunshine Project between 1974 and 1979, revenues from these same tax sources in 1980 were expected to provide ¥118 billion earmarked for alternative energy R&D. The Electric Resources Development and Promotion Tax was raised by over 350 percent, from ¥.085 to ¥.30 per kilowatt hour; and although the Petroleum Tax remained at 3.5 percent of retail sales, its allocation was changed to permit MITI to use an estimated ¥35 billion for alternative energy R&D in 1980 alone (Tsūshō Sangyōshō Shigen Enerugīchō Sekiyū Daitai Enerugī Taisakuka, June 1980b, pp. 10–12).[12] In addition, the MOF consented to establish four new special sub-accounts to facilitate the R&D effort. The funds generated from these tax increases are allotted to these new special sub-accounts in roughly equal measure for nuclear and nonnuclear alternatives to petroleum. In 1980, the funds together amounted to ¥118 billion, and they are projected to amount to almost ¥3 trillion over the next decade.

At the same time that the financial compromises were struck between MITI and the MOF, the leadership of the LDP was proposing a means to satisfy all parties to the debate. Top party officials met on December 13 to discuss the possibility of transforming the idea of a purely public corporation into a more hybrid combination of public and private enterprise. This sort of hybrid is known as a *dai san sekutā* (third sector) company in Japan, and is frequently resorted to by industry when it seems that government is resisting private sector pressures to create a public corporation, or by government when it seems that industry is unwilling to cooperate with a government proposal for the creation of a public corporation. In this case it was clearly the latter.[13] The "third sector" company, designed to maximize private sector managerial and technological expertise in conjunction with joint public and private sector capital, was an important part of many central government plans during the high-growth decade.[14] The compromise proposal reportedly advanced by an

---

[12] Both of these taxes are paid to the government by the energy *supplier*, not directly by the end user.

[13] For a detailed case of the former, see Richard J. Samuels, "The Politics of Regional Policy in Japan" (Ph.D. dissertation, MIT, Department of Political Science, 1980).

[14] For the relationship between "third sector" firms and other forms of more purely public or private enterprise, see Chalmers Johnson, *Japan's Public Policy Companies* (Washington, D.C.: American Enterprise Institute for Public Policy Research, 1978).

unidentified LDP leader on December 13, although palatable to industry leaders, was strongly opposed by Uno Sosuke, Director General of the AMA, and Takeshita Noboru, Minister of Finance (*Nihon Keizai Shimbun*, December 14, 1979). At a meeting with Chief Cabinet Secretary Ito Masayoshi on December 18, they announced that they could not accept this compromise (*Nihon Keizai Shimbun*, December 19, 1979). The Party leadership, however, proved as resourceful as MITI proved tenacious. After public announcements in support of such a quasi-public sector alternative energy corporation by LDP Secretary General Sakurauchi Yoshio and others, MITI Minister Sasaki demonstrated new flexibility. Although the first version of the "third sector" plan served to allay the fears in the business community that MITI would dominate the nation's energy R&D, it had not addressed the issue of fiscal reform, an issue of even greater concern to the MOF and AMA. Apparently under pressure from the LDP, Sasaki announced on December 20 that MITI was abandoning the plan for an Alternative Energy Public Corporation in favor of a "third sector" New Energy Development Organization (NEDO) (*Nihon Keizai Shimbun*, December 21, 1979). To placate private sector opposition, he announced that the new organization would be administered by a policy committee made up of distinguished leaders of industry, government, and the academic world. To placate AMA and MOF opposition, he announced that NEDO would absorb one of the existing *tokushu hōjin* under MITI control, the Rationalization of Coal Industry Corporation, thereby streamlining the MITI bureaucracy.

These proposals, counterproposals, and attempted compromises were made all the more frenetic by impending budget compilation deadlines. The final part of the fiscal 1980 budget calendar is displayed in Table 9.

The MITI proposal was *not* included in the official MOF budget proposal of December 22. The MOF and AMA remained holdouts, preferring the abolition of existing MITI-related *tokushu hōjin* to the creation of a new one. The LDP then tried again, in the midst of the revival negotiations. On December 25, the Administrative and Financial Policy Affairs Research Council within the larger LDP Policy Affairs Research Council suggested even further MITI concessions as conditions for MOF and AMA acceptance of the NEDO plan. In addition to requiring NEDO to absorb the Rationalization of Coal Industry Corporation, the LDP proposed that NEDO also eventually assume responsibility for the government's monopoly of alcohol production. It was becoming increasingly difficult for the MOF and AMA to object on the grounds of administrative irrationality.

Final approval for a further revised NEDO plan was reached at the eleventh hour, on December 29, at an all-night meeting of the Ohira cabinet. It was here that the Prime Minister's twin policy priorities of

Table 9

PARTIAL 1980 FISCAL YEAR BUDGET
CALENDAR

December 22, 1979:	Ministry of Finance Plan Announced
December 23, 1979:	Revival Negotiations Begin
December 26, 1979:	Ministerial Conference
December 27, 1979:	Cabinet Negotiations
December 28, 1979:	LDP Leadership Review
December 29, 1979:	Cabinet Meeting for Decision on Final Government Program

November (fiscal reconstruction and energy policy) came into direct, and final, confrontation in the 1980 budget compilation process. Within two hours after these final negotiations began, they were stalled by AMA chief Uno's intransigent opposition. He reportedly chided MITI for its "greed" in desiring to expand its already large number of twenty-two *tokushu hōjin*, and he accused MITI of seeking merely to create yet additional *amakudari* nests for its retired officials (*Nihon Keizai Shimbun*, December 30, 1979).[15] Further concessions by MITI would clearly be necessary, and Minister Sasaki agreed to additional bureaucratic rationalization. He agreed to combine in a single public policy company two other *tokushu hōjin* under his control: the Small Business Promotion Corporation and the Smaller Enterprise Retirement Allowance Mutual Aid Project Corporation (Takano, 1980). Only then did NEDO become part of the government's official budget proposal to the Diet.

The Diet does not typically pass upon government budget proposals until early spring, and this delay allowed MITI to prepare a new draft of the enabling legislation for NEDO and the rest of its alternative energy policy program. The new MITI draft of its Alternative Energy Law was revealed on February 12, 1980. Although it remained more comprehensive than any previous legislative program for alternative energy R&D, it reflected the many pressures described above, and was clearly less ambitious than the November draft. Whereas the Minister of International Trade and Industry had been afforded supervisory and regulatory powers over industrial energy choices in Articles Three, Five, and Six of the first draft, he was limited in the new version to setting supply goals and guidance with the approval of the Cabinet. Whereas he was initially allowed to set "basic policy" (*kihon hōshin*), he was now in a far less

---

[15] *Amakudari*, literally "descent from heaven," is a term used to describe the recirculation of retired government officials to highly paid positions in the private sector or in public corporations.

commanding position. In this regard, Article Four of the new draft deleted requirements that industry submit energy use plans to MITI, and instead provided only that "those who use energy should try to introduce alternative energy in consideration of supply-demand, technology, and other factors." MITI sanctions for noncompliance, which had been included in Article Eleven, were likewise deleted. What were initially controls became enticements; there is far less regulation and much more inducement to action in the revised version (*Asahi Shimbun*, February 14, 1980). The most interesting aspect of these revisions, especially for students of the Japanese policy process, is the fact that this second draft version underwent only minor additional revisions before Diet passage in May. Although environmental interests within the government succeeded in adding a short environmental protection clause, and although the JSP and Komeito jointly sponsored an amendment concerning whether the "Prime Minister" or the "law" shall guide the new alternative energy program, all major political battles were fought within the government and ruling party before the second drafting of the legislation, well before its submission to the Diet. This is not, however, to be interpreted as a government steamrolling of opposition. Instead, in marked contrast to the U.S. case, the energy R&D issue seems to have generated neither sharp partisan cleavages nor much more than general indifference among the opposition parties in Japan. Although they felt compelled to revise the law in minor ways for reasons of Diet politics, none of the opposition parties have issued detailed energy policy programs of their own. Constituents of these energy R&D battles are only those with direct power to both "give and take." This limitation ensures both the quality of the accommodation reached and the intramural character of energy R&D politics.

The introduction of this new energy policy program raises a number of important questions, not the least of which is: What does the enabling legislation actually enable the government to do? NEDO, which began operations on October 1, 1980, is formally charged with producing a concentrated, large-scale R&D effort in the areas of (1) liquefied coal, (2) geothermal, and (3) solar technologies, and with responsibility for the provision of loans for overseas mining and field surveys. Insofar as NEDO is involved in mining financing, issuing energy development bonds, subsidizing prospecting at home and abroad, and guaranteeing bank loans for energy development, its effort is as much financial as it is scientific or technological. In all these activities, however, NEDO stresses the *commercialization* of alternative energy technologies (Shin Enerugī Sōgō Kaihatsu Kikō, 1980).

But the formal NEDO role, financial or otherwise, is rather more ambiguous than it might at first seem. That ambiguity is due in part to the ambiguity inherent in the "third sector" formula. NEDO has neither a free market nor a governmental mandate. Some press reports suggest that 60 percent of the 337-person NEDO staff will come from the private sector (*Asahi Shimbun*, December 28, 1979). This leaves only about 135 positions for government officials, and if we consider that NEDO is absorbing other existing *tokushu hōjin*, then we must assume at least a restricted government role in the new organization. In fact, MITI went to great lengths to include the role of the private sector in its draft description of NEDO. Reflecting the initial recalcitrance of industrial leaders, MITI proclaimed that "although [NEDO] is established as a *tokushu hōjin*, the vigor of the private sector will be fully utilized" (Tsūshō Sangyōshō, May 1980a). Indeed, this seems to have been an understatement. MITI announced in July 1980 that the chairman of the NEDO Board of Directors would be Doko Toshio, former Keidanren chairman and an initial source of opposition to MITI's original four-point program. Likewise, MITI appointed an Hitachi Vice President for Heavy Industries, Watamori Tsutomu, NEDO President. Both Koko and Watamori are leading proponents of nuclear power, the one alternative to petroleum excluded from the NEDO charter. One might therefore expect NEDO to act as a check on MITI interference with the nuclear power industry. But this apparent capture of NEDO by private industry has not fully convinced all interested parties. Takano (1980, p. 57) quotes one Keidanren official who remains wary:

> The government really has a way with words. They create public corporations and other special legal bodies which, in their first generation, are models of public sector–private sector cooperation. Upon their establishment, these organs' top officers come from private enterprise, but eventually, in their second or third generation, it is the bureaucrats who are placed in the top posts. . . .

Nevertheless, NEDO's *governmental* role remains to be defined.

This raises a second question: Are we to evaluate the 1980 Law as yet another MITI success in the expansion of its energy-related powers? Clearly, MITI's ability to steer an energy-related budgetary increase of three times the total budgetary increase in fiscal 1980 represented an exceptional success, especially given budgetary norms of balance and incrementalism (Campbell, 1977). It seems likely that even the concessions to Keidanren and to the AMA and MOF were fully anticipated by MITI planners. In retreating from an overly ambitious scheme, they may have ended up at their original destination. Yet, they may also have fallen short of total success in what Takano (1980) has described as their "giant plot" to monopolize all new alternative energy revenues. We should be reminded that atomic power research did not receive special attention in the 1980 Law, and is not part of the NEDO mandate. The big gains in the 1980 package were MITI gains, but they remain the lesser part of the total alternative energy R&D effort. Additionally, as noted above, the balance between governmental and nongovernmental control of NEDO remains to be struck.

This then suggests a third question: How does this new package relate to existing institutional arrangements in the alternative energy area? Again, the answers are clouded by ambiguity and uncertainty. One might assume that NEDO would supplant the Sunshine and Moonlight Projects. After all, it exists within the same Ministry, it is largely concerned with the same agenda for nonnuclear alternative energy R&D, and it is funded from exactly the same tax sources. Thst assumption, however, is probably incorrect. MITI officials have tried to explain NEDO as a direct descendant of the Sunshine Project, but as one less concerned with basic research than with development, demonstration, and commercialization. In reality, however, such a distinction is unlikely to prove this clear-cut. Even within MITI there is evidence of bureaucratic struggle. There are already signs of competition between MITI's Agency of Industrial Science and Technology, which supervises the Sunshine Project, and its Agency of Natural Resources and Energy, wherein NEDO resides (Takano, 1980). In addition to the intra-MITI confusion over the new organization, there is also legitimate question about the relationship of the MITI alternative energy package to other, non-MITI alternative energy programs, particularly those of the Science and Technology Agency. In May 1977, the Prime Minister's office sponsored a Science and Technology Conference, out of which emerged the May 1978 "Basic Plan for Energy Research and Development" (Naikaku Sōridaijin, 1980). This was an STA-led effort to coordinate Japanese alternative energy R&D activities, and it remains, even in its third revised form, the most comprehensive statement of the government's programs. But although there clearly should be some connection between the 1980 MITI program and this STA-prepared plan, both of which are designed to elevate and coordinate public sector energy R&D, there is no explicit acknowledgment of any relationship in the documents of either agency. We can expect an even wider exacerbation of the bureaucratic confusion.

In sum, we are left with a very different impression of the energy policy process than that reported elsewhere:

> Energy policy in Japan is administered by MITI . . . with guidance for long-term energy policy prospects from the Advisory Committe for Energy. Close coordination is maintained with the Science and Technology Agency . . . under the authority of the Prime Minister.
> (Hollomon and Grenon, 1975, p. 206)

There is no evidence that the bureaucratic environment in the energy R&D area is any more harmonious in Japan than elsewhere. It is conflict rather than consensus that best characterized these bureaucratic relationships. In spite of our finding that energy R&D does not conform to the general Japanese pattern in which R&D is centered in the private sector, even this "centralized" R&D effort is difficult to clearly profile.

CONCLUSION

To review, there are two fundamentally different conceptions of Japan's energy alternatives. The first is narrowly limited to the diversification of energy supply and supplier. Under this definition of the issue, three policy imperatives seem quite well defined. Japan must first act to reduce the continued high concentration of its foreign suppliers by diversifying its sources of petroleum. This is clearly an optional energy alternative, but, as it is an option limited to petroleum, it was not treated on these pages as an alternative energy option. Secondly, Japan must act to reduce its continued high dependence upon oil by diversifying its primary energy resource mix. There is much debate about Japan's ability to do this. In August 1979, the Advisory Committee for Energy reported a set of energy supply targets to the Minister of International Trade and Industry. These estimates have been widely accepted as authoritative, and are reported as columns 5–7 in Table 10. They have also been criticized as naive and overly sanguine for suggesting that non-oil sources would account for over half of all primary energy supply by the end of this decade, even though they presently account for only one quarter of Japanese primary energy. This would entail more than a doubling of coal use and a near quintupling of Japan's reliance upon nuclear energy. It also assumes that as much as 30 percent of the increase in energy demand through 1995 will be absorbed by energy conservation.[16]

---

[16] Herbert I. Goodman has called this forecast "wildly unrealistic" ("Japan and the World Energy Problem," an occasional paper of the Northeast Asia–United States Forum on International Policy, July 1980, p. 47); but the most outspoken critic of the Sōgō Enerugī Chōsakai projections has been Ikuta Toyoaki, the president of the prestigious Institute for Energy Economics. These projections are based upon what he views as fancifully optimistic growth rates, inflated expectations for nuclear power, and unfounded faith in the continued availability of up to 6.3 million barrels per day of imported petroleum, the target established at the 1979 Tokyo Summit. Ikuta therefore revises government estimates downward by 10 to 40 percent.

Japanese energy resource planning data must be evaluated cautiously. Projections in 1970 of a 60 GW nuclear power capacity by 1985 have been several times revised by several bodies. Current capacity is only 15 GW.

Ikuta's revised projections were first offered to the foreign press on May 6, 1980. The text of his remarks was reprinted by the Foreign Press Center, Number B-80-01. See also Ikuta Toyoaki, "Energy Problem of Japan" (mimeo), May 25, 1980; and Watanuki Joji, "Energy Issue and Socio-Political Implications: Japan's Case" (mimeo), 1980.

Table 10

ACTUAL AND PROJECTED PRIMARY ENERGY SUPPLY IN MILLIONS OF BARRELS PER DAY OF OIL EQUIVALENT*

(Figures in parentheses represent percent of total supply)

	1960	1965	1970	1977	1985	1990	1995
Hydro	.25 (14.7%)	.34 (11.3%)	.36 (6.4%)	.34 (4.8%)	.47 (4.7%)	.55 (4.6%)	.64 (4.6%)
Nuclear	–	–	.02 (0.3%)	.14 (2.0%)	.67 (6.7%)	1.31 (10.9%)	1.98 (14.3%)
Coal (Domestic)	.73 (43.9%)	.65 (21.5%)	.52 (9.1%)	.23 (3.2%)	.25 (2.5%)	.24 (2.0%)	.25 (1.8%)
Coal (Import)	.11 (6.6%)	.26 (8.5%)	.71 (12.4%)	.82 (11.6%)	1.36 (13.6%)	1.88 (15.6%)	2.29 (16.5%)
Oil (Domestic†)	.00 (0.5%)	1.76	4.03	.06 (0.9%)	.14 (1.4%)	.17 (1.4%)	.24 (1.7%)
Oil (Imported)	.56 (33.4%)	(57.6%)	(70.9%)	5.28 (74.5%)	6.30 (62.9%)	6.02 (50.0%)	5.98 (43.1%)
Natural Gas (Domestic)	.01 (0.8%)	.03 (1.1%)	.03 (0.6%)	–	–	–	–
LNG (Domestic)	–	–	.02 (0.3%)	–	–	–	–
LNG (Import)	–	–		.21 (2.9%)	.72 (7.2%)	1.08 (9.0%)	1.21 (8.7%)
Geothermal	–	–	–	0 (0.0%)	0 (0.4%)	.12 (1.0%)	.25 (1.8%)
Synfuel, Solar, etc.	–	–	–	.01 (0.1%)	.09 (0.9%)	.66 (5.5%)	1.05 (7.6%)
Total	1.67	3.05	5.69	7.09	10.01	12.04	13.88

SOURCES: 1960: IEA, *Energy Policies and Programmes of IEA Countries, 1979 Review* (Paris: OECD, 1980), p. 151; 1965 and 1970: Rollomon and Grenon (1975), p. 206; 1977–95: Sōgō Enerugī Chōsakai (1979).

*These figures represent conversions to millions of barrels per day of oil equivalent from several non-equivalent units of measure, and there may therefore be rounding errors in reconversion.

†Figures for 1977–95 include domestic gas production.

The third policy imperative follows from these same data, for even the diversification of supply and supplier leaves Japan dependent upon foreign energy sources. If one excludes the nuclear power option and examines the geographic origins of Japan's remaining alternatives to petroleum, one discovers that even in the most optimistic of estimates, only about 10 percent of Japan's total primary energy will be derived from purely domestic sources (domestic coal, domestic oil, solar, geothermal, etc.) by the end of this decade. Thus, the final imperative involves the long-term reduction of foreign dependence—upon whatever resource or region. In this regard, there is much evidence that Japanese energy R&D is directed at these concerns. The clearest example of the ways in which imperatives to diversify combine with imperatives to develop domestic technologies is that of Japan's quest for nuclear self-sufficiency in the form of the nuclear fuel cycle.[17] The attraction of nuclear power for Japan is obvious; compared to oil or coal, the yield per unit weight of nuclear fuel is orders of magnitude higher. As Japan must import all of its uranium, the immediate problem of supply insecurities would still present itself, although to a lesser extent than in the case of petroleum. But the establishment of a complete nuclear fuel cycle would eliminate supply concerns, and has therefore been accorded high priority. Nuclear fuel cycle related R&D increased by 30 percent between 1977 and 1978, at the same time that nuclear powered electric generation, radiation, and safety related research actually decreased (Sōrifu Tōkeikyiku, 1980). The Japanese government is leading the effort by consistently stressing the development of "domestic" technologies in the recovery of uranium from sea water, uranium enrichment (centrifuge separation), the development of the breeder reactor, and fuel reprocessing (Kagaku Gijutsuchō, 1978; Naikaku Sōridaijin, 1980). The Japanese effort to complete the nuclear fuel cycle highlights the way in which "the substitution of knowledge for resources" (Suttmeier, 1978) might dramatically alter a range of issues in a manner quite unimaginable in the context of a mere diversification of resources.

The broader definition of Japanese energy alternatives thereby presents itself. Technologies currently under development may not only bring Japan self-sufficiency in energy, but may also form part of the core of Japan's next generation of export activity. Given the Japanese capability to commercialize technological developments for industrial growth, it is not inconceivable that Japan could one day transform itself from the vulnerable position of foreign energy resource importer to one of indigenous energy technology exporter. The answer, of course, lies in the Japanese perception of their energy situation: Is it an energy dilemma or an energy opportunity? The evidence on these pages suggest the latter at least as much as the former.

Insofar as the R&D effort itself is concerned, we've seen evidence that two heretofore tacit divisions of labor are changing. The pre-1979 regime, characterized by a virtual public sector monopoly on nuclear R&D

---

[17] The nuclear fuel cycle is "the series of steps involved in supplying fuel for nuclear power reactors and disposing of it after use. It can include some or all of the following stages: mining, refining of uranium or thorium ore, enrichment, fabrication of fuel elements, their use in a nuclear reactor, spent fuel reprocessing, recycling, radioactive waste storage or disposal" (Arrow et al., *Energy*, p. 596).

and by a private sector dominance of nonnuclear R&D, has grown rather more fluid. With the changes accompanying the Alternative Energy Law of 1980, the government finds itself very much at the center of nonnuclear research as well. Moreover, a similar division of labor between MITI and STA is also being redefined. MITI has moved vigorously, if not always successfully, to expand its jurisdiction across the full range of energy R&D areas.

In conclusion, then, in examining the politics of alternative energy R&D in Japan, we have scratched consensus and found conflict, and we have scratched conflict and found consensus. To disengage the two would be both to denude the issue and delude the reader. We are therefore left with the paradox that conflict and consensus in the Japanese policy context, far from being antithetical, seem perfectly compatible; indeed, they seem to be mutually reinforcing. If the politics of alternative energy R&D in Japan is any guide, Japan is neither a monolith of rapturous harmony nor a pit of contentious and self-destructive discord. In itself this is hardly striking, but upon examination of the *quality* of accommodation reached even on bitterly contested issues, one cannot help being optimistic about Japan's energy future.

Appendix

SUNSHINE PROJECT BUDGETS
(in billions of yen)

Energy Source	1974	1975	1976	1977	1978	1979	1980	1974–1980
Solar	0.85	1.10	1.45	1.45	2.05	3.80	9.40	20.10
Geothermal	0.55	1.10	1.55	2.55	3.20	3.55	8.45	20.95
Coal	0.40	.85	.90	1.05	1.45	2.90	8.45	15.95
Hydrogen	0.35	.45	.45	0.50	0.60	0.70	0.95	4.00
General Research	0.25	.45	.55	0.65	0.85	1.00	0.95	4.70
Total	2.4	3.95	4.90	6.20	8.15	11.95	28.20	65.70

SOURCE: Shigen Enerugīcho, *Enerugī Kankei Shiryōshū* [A Compilation of Energy-Related Data], Tokyo, July 1980, p. 88.

BIBLIOGRAPHY

Arrow, Kenneth J., et al. *Energy: The Next Twenty Years.* Cambridge, Mass.: Ballinger Press, 1979.

Campbell, John C. *Contemporary Japanese Budget Politics.* Berkeley and Los Angeles: University of California Press, 1977.

Denki Jigyō Shingikai Jukyū Bukai. *Chūkan Hōkoku* [Midterm Report]. Tokyo, December 1979.

Gerstenfeld, Arthur, and Sumiyoshi Keyi. "The Management of Innovation in Japan—Seven Forces that Make the Difference." *Research Management,* January 1980.

Goodman, Herbert I. "Japan and the World Energy Problem." An occasional paper of the Northeast Asia–United States Forum on International Policy, July 1980.

Hollomon, J. Herbert, and Michel Grenon. *Energy Research and Development.* Cambridge, Mass.: Ballinger Press, 1975.

Ikuta Toyoaki. "Current Energy Situation." Tokyo: Foreign Press Center, 1980a.

_____. "Energy Problem of Japan." Mimeo, 1980b.

Institute for Energy Economics. "New Energy Development in Japan." Tokyo, September 1980.

International Energy Agency. *Energy Policies and Programmes of IEA Countries.* Paris: OECD, 1980a.

———. *Energy Research, Development and Demonstration in the IEA Countries.* Paris: OECD, 1980b.

Johnson, Chalmers. *Japan's Public Policy Companies.* Washington, D.C.: American Enterprise Institute for Public Policy Research, 1978.

Kagaku Gijutsuchō. *Kagaku Gijutsu Hakusho* [Science and Technology White Paper]. Tokyo, 1978.

Kagaku Gijutsuchō Keikakukyoku Chōsaka. *Kagaku Gijutsu Kihon Dēta Shū* [A Compilation of Basic Science and Technology Data]. Tokyo, February 1980.

Kagaku Gijutsuchō Kenkyū Chōseikyoku. *Shōwa 54 Nendo Kagaku Gijutsu Shinkōhi Nado No Gaiyō* [An Outline of 1979 R&D Promotion Expenditures]. Tokyo, January 1979.

Kagaku Gijutsu Kaigi. *Shimondai 6 Go "Chōkiteki Tenbō ni Tatta Sōgōteki Kagaku Gijutsu Seisaku no Kihon ni Tsuite" ni Taisuru Tōshin* [A Report to the 6th Deliberative Conference Concerning the Long-Term Prospects for the Basis of Science and Technology Policy]. Tokyo, 1977.

Kaya Yoichi. "Japan's Energy Consumption Structure and the Direction of Energy Conservation." In *The Wheel Extended*, 9:2 (Autumn 1979), 1–11.

Ministry of International Trade and Industry. *Promotion of the Moonlight Project: Research, Development and Demonstration of Energy Conservation Technology.* Tokyo, 1979.

———. "Sunshine Project for 1980s." In *Sunshine Information Center News* (1980a), pp. 2–11.

———. *The Vision of MITI Policies in the 1980s.* Tokyo, 1980b.

Naikaku Sōridaijin. *Enerugī Kenkyū Kaihatsu Kihon Keikaku* [Basic Plan for Energy R&D]. Tokyo, August 11, 1978; April 19, 1979 (revised); July 15, 1980 (revised).

National Science Board. *Science Indicators 1978.* Washington, D.C.: U.S. Government Printing Office, 1979.

Nihon Enerugī Keizai Kenkyūjo. *80 Nendai no Enerugī Seisaku no Kadai* [Energy Policy Problems for the 1980s]. Tokyo, 1980.

Noguchi Yukio. "A Dynamic Model of Incremental Budgeting." In *Kagaku Gijutsu to Seisaku ni Taisuru Gakusaiteki Kokusaiteki Sekkin* [An Interdisciplinary and International Approach to Science, Technology, and Policy], ed. Inose Horoshi. Tokyo: Ministry of Education, 1980.

Samuels, Richard J. "The Politics of Regional Policy in Japan." Ph.D. dissertation, MIT, Department of Political Science, 1980.

Sawa Takamitsu. "Enerugī Kiki to Keizaigaku" [Economics and the Energy Crisis]. *Nikkei Business*, Tokyo, June 2, 1980.

Shigen Enerugīcho. *Enerugī Kankei Shiryōshū* [A Compilation of Energy-Related Data]. Tokyo, July 1980.

Shin Enerugī Sōgō Kaihatsu Kikō. *Shin Enerugī Sōgō Kaihatsu Kikō no Gaiyō* [An Outline of the New Energy Development Organization]. Tokyo, 1980.

Sōgō Enerugī Chōsakai. *Chōki Enerugī Jukyū Zantei Mitōshi* [Provisional Long-Term Energy Supply and Demand Outlook in Japan]. Tokyo, August 1979.

Sōgō Kenkyū Kaihatsu Kikō. *Enerugī o Kangaeru* [Thinking About Energy]. Tokyo, 1979.

Sōrifu Tōkeikyoku. *Shōwa 54 Nen Enerugī Kenkyū Chōsa Kekka no Gaiyō* [An Outline of the Results of the 1979 Energy Research Investigation]. Tokyo, February 1980.

Suttmeier, Richard P. "Japanese Reactions to U.S. Nuclear Policy: The Domestic Origins of an International Negotiating Position." *Orbis*, 22:3 (1978), 651–680.

Takano Takeshi. *Tsūsanshō no Yabō* [MITI's Ambitions]. Tokyo: Weekend Books, 1980.

Tsuru Shigeto. "The Energy Prospect for Japan." *Japan Quarterly*, 27:1 (January–March 1980), 15–19.

Tsūshō Sangyōshō. *Shin Enerugī Kaihatsu Suishin no Chūkakutai ni Tsuite* [Concerning the Central Organ for Promotion of New Energy Development]. Tokyo, June 1980.

Tsūshō Sangyōshō Shigen Enerugīchō Daitai Enerugī Taisakuka. *Shōwa 55 Nendo Sekiyū Daitai Enerugī Kankei Yōsan no Gaiyō* [An Outline of the Alternative Energy-Related Budget for 1980.]. Tokyo, May 1980a.

Tsūshō Sangyōshō Shigen Enerugīcho Sekiyū Daitai Enerugī Taisakuka. *Daitai Enerugī Taisaku no Suishin ni Tsuite* [Concerning the Promotion of an Alternative Energy Policy]. Tokyo, June 1980b.

Watanuki Joji. "Energy Issue and Socio-Political Implications: Japan's Case." Mimeo, 1980.

INSTITUTE OF EAST ASIAN STUDIES PUBLICATIONS SERIES

China Research Monographs

1. James R. Townsend. *The Revolutionization of Chinese Youth: A Study of Chung-Kuo Ch'ing-nien*, 1967 ($3.00)
2. Richard Baum and Frederick C. Teiwes. *Ssu-Ch'ing: The Socialist Education Movement of 1962–1966*, 1968*
3. Robert Rinden and Roxane Witke. *The Red Flag Waves: A Guide to the Hung-ch'i p'iao-p'iao Collection*, 1968 ($4.50)
4. Klaus Mehnert. *Peking and the New Left: At Home and Abroad*, 1969*
5. George T. Yu. *China and Tanzania: A Study in Cooperative Interaction*, 1970*
6. David D. Barrett. *Dixie Mission: The United States Army Observer Group in Yenan, 1944*, 1970 ($4.00)
7. John S. Service. *The Amerasia Papers: Some Problems in the History of US-China Relations*, 1971 ($4.00)
8. Daniel D. Lovelace. *China and "People's War" in Thailand, 1964–1969*, 1972*
9. Jonathan Porter. *Tseng Kuo-fan's Private Bureaucracy*, 1972 ($5.00)
10. Derek J. Waller. *The Kiangsi Soviet Republic: Mao and the National Congresses of 1931 and 1934*, 1973 ($5.00)
11. T. A. Bisson. *Yenan in June 1937: Talks with the Communist Leaders*, 1973 ($5.00)
12. Gordon Bennett. *Yundong: Mass Campaigns in Chinese Communist Leadership*, 1976 ($4.50)
sp. John B. Starr and Nancy A. Dyer. *Post-Liberation Works of Mao Zedong: A Bibliography and Index*, 1976 ($7.50)
13. Philip Huang, Lynda Bell, and Kathy Walker. *Chinese Communists and Rural Society, 1927–1934*, 1978 ($5.00)
14. Jeffrey G. Barlow. *Sun Yat-sen and the French, 1900–1908*, 1979 ($4.00)
15. Joyce K. Kallgren, Editor. *The People's Republic of China after Thirty Years: An Overview*, 1979 ($5.00)
16. Tong-eng Wang. *Economic Policies and Price Stability in China*, 1980 ($8.00)
17. Frederic Wakeman, Jr., Editor. *Ming and Qing Historical Studies in the People's Republic of China*, 1981 ($8.00)
18. Robert E. Bedeski. *State Building in Modern China: The Kuomintang in the Prewar Period*, 1981 ($8.00)
19. Stanley Rosen. *The Role of Sent-Down Youth in the Chinese Cultural Revolution: The Case of Guangzhou*, 1981 ($8.00)
20. Prudence Chou. *Lao She: An Intellectual's Role and Dilemma in Modern China* (forthcoming) ($8.00)
21. James Cole. *The People Versus the Taipings: Bao Lisheng's "Righteous Army of Donagan,"* 1981 ($6.00)
22. Dan C. Sanford. *The Future Association of Taiwan with the People's Republic of China* (forthcoming) ($8.00)

---

*Out of print. May be ordered from University Microfilms, 300 North Zeeb Road, Ann Arbor, Michigan 48106.